BOOM BABY!

The Sudden, Surprising Rise of the
INDIANA PACERS

Conrad Brunner

MASTERS PRESS

A Division of Howard W. Sams & Co.

Published by Masters Press
(A Division of Howard W. Sams & Co.)
2647 Waterfront Pkwy. E. Drive, Suite 300
Indianapolis, IN 46214

©1994, Conrad Brunner

Interior design: Leah Marckel

Cover design: Phil Velikan

Interior photos provided by the Indiana Pacers' team photographer Frank McGrath

Editor: Susan M. McKinney

Proofreader: Phyllis L. Bannon and Heather Seal

"Boom Baby!" is a trademark of Bobby Leonard Enterprises, used with permission

Library of Congress Catalog Card Number: 94-68643
ISBN: 0-57028-036-3

Foreword

I've had a lot of teams I'm really fond of and really proud of what they accomplished. I would suspect that coaching the 1993-94 Indiana Pacers was one of the most enjoyable experiences of my life because of how the team came back. I kind of had that situation at UCLA, at Kansas, At New Jersey — a number of teams that have come from the dead — but last year would be hard to top, I think, because of what the team did and the acceptance locally and nationally.

I don't like to compare one group to the next because that's not fair. But I don't think I've been around a team on any level that got along any better. I don't think I've been connected with a team that had better leadership from its players — Byron (Scott), Sam (Mitchell), Vern (Fleming), LaSalle (Thompson), Derrick (McKey), Reggie (Miller). I've never been around a group like that in my whole career.

When I got this job, Donnie (Walsh) more or less said, "Larry, I don't know if the guys can play or not. I have had different coaches give different opinions." And he had certain ideas about whether certain guys could play, but he really wanted to see. So he wanted me to evaluate them and that was the only thing we talked about. We didn't make goals publicly or within the organization about what we wanted to do. The only goal we made publicly was to play hard and try to play the right way. Privately, with the team, I was saying, "Let's try to win, and we'll evaluate at the end of the year whether we played up to our potential or not based on how far we went and how well we did." I didn't think about anything else but that.

I didn't think I was inheriting a contender, because I wouldn't have been the coach. I don't think they would have made a change. But I didn't worry about it. I was excited about working for Donnie and being in Indiana because of the interest. I had some ideas about some of the players but I hadn't seen them enough to really understand. I was anxious my first year to evaluate them and see where we needed to go, see who could play in a style I felt comfortable coaching.

From my perspective, our success was a wonderful thing because I'm an ABA fan, my background goes back to the ABA, so whenever the Pacers, San Antonio, New Jersey or Denver happens to succeed, I get pretty excited and this was the first time all four ABA teams made it to the playoffs.

In a state like Indiana, that obviously has always loved basketball and has a rich tradition from high school right on up, it's really important, I think, to be accepted, finally. It was nice to be part of that because, in the ABA days, the Pacers were the marquee franchise and that hadn't been the case for the team since moving to the NBA.

I was always hoping when I go there, because we're in an area that absolutely goes bonkers over basketball and appreciates it, that we would be accepted. I was kind of disappointed early, and surprised, to be honest, and then I was pleasantly surprised later.

Ever though we weren't winning early, everywhere we went I heard comments from people about how hard the guys tried, how unselfishly they played. And I thought that might be enough, but, obviously, you have to win. It's not always that way in our league.

Just look at where we finished, attendance-wise (though they set a club record with an average of 13,264): the Pacers ranked 23rd in the NBA. There's a lot of teams in our league that have not done as well and don't compete like we do that did better. I was kind of disappointed, but it turned out. At the end, I've never seen a crowd like that, and I've been in some pretty unbelievable places.

From a coaching standpoint, to be a part of a real team, to see so many guys contribute in so many different ways was really meaningful to me because I love to teach and I love this game because it's such a team game. And I saw that night in and night out from this club, guys making sacrifices and playing the right way and playing hard. I was hopeful when I got this job that the people of the state would be proud of us for that. When you look at the playoffs and the enthusiasm generated, it was the case.

What were the keys to our turnaround? Byron coming, that was as significant as anything. Reggie's unselfishness. When your best player makes sacrifices like he did, it's really significant. The way Derrick came and fit in, replacing a tremendously popular player. How we reacted to injuries, always having somebody step forward to make a contribution. You can cite Sam, from not playing, taking over for Dale (Davis) who, at that time, probably was our best player, and the team didn't skip a beat. I think Rik (Smits), the way he was accepted by the team, after a really bad period, and his emergence was a tremendous factor.

Obviously, the Houston game (a 119-108 road victory on Jan. 29 that started the Pacers' second half surge) was significant because it showed the character of the team. We won coming off five heartbreaking losses in a row. Instead of worrying about the five losses, and saying "Oh, shit, we're playing a great team," we showed just why we were able to go from 16-23 to accomplish what we did. That was really of more significance than just a win.

And to me, personally, it was the staff, the way they meshed. Gar (Heard) sat back and let Bill (Blair) do his thing. The way they accepted each other and the contribution they made was really big. I think for me, personally, that was a great situation. I could coach and teach and hand them some responsibilities that took a lot of pressure off of me.

I've been asked to write these before, but always turned the offers down. But the fact Conrad Brunner wrote this book, obviously is significant to me because he was with the team from day one, so he had a perspective that was unlike most.

Larry Brown

Preface

When it comes to Bobby "Slick" Leonard, there never is a shortage of stories to tell, which makes for a great deal of anticipation over his promised autobiography.

Most deal with his legendary reputation as an off-the-cuff, free-wheeling head coach who spent as much time with his players off the floor as on. Some deal with his overlooked talent for improvisation during a game — particularly in the closing seconds, when he would invent plays, or implement one he drew up on a cocktail napkin the night before. However he did it, he worked wonders with the old Indiana Pacers of the ABA, winning three championships in four years.

There is far more to Leonard, though, than his reputation. After all these years, he still cares passionately about the Pacers. As a broadcaster and analyst, he eschews any pretense of objectivity, openly rooting for the team on the air, patting players on the back as they come to the huddle during timeouts, standing and clapping when he wants to cheer them on.

At one point during last year's Eastern Conference championship series with New York, he had to leave his broadcast partner, Mark Boyle, alone for nearly six minutes of a game because his nerves had gotten the best of him, and he had to head outside for a smoke.

The most pertinent story to this book, though, is of its title. Leonard's trademark phrase "Boom Baby!", emoted when a Pacer hit a three-pointer or threw down a big dunk, became the rallying cry of the 1993-94 Indiana Pacers, appearing on T-shirts, hankies, bumper stickers, business marquees, and even in a song.

Though Slick had planned to use "Boom Baby" as the title for his life story, he readily agreed to let us use it for this story of the most remarkable season in the Pacer's NBA history. What "Rip City" is to Portland or "Yes" is to New York, "Boom Baby" has become to the Indiana Pacers.

It is fitting that the rise of these new Pacers to prominence in the NBA is so readily identified by the words of a man who made the old Pacers a team indelibly etched into the city's conciousness.

We thank Bobby Leonard for "Boom Baby," and much, much more.

To Richard Jens Brunner, 1954-1972.
He would've been the first newspaperman in the family.
Hopefully, I'll be the last.

Table of Contents

BOOM BABY!

The Sudden, Surprising Rise of the
INDIANA PACERS

1 From ABA to MIA

The party, much like the season it honored, was impromptu.

Thousands spilled out of the plaza adjacent to the Indianapolis City Market and into the streets, dozens more craning from open windows in neighboring office buildings, to celebrate an awakening.

After years of dormancy, the NBA finally was alive and well in Indianapolis.

A tradition of success that had died nearly two decades before, in a different league, in a different time, had sprung to life without warning. The little team that could, the Indiana Pacers, had risen from a 16-23 record in late January to within 35 seconds of a berth in the NBA Finals.

And now, they were talking about wanting more. The city actually wanted a downtown parade. But when representatives approached club president Donnie Walsh, he cooled them down slightly. Parades, he said, were for champions.

Come back next year.

There were tributes from Mayor Stephen Goldsmith, owner Melvin Simon and Walsh. All the players, and most of their wives or girlfriends, crowded onto the stage to join the party.

One who couldn't be there was the man who played the single biggest role in making the event possible.

The coach, Larry Brown, was in a hospital recovery room after having surgery to replace his right hip.

Finally, the crowd got what it wanted. The last man to the microphone was the first in their hearts.

It was Reggie Miller, the sudden superstar.

Fresh off his appearance on the Late Show with David Letterman the night before, Miller — introduced as "Mr. TV star" by Vern Fleming — told the throng estimated in excess of 5,000 exactly what it wanted to hear.

"We were 30 seconds away from playing Houston in the NBA Finals," Miller said. "The taste of winning is in all of our mouths.... We're definitely going to be back."

For a franchise that had all but engraved "Wait till next year" over the entrances to Market Square Arena for its habitual mediocrity — if the team was lucky — that phrase had taken on an entirely new, strangely optimistic tone.

* * *

In a state where basketball is a religion, the Pacers had, over time, managed to convert what once had been a burgeoning congregation of faithful into a cynical aggregation of agnostics.

It wasn't easy. It took a combination of bad decisions, bad judgement and bad luck to bring about the degeneration of a dynasty.

The Pacers had the proudest name in the old American Basketball Association, winning three championships in four years, producing three MVPs (Mel Daniels twice and George McGinnis once) and four all-ABA players (Daniels four times, McGinnis and Roger Brown thrice and Bob Netolicky once).

They also had a roman candle of a head coach, Bobby "Slick" Leonard, a former star for Branch McCracken at Indiana University who was a colorful, volatile and brilliant leader for this wild bunch.

In the new frontier of professional basketball, these were the cowboys, riding hard, shooting fast and roping in herds of followers. They played in the old State Fairgrounds Coliseum, which had a capacity of less than 10,000 but regularly housed standing-room-only crowds.

To this day, the franchise's only retired jerseys belong to McGinnis, Daniels and Brown. The only banners that hang alongside them in Market Square Arena are from the ABA championship years of 1970, '72 and '73.

That's because when the red, white and blue ball was deflated for good in 1976, so, too, were the Pacers.

Even before the merger, the franchise was struggling financially. The original ownership group sold in January of 1975 to another headed by Tom Binford, widely known as chief steward of the Indianapolis 500.

The franchise was saved, but the glory days were over. After one last trip to the ABA championship finals in 1975 (a 4-1 loss to Kentucky), McGinnis jumped to the NBA, lured by Philadelphia's six-year, $3 million contract.

This was a devastating loss. The Pacers didn't just lose a star player, they lost a local icon.

McGinnis was deeply rooted in the community. He played at Washington High in Indianapolis, then moved on to Indiana University. When the Pacers signed him after his sophomore season with the Hoosiers in 1971, it was regarded as a coup not just for the franchise but the fledgling league.

In their final ABA season, they posted their first losing record in eight years (39-45) and were eliminated in the opening round of the playoffs.

The ABA-NBA merger then exacted more severe tolls.

The Pacers had to pay a $3.2 million entry fee and, with the three other remnants (Denver, San Antonio and New Jersey) had to come up with $3.3 million to settle with Kentucky Colonels owner John Y. Brown, who pocketed a healthy sum for nothing more than going out of business.

No one, though, was more shrewd than the co-owners of the last remaining ABA franchise, the St. Louis Spirits. Instead of accepting a one-time cash settlement, brothers Ozzie and Dan Silna negotiated a deal that would bring them one-seventh of the combined annual national television revenues from the four surviving teams.

Inexplicably, there was no expiration date on the agreement, so it is a price the Pacers, Spurs, Nuggets and Nets are still paying.

Though none of the former ABA teams would share in NBA television revenues for two years, the Silnas have come out millions ahead.

In the 16 years since the Pacers began receiving television revenues, they have paid the Silnas slightly more than $7 million, including $1.3 million for the '93-94 season alone.

Quadruple that, and the Silnas have taken home more than $28 million from the former ABA teams, a staggering total.

For the Silnas, going out of the basketball business proved a wildly profitable venture.

For the Pacers, staying in it proved costly. They have yet to show a profit after any of their NBA seasons.

There was one other codicil of the merger agreement: none of the new teams could participate in the 1976 draft.

That was particularly painful for the Pacers, who missed the opportunity to pick any of the three first-rounders from Indiana University's 1976 national championship team — forward Scott May (who went No. 2 to Chicago), guard Quinn Buckner (No. 7 to Milwaukee) and forward Bobby Wilkerson (11th to Seattle).

None of the three became major stars, but all were solid pros. In a market that needed every draw it could get, any of them would have provided a needed lift.

Underfunded and unprepared for what was to come, the Pacers struggled mightily. The battle to stay afloat financially — at one point, the community actually hosted a "save-the-Pacers" telethon — proved as tough as the competition on court, and led to some necessarily short-sighted decisions that proved disastrous.

Before the 1978-79 season, ownership invited UCLA's Ann Meyers, widely recognized as the best female player in the country, to become the first to try out for an NBA team. She didn't last long, and the anticipated publicity bonanza did more harm than good to the struggling franchise's image.

From 1977-85, the club's various forms of management made an astonishing 45 trades — an average of five per year. The decision making turned out to cost the franchise chances for greatness. Imagine Larry Bird, Michael Jordan, Patrick Ewing and Alex English as teammates on the Indiana Pacers. It would have been the original dream team.

With a little luck and a lot of foresight, it could have happened.

In 1978, the Pacers held the No. 3 pick in the draft and could have used it on a skinny junior from Indiana State named Larry Bird. At the time, though, the level of Bird's future greatness was anything but certain, and the Pacers were in need of immediate help up front.

There was one other mitigating factor. The Pacers would have had until the 1979 draft to sign Bird, or else lose his rights. A franchise already short on cash feared wasting a pick on a player they could scarcely afford to pay.

Bird was bypassed in favor of Kentucky bruiser Rick Robey.

One year later, Robey and Bird, taken with the sixth pick, were teammates in Boston. Robey was dealt to the Celtics midway through his rookie year for Billy Knight, whose best years were behind him.

Another failed attempt at reclaiming the past came in 1980 when English, a promising young small forward, was shipped to Denver for an aging McGinnis. English scored more than 25,000 points in a 15-year career. McGinnis would retire in 1982.

On June 5, 1981, the Pacers made a deal that seemed harmless at the time, sending their 1984 first-round pick to Portland for journeyman center Tom Owens. After playing one season with the Pacers, Owens was traded to Detroit for a second-round pick.

The draft pick in Portland's hands turned out to be the second overall in 1984. Jordan went third.

Small wonder, then, that from 1976 through 1986, the Pacers averaged 31.5 wins and made the playoffs just once. Jack McKinney took them to a 44-38 record before a first-round sweep at the hands of the powerful Philadelphia 76ers in 1980-81.

It wasn't much, but it would stand as the best season in club history for 13 years.

This was a franchise cursed not only by poor decisions, but simple bad luck.

In 1983, the Pacers lost a coin flip with Houston for the top pick. The Rockets got Virginia's 7'-4" center Ralph Sampson and reached the NBA Finals three years later. The Pacers settled for Missouri center Steve Stipanovich, a solid, unspectacular player who had one thing in common with Sampson — both were forced into premature retirements due to degenerative knee problems.

In the 1985 lottery, the Pacers again finished a distant second as another franchise center, Ewing, went to New York, which drew the top pick. Oklahoma forward Wayman Tisdale was the Pacers' prize at No. 2, but he was no consolation.

The following season, the team lost one of its cornerstones. Clark Kellogg, who had averaged better than 20 points and 10 rebounds as a rookie in 1982-83, was forced into early retirement with serious knee problems.

Fate struck again in 1988, the year of the one-man draft. The one man was Danny Manning and the No. 1 pick wound up in the hands of the L.A. Clippers. Used to this business of settling for leftovers — and acutely aware they had lost two previous chances to draft a franchise center — the Pacers took a flyer on 7-4 Dutchman Rik Smits of Marist with the second pick.

Admittedly a project, Smits' role took on an unexpected urgency in his first training camp when Stipanovich, like Kellogg, saw his career come to an unexpected end.

In 1983, real estate developers Mel and Herb Simon purchased the team for $6 million to save the franchise for Indianapolis. The club's ownership had changed hands three times in the previous eight years. Attendance had bottomed out to an average of 4,814 in the 1982-83 season.

Rumors of a move to a larger market were ever-present, and would be for the next decade. In general, it was a franchise very much in disarray.

To their credit, the Simons moved slowly. They organized the business side of the operation first, bringing an air of professionalism to the offices. Three years after they bought the team, they got directly involved in the basketball decision making.

Donnie Walsh, who had been an assistant coach to George Irvine, leapfrogged all the way to the general manager's position in a massive front-office reorganization on April 21, 1986.

Bob Salyers, who had been the club's president and general manager for three years, was named legal counsel. Wayne Embry was asked to remain as a consultant but did so only briefly. He soon would leave to take the general manager's job in Cleveland.

Irvine, who had produced 48 victories in two seasons, was kicked upstairs to a position at Walsh's right hand.

* * *

Walsh was unlike anything this franchise had seen.

He was a basketball man, true, but also a lawyer, a philosopher and a tireless worker who subsisted, it seems, on a steady stream of cigarettes and diet colas.

He also had a mission: to make professional basketball work in Indianapolis. He savored the challenge, because so many before him had said it couldn't be done.

Born in Manhattan, Walsh was the eldest of five siblings, with two brothers and two sisters. His father was a Navy dentist, so the family lived a solid middle-class existence.

One of his sisters would marry a millionaire. His brother, Jimmy, would hit it big in the cellular phone industry and retire with millions before he reached 40.

In the Walsh family, though, Donnie remained at the top of the tree. "I'm the oldest," he said. "That's the way our family works."

A high school basketball star at Fordham Prep (he battled Long Island's Larry Brown for headlines), Walsh was offered a scholarship by North Carolina's Frank McGuire.

In those days, that simply was an offer no young man could refuse.

After a year at prep school, Brown joined Walsh at North Carolina. Another prominent member of that team was Doug Moe.

The three became friends for life.

Walsh was a solid player, but nothing special. McGuire left for the NBA Philadelphia Warriors in 1961 and was replaced by Dean Smith. McGuire came calling in '62, using an 11th-round draft pick on Walsh.

No fool, Walsh understood this was little more than a courtesy. In what was then a nine-team NBA, an 11th-round pick had no chance.

Brown and Moe were bigger stars who would go on to successful playing careers in the ABA.

Walsh decided to enter law school because, he said, "I didn't know what else to do."

Smith asked Walsh to stay on as a graduate assistant, to keep his hands on the game. Despite other intentions, he never would really let go.

He married his longtime sweetheart, Judy (they met when Walsh was 14 and she was 12), during his second year of law school and eventually rose to become associate editor of the Law Review. With those responsibilities, he was forced to give up his part-time coaching job.

His new passion was the law.

"It was the first time I really started to think on my own," he said. "It revived me as a student and opened me up intellectually." After graduation, he had two remarkable job offers. One was to join Richard Nixon's New York law firm. The other was with the U.S. Justice Department's honors program.

"Had I gone either route," Walsh said, "I would've been in on Watergate, on one side or the other."

He was on the verge of accepting the Nixon offer when a funny thing happened on the way to judicial fame and fortune. Walsh was walking through the offices after meeting Nixon when he noticed a group of young lawyers about his age huddled in a windowless library poring over a stack of books. At that point, he re-thought his career choice and decided not to practice law.

"It was a dumb decision at the time," he said, "but I couldn't see doing it."

He stayed in Chapel Hill as Smith's assistant, but not for long. McGuire, who did not go with the Warriors when they left Philadelphia for San Francisco before the 1962-63 season, took the head coaching job at South Carolina. He promptly hired Walsh.

The McGuire-Walsh tandem remained intact for 12 years and it was in Columbia that Walsh sensed his future would not be in coaching. McGuire was a head coach who really did not need an assistant on the floor. Walsh organized the recruiting and, in essence, served as the basketball office's liaison in all business matters.

It was his first real exposure to the administrative side of the sport, and it was an enlightening experience.

It also was frustrating. Walsh had a wife and five kids to think about, and he had spent a dozen years as an assistant college coach.

And it wasn't like he didn't have options.

Walsh took and passed the bar exam and was prepared to resume the career that had been interrupted in 1965, when another voice from the past spoke up. Brown and Walsh hadn't maintained close contact over the previous decade — in fact, they had scarcely spoken since Walsh left Chapel Hill — but when he had a vacancy on his Denver Nuggets staff in 1977, Brown called Walsh.

Brown also hired his former Virginia Squires teammate, George Irvine.

His first exposure to pro basketball turned out to be a revelation for Walsh. There was more to the game, he saw now, than coaching and playing. The idea of becoming an administrator had allure. He would use his time on the bench to absorb knowledge toward that end.

He also learned a valuable lesson about the nature of Brown, one that would pay off years later.

Convinced the Nuggets were one piece away from real contention, Brown decided that piece was McGinnis, who had starred three years for Philadelphia.

On August 16, 1978, the Nuggets sent Brown favorite Bobby Jones and Ralph Simpson to the 76ers for McGinnis.

By August 17, 1978, Brown wanted McGinnis gone.

"We went to our first practice, and the players were running some line drills and George was cutting the corners," Walsh said, recalling the day after the trade. "Larry came out of the practice and, as he was walking off the court, he said, "We've got to have a meeting. We've got to trade McGinnis."

"He called a team meeting in which he told McGinnis that if he wouldn't put out, he couldn't play for Larry. George just looked up and said, "OK, then, you'd better trade me." Larry said "You've got it," and stalked out of the room." McGinnis was not a practice player and Brown was very much a practice coach. The two would never be compatible.

Oddly enough, McGinnis lasted longer with the Nuggets than Brown.

While Walsh loved the pro game, Brown did not. He left the Nuggets with no explanation midway through the 1978-79 season. Though Denver finished 19-10 under Walsh and made the playoffs, Walsh had no desire to take up coaching full time. Still, he accepted a two-year contract.

Brown would wind up at UCLA.

In his only full season with Denver, Walsh saw a team full of disparate personalities fall apart. It was the beginning of the end for the brilliant David Thompson, who missed 43 games that year with a foot injury but had a greater problem: drugs. He would have one more productive season before rapidly declining into a shadow of his former self.

Through the 30-52 year, though, Walsh caught a glimpse of hope, courtesy of the Pacers. He had a hand in the trade that sent McGinnis back to Indiana for English. It was his first major success, though shared with Nuggets general manager Carl Scheer, and it fueled his hunger for more.

"That's when I really knew I wanted to do this," Walsh said."I didn't have the talents to coach. A coach has to be single-minded. I had a broader base of knowledge, more interests."

When the '80-81 team started 11-20, Walsh was replaced — at no objection — by Moe, who he had hired as an assistant late in the previous season.

After briefly returning to coaching as Moe's assistant the following year, Walsh gave it up. He made some money putting together real estate deals in South Carolina, but was unfulfilled.

"I was very unhappy," he said. "It made me confront a lot of things about myself. I had to make real hard decisions that turned out to be the key to my happiness.

"From that point on, I've been secure with myself and the way I am. My happiness doesn't depend on a job or a person or what city I'm in, but what is going on inside of me."

The problem Walsh had to address was alcoholism.

He didn't touch a drop until his junior year of college, then began to drink more heavily through four years of law school when the norm was to study hard all week and, as Walsh put it, "get zonked on the weekend."

After his first four years with McGuire at South Carolina, he gave it up entirely. "It made everybody around me happy," Walsh said, "but it didn't solve anything inside of me."

In Denver, he began drinking again.

Out of basketball and uncertain if he ever would get back in, Walsh checked into a treatment center. He admitted to himself that he was an alcoholic, and has been recovering ever since.

"Those four weeks in treatment changed my life," he said. "It filled in all the holes of why I'm like I am. Nobody made me go in. I went in there to find out. I was serious about it.

"When I walked out of there, I knew what the answer was for me and what I had to do for the rest of my life."

He was scanning the atlas for a route back into basketball when Irvine called. Walsh's former assistant in Denver had been hired to replace Jack McKinney with the Pacers in 1984 and needed a right-hand man. It turned out to be Walsh's big break.

Two years later, he was in the position he had craved: general manager of an NBA franchise. He had Irvine at his side as the head of basketball operations to provide support.

"I always wanted to be a general manager, and now, I had it," Walsh said. "It was kind of like (the movie) 'The Candidate'."

"Now what?"

* * *

The job facing Walsh and Irvine was monstrous: to take a franchise that had spent two decades as an NBA laughingstock and make it not only respectable but successful.

All too aware of the franchise's lurid history of personnel decisions, Walsh outlined a philosophy: build through the draft, be conservative with trades and free agent signings and establish credibility for the club within the league.

"I thought it would take four years to accumulate the talent, then you'd have to play together for a certain amount of time," he said. "I was thinking it would take seven or eight years to get to the top of the league."

He also was thinking that, by then, he would no longer be around.

"I really thought," he said, "I would be an interim guy here."

His first two moves had a far greater impact than even Walsh expected, and went a long way toward securing his long-term future.

He hired Jack Ramsay as the head coach, then scored another coup by taking Auburn forward Chuck Person with the fourth pick in the 1986 draft.

Walsh had snowed the rest of the league into believing he would go big, dropping the names of North Carolina State's Chris Washburn and Memphis State's William Bedford.

The Knicks, firmly believing they would be able to draft Person with the fifth pick, were stunned when Walsh made his move — as were assembled Pacer fans, who lustily booed the selection when it was announced at Market Square Arena.

New York settled for Kenny Walker, who could not solve a small forward problem that plagued the Knicks for years to come.

Ramsay's professorial guidance and Person's rookie brilliance combined to make the Pacers one of the league's great success stories. They improved by 15 victories, to 41-41, and returned to the playoffs.

Person was the league's rookie of the year and truly looked like a superstar in the making.

It seemed the franchise had turned the corner.

As it turned out, success had come too quickly. Person's ego ran out of control and he challenged Ramsay's authority, effectively splintering the team. The Pacers missed the playoffs in '87-88, and Ramsay was gone after an 0-7 start the following year.

Walsh eventually settled on the flamboyant Dick Versace, a coach who proved to have greater style than substance. But he also made two monumental trades.

First, he sent Tisdale, a talented player who could amass statistics but not victories, to Sacramento for LaSalle Thompson and Randy Wittman. Thompson filled the void created by Stipanovich's early retirement.

Wittman, a former Indiana University star, was a solid backup with designs on becoming a coach. That type of player would be good for chemistry.

Two days later, on February 22, 1989, Walsh stole Detlef Schrempf from the Dallas Mavericks for Herb Williams, another player who seemed more interested in stats than standings.

The team went 22-31 for Versace to finish 28-54.

With the influx of new talent, plus an incoming lottery pick, No. 7 overall, the future was starting to brighten once more.

There was division in the front office over who to draft. Everyone agreed point guard was the greatest need, but that was about all. Versace wanted Tim Hardaway, the gritty point guard from Texas El-Paso. Others liked Pooh Richardson, UCLA's smooth playmaker.

Walsh wanted George McCloud. He thought the 6'-8" Florida State star could be, if not the next Magic Johnson, then a poor man's version of the Laker legend.

That turned out to be one of Walsh's biggest mistakes.

Still, the team broke out to a 19-9 start in 1989, gracing the pages of Sports Illustrated for the first time in years. The fans, having been teased and let down before, remained skeptical. With good cause, as it turned out.

Versace, nicknamed Dick Verbose, among other things, was in over his head and quickly alienated the team, which fell apart. The Pacers limped into the playoffs with a disappointing 42-40 record — still the franchise's best in nine years — but were quickly swept by Detroit.

After a 9-16 start in 1990, Versace was given the opportunity to pursue his first love, television, on a full-time basis. He was replaced by Bob Hill.

An outgoing, likeable everyman as an assistant, Hill clearly was the players' choice. His hiring lifted the veil of excuses the players had hidden behind for years. Hill was their coach. If they failed him, it was their fault.

The relationship worked wonders, at first. The Pacers went 32-25 for Hill, who turned the team over to young point guard Micheal Williams, and returned to the playoffs, where they faced Larry Bird and the Boston Celtics in the first round.

Would this be the long-awaited breakthrough?

When Person scored 39 points, including a playoff-record seven three-pointers, to lead the Pacers to a 130-118 victory in Game Two in Boston Garden to even the series coming back to Market Square Arena, it looked more possible than ever.

But the Pacers were new to the experience, while Boston had been through it all before. The Celtics knew Indiana was celebrating a little too soon, anticipating a little too much.

Person, who averaged 31 points in the other four games of the series, would produce just six in Game Three. The Pacers quickly lost the homecourt advantage they had held so briefly, 112-105.

The final two games produced the highest level of basketball the Pacers had ever seen. They rallied themselves to win Game Four 116-113, sending the series back to Boston for the decisive fifth game.

In the second quarter, Bird dove for a loose ball and smacked his head hard on the Garden parquet. When the teams came out after the break, Bird was still in the locker room. He emerged in the third quarter, with the Celtics trailing, and proceeded to take over the game to swing momentum back to the home team.

Still, it boiled down to one last shot from Person in the closing seconds, an off-balance three-pointer over two defenders that missed, and the Celtics had survived, 124-121.

Bird was so impressed by the Pacers, he offered a statement that proved damning: "If they don't win 50 games next year, something's wrong."

For Hill's Pacers, it wasn't so much that something was wrong, but not enough things were right.

In many ways, that playoff series offered false hope. They now believed themselves to be better than they were because of their abundance of offensive talent. When it came time to make hustle plays, defend and rebound — the things that win rings — they came up woefully short.

They struggled to a 40-42 finish in the 1991-92 season and earned a rematch with Boston that was a typical sequel: all hype. Boston won easily in three games, forcing Walsh to face the reality that the team he had built simply was not good enough.

That summer, he made the most difficult move of his career, trading Person and Micheal Williams to Minnesota for Pooh Richardson and Sam Mitchell. Person was Walsh's first draft pick and the two had developed what resembled a father-son relationship. Williams had proved a shrewd free agent signee two summers before.

Richardson, who had been the biggest star for the expansion Timberwolves, was supposed to solve the perpetual point guard problem in Indiana. Mitchell, who had been an undersized 6'-7" power forward in Minnesota, would be a tough-minded role player.

The draft produced 6'-11" Dale Davis, an agile, athletic power forward who lacked an offensive game. On this team, that hardly would be noticed.

It all led into the 1992-93 season, the beginning of the end for Hill.

In many ways, for the franchise, it was the end of the beginning.

2 Stormy Seas

Donnie Walsh doesn't take much time off. As president of the Indiana Pacers Corporation, which not only runs the NBA team but manages Market Square Arena, it is one luxury item he scarcely can afford.

When he returned from a short break immediately after the conclusion of the 1992-93 season, he wondered if the few days away from his desk were worth the overflowing in-box of problems he now faced.

"I picked," he said, "one hell of a week to go on vacation."

In Walsh's absence, the franchise sent an unofficial emissary to see if Kentucky's Rick Pitino would be interested in returning to the NBA not only as head coach, but also general manager.

The Atlanta Hawks had been the first to contact Pitino, with reports of a $2 million per year offer being discussed.

"He's probably on most everybody's wish list," said Kentucky athletic director C.M. Newton. "What of it?"

For Pitino, this meant another rite of summer: calling a press conference to deny all the rumors and re-state his commitment to the Wildcats.

"You don't ever leave happiness," Pitino said.

Walsh and the Pacers were still trying to find some.

That season followed what had become the team's pattern under coach Bob Hill, a wretched start (22-28) followed by a desperate climb toward respectability.

They won 19 of their final 32 games to finish .500, but needed a 94-88 win at home against Miami in the regular-season finale to finish 41-41 and tie Orlando for the final playoff spot.

It took five tie-breakers to determine who would go to the playoffs to face New York, and who would go into the lottery.

The first tie-breaker, head-to-head results, settled nothing. The Pacers and Magic split four games.

The second was their records against the Eastern Conference. Both teams were 27-29.

The third, records within the division, was bypassed because the Pacers competed in the Central, the Magic in the Atlantic.

The fourth, records against Eastern Conference teams in the playoffs, also produced identical 13-17 marks.

And so it came down to the fifth: point differential in games against each other.

None of the games were close. Orlando's two victories were by 14 and 13 points. The Pacers won twice by 16. The final tally, then, had the Pacers outscoring the Magic by a paltry five points over four games.

The Pacers thus drew the privilege of facing the top team in the Eastern Conference, the 60-22 Knicks, while Orlando headed to the lottery again.

For an Indiana franchise thoroughly used to bad fortune, this turned out to be an unusually cruel twist of fate.

Orlando, which was bestowed behemoth Shaquille O'Neal in the lottery the previous year, beat the longest of odds and drew the No. 1 pick again. The Magic shrewdly parlayed it into three future first-rounders plus guard Anfernee Hardaway in a trade with Golden State, which paid a steep price for Chris Webber.

"If we'd been in the lottery," said Walsh, reaching for a rationalization, "our ball wouldn't have been drawn."

Six months of games, of the emotional investment a franchise puts into a season, had boiled down to a difference of less than a couple of garbage-time three-pointers.

It wasn't right.

This, the league recognized, albeit too late to help the Pacers.

Not only did the NBA rewrite the fifth tie-breaker — which now compares records against playoff teams in the opposite conference — it radically altered the lottery procedure to further reduce the odds of a team with one of the better records winding up with the top pick.

In their own way, then, the Pacers had a major impact on the NBA that season. It just would not come on the court.

In the first round of the playoffs, they dropped the first two games in Madison Square Garden, then came home to an apathetic public. Only 11,380 bothered to show up at Market Square Arena for the Pacers' 116-93 drubbing of the Knicks — the game marked by John Starks' fabled head-butt of Reggie Miller. That victory did little to stir the populace.

For Game Four, attendance was 13,059. With Miller again torching the Knicks (he would wind up with 33 and averaged 31.5 in the series), the Pacers built a 72-60 lead in the third quarter, but the Knicks scored 10 straight points to make it a two-point game heading into the fourth.

With less than a minute left in regulation, the Pacers led 94-92, but Starks drove and fed Charles Oakley for a layup that forced overtime. There, Glenn "Doc" Rivers — who had come to New York in a trade with Larry Brown's Los Angeles Clippers — took over, hitting a trio of three-pointers in the extra period to carry the Knicks to a 109-100 victory.

"We proved we're a little better than most people thought," said coach Bob Hill. "I'm proud of this team."

For the players, the sense of accomplishment for extending the powerful Knicks to four difficult games was numbed by the reality of their situation. It was the fourth straight year the Pacers had lost in the first round.

Only once, in the compelling series with Boston in 1991, had they pushed it as far as five games.

In six playoff trips spanning 13 years, the Pacers had produced a record of 4-17, easily the worst of any NBA franchise with the exception of the most recent wave of expansion teams.

"We gave them a good run and we played some good basketball," said Detlef Schrempf, "but we lost, so we're still in the same boat."

And the usual course was charted: stormy seas.

The day after Walsh returned from his vacation, Hill was fired despite a 113-108 record and three straight playoff trips. There was no failure in Hill's tenure. There just wasn't enough success.

Reaching the playoffs every year is only meaningful if a team can realistically expect to compete for a championship. Otherwise, all a playoff spot does is ensure mediocre draft position, dooming the team to repeat its cycle.

The Pacers had become Sisyphus, perpetually unable to roll their boulder over the crest.

"The easy answer is to say, 'Let's go get a superstar,' " Walsh said. "OK, how do you do that? Look at the Dream Team. Only one of those guys has ever been traded (Charles Barkley from Philadelphia to Phoenix). Once they become superstars, they just aren't available."

Coaches, on the other hand, seem always to offer an abundant market.

"That's what they do here," said Hill. "The history of this franchise has been, 'We didn't do well enough, let's change coaches.' This place has been a graveyard for coaches."

Walsh wondered if he, too, had reached the end of the line.

He had hardly gotten a ringing endorsement from club co-owner Herb Simon the day before the Hill firing.

Asked about Walsh's job security, Simon said, "I'd like to see his report on the team. Personally, I'd like to be associated with him for a long time, but there are other considerations."

Walsh, who had fought for years to establish a niche for professional basketball in a market dominated by high school and college hysteria, sounded like a man on the ropes.

"I haven't spoken to the Simons about my job," he said May 18, the day Hill was fired, "but, from what I read, my job is open."

"I put the coach and the team together . . . If they feel that they have to replace me and that will improve the situation, that's their decision and I'll accept it."

"I've liked being with the Indiana Pacers. I've enjoyed working with Herb and Mel Simon. I like living in the city of Indianapolis. But the foremost reason that I'm here is to try to make this a better basketball team."

"That's the number one thing I want to see here. And if it has to happen without me, then that's the answer and I'll accept it. But until I get a decision from ownership, I have my responsibilities and this news conference is the beginning of my responsibilities for next year."

Walsh's back clearly was against a wall of his own construction. He had to present ownership with a plan for decisive action and make bold moves.

The race against mediocrity was starting to look like it was being run on a treadmill. That, Walsh realized all too well, would mean no winner.

He would need to obtain an impact player, an impact coach, or both.

Quickly.

* * *

Herb Simon had to determine if he needed a new general manager. Walsh's record was much like that of the team: in trades, drafts and contract negotiations, he was right around .500.

At this point in the franchise's development — Walsh's original five-year plan had stretched to seven, with no end in sight — Simon was growing weary of mediocrity. He had several close friends who also were NBA owners, including the L.A. Clippers' Donald Sterling and Philadelphia's Harold Katz, and they both were men who more often erred on the side of aggression.

Simon was a far more patient man. Through his experience as a real estate developer, he had learned that not every shopping mall could be built on schedule, but that did not mean the project should be abandoned. He understood the unpredictable nature of both his businesses.

He also was fiercely loyal. Walsh had served him well, bringing his franchise out of the muck and cleaning it up nicely. He wanted to hear what Walsh had to say about his plans for the summer before he made any decision about a change in management.

Not that Simon was above dangling a few lines to see what he might catch. Pitino couldn't be landed.

What about Larry Bird?

The one man whose legend in Indiana exceeded that of Bobby Knight, Bird's bad back had required career-ending surgery. Simon did more than wonder if Bird might consider a return to his home state to take up coaching. And, if it took that to get him to come, serving as general manager.

"I just called him to see what he'd think," said Simon. "He said his back wouldn't let him do it." With Pitino and Bird scratched off his personal list, Simon wanted to see who Walsh recommended.

Since the master stroke of hiring Ramsay in '86, Walsh had not gone for marquee names. Versace was a relatively obscure assistant coach with Detroit when Walsh picked him over NBA veteran Bill Blair. Hill, too, was known mainly as somebody else's assistant — to Brown at Kansas, to Hubie Brown with the Knicks, and then to Versace.

It was clear from Walsh's recommendations that there would be no more gambling. His list had nothing but sure bets.

He figured if ownership was willing to throw $2 million at Pitino, he had a mandate to go after coaching talent that would command top dollar.

Lenny Wilkens was available after seven seasons in Cleveland, three of which produced 50 (or more) victories. So was Mike Fratello, who had rebuilt a young Atlanta team into an annual contender in the late-1980s. Former Houston and Milwaukee coach Del Harris, a native of Orleans, Indiana, also was an option.

Jim Lynam, the Philadelphia general manager, wasn't interested in coming back as a coach. Don Nelson, thought to be dissatisfied with his power base in Golden State, likewise rebuffed initial overtures.

There was one other name, but it came with an asterisk. There were rumors floating around the league that Brown might be free of his obligation to the Clippers. Walsh was unsure of Brown's status, but it merited checking out.

* * *

Brown was the most successful coach the Clippers had hired since moving West from Buffalo. He replaced Mike Schuler midway through the 1991-92 season and finished 23-12 to produce a 45-37 record, the best since Jack Ramsay took the 1975-76 Buffalo Braves to a 46-36 mark.

He entered the 1992-93 season with a number of players facing uncertain futures, primarily franchise cornerstone Danny Manning, who was scheduled to become an unrestricted free agent on July 1, 1994. Point guard Mark Jackson would be given an extension. Ken Norman was in the final year of his contract and would wind up in Milwaukee. Ron Harper would become a free agent at the same time as Manning.

The relationship between Brown and Manning had soured. At one point, the two got into a shouting match that went from the team bus into a hotel lobby. After four years at Kansas and one and one half in L.A., it seemed obvious the ties between the two had been severely frayed.

It became just as obvious to Brown that Manning would not re-sign with the Clippers, so he pressed management to avoid a festering situation by trading him prior to the February 25, 1993, deadline.

"We needed to move on," said Brown, "and have a plan."

Several alternatives were discussed, but one stood out. The night before the deadline, Brown thought the Clippers had a three-way deal with Dallas and Golden State.

The Warriors would get Manning. The Mavericks would wind up with Sarunas Marciulionis and Chris Gatling. The Clippers would get the rights to unsigned rookie Jim Jackson and a 1993 first-round pick from the Warriors (that turned out to be Chris Webber).

It never happened.

Brown said he was left alone in a conference room while the franchise's three executive vice presidents, Andy Roeser, Elgin Baylor and Harley Frankel, met privately. When they returned, they told Brown there would be no deal. Manning would stay for the time being.

Not having the cooperation of management made the situation intolerable for Brown. He called for a meeting with owner Donald Sterling and submitted his resignation, effective at the end of the season. Sterling, who wanted Brown to stay, met with the coach's agent, Joe Glass, to offer a proposal.

Brown would stay on to coach as long as he wanted, then move into management. "I would say," Glass said, "it was a lifetime deal."

Weeks passed, and the proposal never turned into a firm offer. Sterling then came back with a different idea, a one-year deal. Brown thought that would be workable, under certain circumstances: namely an organization-wide agreement on how the team would be run.

Again, no written offer was forthcoming.

After the Clippers, who finished 41-41, were beaten 84-80 by Houston in the fifth game of their first-round series, Glass sent Sterling a confirmation of Brown's February letter of resignation.

It was a particularly odd situation. Sterling didn't want Brown to leave. Brown didn't want to leave. And yet, the two could not agree on circumstances under which he would stay.

"There's a big difference in being a successful builder and being a successful basketball entrepreneur," Glass said. "When you're a builder, you're dealing with brick and mortar, which have no feelings. People, you have to deal with differently."

For Brown, who still maintains a home in Los Angeles, it was a particularly frustrating experience.

"I liked Los Angeles. I honestly thought that would be my last job," Brown said. "What I didn't like was we couldn't make a decision, we had no chain of command, we had no gameplan."

Adding to the confusion, Brown and his wife left immediately after the season for a vacation in Hawaii. There had been no announcement of his departure from the Clippers.

Walsh, who wasn't yet sure if he could formally contact Brown, couldn't resist the line: "Here today, gone to Maui."

* * *

Simon was impressed by Walsh's presentation, with one exception. The one name on the list he had reservations about was Brown. Though highly successful, the coach had a reputation as a vagabond. Not only that, he seemed wedded to the passing game offense.

One of the great revelations of the previous season had been that the Pacers, as constructed, simply were not a passing-game team. Lacking instinctive players, they needed the structure of set plays. Hill, also a passing-game enthusiast, didn't realize this until very late in his tenure and, by then, it was too late.

The May 26 meeting didn't settle the coaching situation, but it did resolve that of Walsh.

"I told him he doesn't have to worry about his status," said Simon. "He'll be here for the whole season, as long as he wants. Next year, we'll re-evaluate again."

How did Walsh read it?

"I'm going to run the franchise," he said, "until somebody tells me to stop running the franchise."

To get a top head coach, he had to sprint.

The Atlanta Hawks moved quickly and hired Wilkens, who had thought he was the Clippers' top candidate to replace Brown.

That sent Walsh and the Simons to Los Angeles to sit down with Brown, who had become Walsh's top choice when it became clear he was free from the Clippers. Brown, more of a teacher than a psychologist, didn't know if he wanted to stay in the NBA. After meeting the Pacer owners at the Ritz-Carlton Hotel in Santa Monica, he wasn't sure he'd get the opportunity right away.

"I wasn't completely comfortable I was the guy they wanted," Brown said. "I knew how Donnie felt about me, but I didn't know how they felt about me. I'd never really been interviewed for a job before, and I could tell they were trying to learn about me."

Walsh convinced the Simons that Brown was the right man for the job; he had a history of pumping life into dormant teams.

"They'll love him," Walsh said. "But he'll drive me nuts. He'll be after me every day to get this guy or that guy."

A week after the meeting in L.A., on June 7, Brown was introduced as the Pacers' fourth head coach in six years. He had signed a five-year, $6.3 million contract, easily the richest ever bestowed upon a coach by this franchise. In it, there was a two-year escape clause. After the 1994-95 season, either party could terminate the contract at no penalty.

"I'm hopeful this will be my last stop," Brown said, "but I've said that before."

Brown immediately stated what would be his mantra throughout the summer, training camp, the preseason, the regular season and the playoffs. He was, above all else, consistent.

"You win in this league," he said, "by playing hard every night, defending and rebounding the ball. . . . As a coach, you build character by putting people on the floor who want to defend, who want to do the little things it takes to succeed."

Both Brown and Walsh made it clear that hiring a coach was merely the first step in reorganizing the team.

"We have some terrific players here," Brown said. "I have to find out what I can do to help them get better, and we're going to all have to find out what areas we have to improve on.

"But it's obvious to me you can't stand pat and be successful in this league. Even the teams that have won have made changes."

That, the players expected.

"I don't know what their plans are," said Detlef Schrempf, who had requested a trade the summer before. "I'm sure they still want to make some changes within the team. I'm sure any coach would want to do something because we've had the same bunch together for a while now and we haven't taken the next step."

Just exactly what else the hiring of Brown would mean was a mystery to all except one.

Greg Dreiling had played for Brown at Kansas, and was the starting center on the 35-4 team of 1985-86. He had come to the Pacers as a second-round pick following that year and had been with the team ever since. He didn't know it at the time, but his days with the team were numbered.

"I know when he came to Kansas, at first the team fought what he wanted," Dreiling said. "He wanted it to be like a family, guys who cared about each other all the time.

"When the guys started listening to that, they saw how much he was right about in the basketball arena. By my senior year, we were a very good team and we were very, very close on and off the court."

Everyone agreed on one thing: the 1993-94 Indiana Pacers would be different.

Whether they would be better was up for discussion.

3 Hello, Larry

If they couldn't obtain an impact player, the Pacers would at least have an impact coach.

With one exception (UCLA), every team Larry Brown had coached, ABA, college and NBA, posted its best-ever record.

The Carolina Cougars were 35-49 under Tom Meschery in 1971-72. Brown took over and, with the addition of former Tar Heel Billy Cunningham—legally forced to fulfill his earlier commitment to the ABA team—they improved by 22 victories the following year to post the best record in the ABA. For that, Brown was named coach of the year.

Brown inherited the Denver Nuggets from Alex Hannum, who had gone 37-47 in 1973-74. With another North Carolina import, Bobby Jones, playing a major role, the Nuggets jumped to 65-19 in '74-75, once again, the ABA's best record.

The next year would bring his first, and only, trip to a professional championship series. With yet another imported Carolinian (albeit N.C. State), David Thompson, the Nuggets reached the last ABA championship series ever played. In a remarkable series that pitted Thompson against Julius Erving's New York Nets, Denver was beaten in six games.

After the ABA-NBA merger, he stayed with the Nuggets two and one half years before leaving the team in Walsh's hands.

He then headed to UCLA for two successful years, including a berth in the NCAA championship game in 1980, before leaving for the NBA's New Jersey Nets.

Too quickly, as it turned out.

He was hired by athletic director J.D. Morgan, who had a tremendous influence on Brown. When Morgan died of heart problems during the 1980-81 season, Brown was confused about what to do.

"I don't think I ever would have left had he stayed," Brown said, "but when I left, I knew I made a mistake."

The Nets had been wretched the year before, going 24-58 for Kevin Loughery and Bob MacKinnon. Brown pushed for sweeping changes. High-scoring guard Ray Williams was signed away from the rival New York Knicks. Two first-round picks brought Maryland teammates Buck Williams and Albert King. They weren't from Carolina, but at least they came out of the Atlantic Coast Conference. The Nets went 44-38, a 20-game improvement that, at the time, was the biggest in NBA history.

The Nets were on their way to even bigger things the next season. When word leaked that Brown had applied for the job at Kansas, he was relieved of command by owner Joe Taub with six games left in the regular season. The Nets, 47-29 at the time, went 2-4 for Bill Blair and were swept out of the playoffs in the first round by the Knicks, a bitter disappointment. It would be Blair's only head coaching opportunity in the NBA, and he had been betrayed by circumstance.

Professionally, Brown had a great run at Kansas. Personally, he was going through problems with his second wife that would end in divorce.

The Jayhawks won the Big Eight tournament his first year, lost in the second round of the NCAA tournament to Chuck Person's Auburn team in 1985, won the Big Eight and went to the Final Four to finish 35-4 the following year. After being eliminated in the Sweet 16 in 1987, Brown and Danny Manning won the national championship in 1988.

Then came an unexpected chance to correct his one great mistake. UCLA called and wanted Brown back. Once again, though, the timing was terrible. Shortly after the Jayhawks won the title, Brown was on a plane to Los Angeles.

He was torn between the euphoria of the moment at Kansas, and his strong feelings for UCLA. But officials at UCLA wanted a quick decision, which Brown wasn't prepared to make.

He wound up back in the refuge of the NBA, with San Antonio.

There, he experienced the only losing season in his 22-year career, a 21-61 record in 1988-89, but the franchise had an ace in the hole. David Robinson, taken with the No. 1 pick in 1987, would be available for the 1989-90 season after he finished his commitment to the U.S. Navy.

With Robinson and fellow rookie Sean Elliott leading the way, the Spurs broke Brown's old record. They improved by 35 wins to 56-26, taking the Midwest Division. In the postseason, the Spurs swept the Nuggets, then faced a Portland team that had improved by 20 wins in Rick Adelman's first season.

The two emerging powers waged a seven-game war, with Games Five and Seven in Portland going into overtime. They both also went to the Trail Blazers, who would advance to the NBA Finals.

After another division title and 55 victories the following year, the Spurs entered the playoffs with high expectations. They were upset by seventh-seeded Golden State in four games. That set the stage for what would follow.

When the team sputtered to a 21-17 mark early in the 1991-92 season, Brown was fired for the first time in his career. He didn't stay out of work long. The Clippers, going nowhere under Mike Schuler, snapped him up and went 23-12 the rest of the way to finish 45-37 and reach the playoffs. It was the best season since the franchise had been located in Buffalo and the team coached by Jack Ramsay.

What sticks out, of course, is the number of opportunities Brown has taken. His reputation as a vagabond was so well-known, that sometimes it seemed as if he was singlehandedly responsible for keeping the word "peripatetic" in general circulation. Brown's friends know someone who is deeply rooted, though not in a place. Brown's home is, and always will be, on a basketball court.

"You don't get to the core of Brown," Walsh said, "until you focus on what he does on the floor.

"I've been saying things like, 'He's among the best,' or 'I haven't seen many better,' but the reality is, he is the best. He is. He's phenomenal."

Those same friends find it difficult to describe Brown in personal terms.

"It's difficult to separate him from basketball," said Doug Moe. "Larry's got a heart of gold. He's a terrific guy. He always wants to do the right thing, be nice to everybody. He's never on time, except when it comes to basketball. In this business, you make a lot of money, but money doesn't mean anything to Larry. It doesn't motivate him. He's always looking for Utopia."

Could Indiana be it?

"He could be there forever," Moe said, "but don't bet on it."

It is rare to find someone in basketball who lacks an opinion on Brown, for his is an image national in scope, enigmatic by nature and confusing to the casual fan.

A relative few, however, have come across Harv. Harv is a much easier man to decipher, and befriend.

"The only people who you hear of that don't like Larry are the ones who don't know him," said Moe, one of many introduced to NBA coaching by Lawrence Harvey Brown. "To me, he's more Harv than anything else. He's a really down-to-earth, normal guy that people try to make into something else."

Irvine supported Moe's analysis.

"He's definitely shy," he said. "He's more comfortable in the simple things of life than in trying to wheel and deal. He's going to tell you what he thinks, but he's not a manipulator. When he says something, you know what he means. He's really one of the more honest guys I've ever been around."

This would be Brown's fifth NBA team — the third in three seasons — and his eighth head coaching job.

That he has never failed somehow is tainted, in the eyes of critics, by his inability, or unwillingness, to stick around. His friends point out Brown spent five years with the Denver Nuggets and five at Kansas, lengthy tenures in today's world of the coach du jour.

The greater reality is Brown simply hasn't waited to get fired, an inevitability of his profession he has avoided all but once, when the ax fell in San Antonio.

"Other coaches do the same thing," Walsh said, "but Larry's been successful everywhere he's been so people say, 'Geez, why did he leave?' And he has always been in top-level jobs."

Still, Brown can not escape the reputation. His father was a traveling salesman, after all.

"Right off the bat, I was perceived as a wanderer," Brown said. "I think I've ticked people off because I wasn't fired and they've been mad at me for leaving.

"I'd like to be like coach (Dean) Smith or Bobby (Knight) and stay in one place forever, and maybe I'm still looking for that place. But that doesn't make me a bad person. . . . My career has been so different from anybody else's, people maybe shake their heads and wonder how he could keep doing this."

The answer is clear: if he can coach it, he will come.

This is a man, as he put it, "consumed by this thing," even at the age of 54, even after his 22nd season. The desire to coach, the energy to produce, has yet to diminish.

"You're not going to see a public persona with him," Walsh said. "He's pure basketball. That's what he does. Wherever he is, whatever he does, it's all basketball.

"Privately, I think most of the people he's worked for really like him and that's why they don't want him to leave. He really, truly has a talent for coaching, which I saw when I first got with him. He starts from a teaching standpoint and he really knows what he's talking about. . . . And, he pushes teams, he really pushes.

"As a matter of fact, he pushes so hard, after three or four years, they need to leave each other."

For a coach of Brown's caliber, there always will be another team that needs re-building, another city that needs revitalizing, another program that needs instant credibility.

"Basketball is his life," said Moe. "He'll die coaching. He's just one of those guys that will coach until he can't coach anymore."

It doesn't matter what level, though he has spent most of his career in the ABA, then NBA, he doesn't see himself as a pro coach.

"I've always had reservations about that," he said. "I've always looked at myself as a teacher, and I still don't know if this is the proper forum to coach and teach the way I feel the most comfortable.

"I love the game because it is basketball and there are no outside distractions — recruiting, going to class, summer jobs — and it's basketball in the purest sense. But you're dealing with older guys that have families and have business. They're mini-corporations.

"I never get the feeling you can develop relationships like you can in high school or college, which is important to me."

Brown frequently has said his ultimate career goal is to wind up in a high school gym, teaching and influencing teenagers. And he's serious.

"When I'm finished with this, I'd kind of like to go back and do things for kids the way things were done for me," Brown said. "I've had so many people do things that helped put me in this position, and most of them were coaches. I love the game. I'd love the opportunity to sit down and teach and watch kids grow."

Brown's father died of a heart attack when Larry was seven years old. Growing up as a player, coaches became his role models. When he became a coach, he felt much of that same responsibility. He wants to be more than a boss to his players. He wants them to trust him, to confide in him, to stand up to him when they feel their cause is just. Most of all, he wants them to listen, and learn.

"The frustration I have is we don't have enough time (to teach)," he said. "I don't blame NBA players. It's society. People don't look at coaches the same way they did when I was growing up.

"You look at Bobby (Knight) and Gene (Keady). Those are two tough guys and disciplinarians. But I'd take their kids any time because they've been coached.

"I've found pros receptive to coaching, but they can't feel it's criticism. . . . Deep down, they will respect you if they feel you care about them."

As a professional player — "one of the last of the pure point guards," said the Pacers' veteran scout, Al Menendez — Brown led the ABA in assists three straight years and was the MVP of the league's first All-Star game, a feat he later apologized for because his team lost. He lost one championship, with New Orleans in 1968, but won the next year when the Oakland Oaks beat the Pacers in five games.

As a coach, he reached the NCAA Final Four with UCLA in 1981 in Indianapolis (losing to Louisville in the championship game) and won a championship with Kansas in 1988, but his previous three shots at the NBA title had ended in the first round.

"The only thing left undone for him," said Walsh, "is an NBA championship. "

He also has a personal mission to win the title with an ABA remnant. He got to the Western Conference finals with Denver in 1978, reached the playoffs in 1982 with a New Jersey team that had been wretched the year before, and won a Midwest Division title with San Antonio in 1990.

The Pacers, who owned the ABA, had never gotten out of hock in the NBA. This was his challenge, to reclaim respect for the franchise and, ultimately, the league that spawned it.

"Toward the end, I thought our league was better than the NBA," he said. "I'm appreciative of the fact they took four teams into the league, and they recognized some of our rules that were good. But there has never been the camaraderie that we had. "

Brown didn't know it at the time but, with the Pacers, he would be able to develop the kind of close player-coach relationships he so cherishes, and would be surrounded by friends in management.

In many ways, it would turn into the closest thing to Utopia he had yet experienced in the NBA.

* * *

To begin the process of evaluation, Brown first met with the players individually. He tested them by telling them things he thought they might not like to hear. In their reactions, he would learn much about their attitudes.

The two strongest personalities on the team got the stiffest tests.

Knowing Reggie Miller's reputation was that of a player who eschewed defense and who never had assumed a mantle of leadership, Brown demanded those two things. "You're probably not going to like this," Brown said to begin the discussion, then laid out his demands. Miller would be a more vocal leader and he would think primarily of stopping his man, rather than outscoring him.

"Reggie said he'd do anything," Brown said. "He thought he knew what it took to win, but he said, 'Show me.' "

The coach knew Schrempf had spent two years as the game's best sixth man before moving into the starting lineup for 66 games at small forward the previous season. An intensely proud player, Schrempf felt his role should've been firmly established, not up for examination. But Brown hedged about his plans for Schrempf, hinting that he might return to the bench. Because Schrempf was primarily a post-up scorer, Brown said, he took opportunities away from center Rik Smits and power forward Dale Davis. He wasn't sure if Schrempf could play small forward the way Brown wanted the position played.

"I thought Detlef looked at me real suspiciously, about my motives," Brown said. "I frankly felt Detlef would be a real asset to the team. But my feeling was Dale and Rik were two of the most important parts of the team. In order for those guys to play a lot, Detlef had to be the small forward.

"I don't know if Detlef really felt comfortable with our conversation. He called me up and said, "I get the feeling you might not want to start me." I said, "I don't know if that's true, but you're going to play the most minutes on the team. I don't care who starts, it's who finishes and plays the most."

Schrempf took that as a clear signal Brown not only lacked faith in him as a small forward — he had, after all, made the All-Star team at that position in '92-93 — but as a starter.

He told Brown he would not accept a return to the bench.

"If I'm playing on a contending team with an All-Star in front of me, I'd have no problem," Schrempf said. "I've made enough sacrifices. I don't see anyone we have who deserves to start in front of me, so I said no. No way."

There was another factor standing between Brown and Schrempf: a scenario eerily similar to that involving Manning and the Clippers.

Schrempf, entering the fifth year of a 10-year contract, could opt for unrestricted free agency after the season. He had requested a trade the summer before and maintained an off-season home in Seattle. The Pacers feared he would sign with the SuperSonics.

Two years before, the Sonics had offered Derrick McKey for Schrempf, a deal that never really left the table. Brown now knew it, and several other possibilities, would have to be considered more seriously.

Miller passed his test, but Schrempf's grade was incomplete.

Brown also had to establish a philosophy for this team. Everything would start with defense, that much he knew. He was more uncertain about the offense. A passing-game specialist, and ardent believer, all Brown had heard was that the Pacers simply were not a passing-game team.

Hill had tried to employ it the previous season. Not until he abandoned the passing game did the Pacers turn things around.

"He told me he's coming off it," said Walsh. "He'll use it as a part of his repertoire, which is good. I don't think this is a passing-game team. But, through the course of the season, there are times you need a free lance offense to get some movement.

"He's more defensive-oriented. His thinking is from the defensive end. He's not out there thinking, 'How am I going to get points?' He thinks, 'How will I defend?' From the defense, he wants to get points."

Brown had to see for himself. "I think our game is changing a lot," he said. "The reason I like the passing game is that every day in practice, you have to guard against it.

"I do know we will try to run. I do know they've been well-coached. I'm going to try to put these guys in a position where they do the things they do best. We're all going to have to learn to guard every night. We'll all have to become a better rebounding team. It doesn't take great skills to do either of those two things."

Another of Brown's immediate tasks was to assemble a staff. With the Clippers, he had longtime assistant R.C. Buford, Quin Snyder (his son-in-law, married to Brown's daughter Kristen), John Hammond and Mack Calvin.

None would come with him to the Pacers.

From Hill's staff, Ed Badger, Randy Wittman and Bob Ociepka were in limbo. Badger had another year on his contract and would wind up with a bureaucratic title, special assistant to the president. Oceipka latched on with the L.A. Clippers and Wittman headed to Dallas to join up with fellow Hoosier Quinn Buckner.

Brown wanted assistants who had been head coaches and wanted to be head coaches again.

His first choice was Doug Moe, who had been fired after going 19-37 in his first season with Philadelphia and was widely thought to be in no mood to return to anyone's bench. "I don't want Doug to do it," Brown said, "unless he absolutely wants to."

He didn't. When Moe met with Brown, he said he only wanted to work the home games. That wasn't enough of a commitment to satisfy Walsh.

After talking to a Rolodex full of candidates, Brown settled on Garfield Heard and Bill Blair.

Fired after the Mavericks' 11-71 season, Heard brought a quiet nobility to the bench. He would work with the big men.

Blair, who had been a Washington assistant the previous seven seasons, nearly had become the Pacers head coach three years before, when Walsh instead hired Versace. Though he had not maintained a relationship with Brown since their turbulent breakup in New Jersey, when Blair called, Brown was anxious to listen. The two had a history.

When Brown was with Denver, Blair was the head coach at Colorado University. The two became close, and Blair was at the top of Brown's list when he went to the Nets.

With two veterans lined up, Brown went for a prospect. He hired former Duke defensive wizard Billy King, who had spent the last four years as an assistant at Illinois State. King, 27, was the national defensive player of the year in 1988 and had stayed in shape. In this strange season, that would pay off.

The first set of personnel decisions involved the roster, namely, free agents George McCloud and Greg Dreiling.

McCloud had his big chance in '92-93, when Hill basically handed him the starting small forward job coming out of training camp. He let it slip away. When the Pacers made him a 1989 lottery pick out of Florida State, every aspect of McCloud's game was questioned but one, his shooting.

If nothing else, the Pacers could count on that. Or so they thought.

McCloud proved incapable of playing the point, but was a solid ballhandler for his size and a good passer. His defense was adequate, but he had a thing against rebounds.

With all of that, had he been even an adequate shooter, McCloud would've had a long NBA career. In four seasons, though, he shot 39 percent. The Pacers would make no attempt to re-sign him.

Dreiling, the quintessential slow, white backup center, had been with the team since '86 and seemed to have a strong relationship with Brown. He became expendable, though, when athletic big man Antonio Davis was signed as a free agent. He, too, would be allowed to leave.

The next step would be Brown's first draft with the Pacers.

Brown likes his rosters to comprise at least five big men capable of defending the low post at either power forward or center (they had Dale Davis, Antonio Davis, Rik Smits and LaSalle Thompson), three point guards (they had Pooh Richardson and Vern Fleming) and five athletes to fill in the "skill" positions.

This was the strength of the team. They had Miller, a former All-Star, at shooting guard. They had Schrempf, a 1993 All-Star, at small forward.

But there wasn't much depth.

Malik Sealy, a first-round pick in '92, never gained Hill's confidence and remained a question mark. The team wanted to see if he could shoot well enough to be a backup to Miller. He had virtually every other element they desired. He probably was the fastest runner on the team. Not a dribble-penetration creator, he could put the ball on the floor two or three times and get into the lane for a shot. He was a sneaky offensive rebounder, able to rise out of a crowd of more earthbound bodies to snatch the ball. Most importantly to Brown, Sealy had the mental toughness and physical attributes — long arms and quick feet — to be an excellent defender. Determining Sealy's role would be one of the major projects of the preseason.

Kenny Williams, a 6-9 pogo stick of a small forward, would also need a long look. A raw player but gifted athlete, Williams was taken with a second-round pick in 1990, right after Antonio Davis, despite his near-total lack of collegiate experience. One of the nation's most highly recruited players as a senior at Northeastern High in Elizabeth City, North Carolina, Williams settled matters by signing with North Carolina.

He was thought to be a prize for the Tar Heels, a member of one of the most impressive high school All-America teams ever. The other first-teamers were Alonzo Mourning of Chesapeake, Virginia, Shawn Kemp of Elkhart, Indiana, Billy Owens of Carlisle, Pennsylvania, and Chris Jackson (now Mahmoud Abdul-Rauf) of Gulfport, Mississippi. It was a powerful class. Of the 20 players named to the first four All-America teams that year by Street & Smith's yearbook, 14 currently are in the NBA.

Among the honorable mention selections was a 6-7 forward for Tolentine High in the Bronx. Sealy, his name was.

Poor grades kept Williams from ever attending Carolina. He enrolled at Barton County Community College in Great Bend, Kansas, and played one year. He transferred back to his hometown school, Elizabeth City State, but had to sit out the '89-90 season with more academic problems.

When the Pacers drafted him, he had exactly one season of junior college experience. At age 21, he was one of the youngest players ever to make the roster.

Three years later, the team still was waiting for Williams to grow up. A leaper in the class of a young Dominique Wilkins, Williams never really developed the other areas of his game. He could hit a 15-foot jumper and his legs enabled him to get rebounds, but his defense was atrocious. It didn't help matters that, in three seasons, he had played for two head coaches (Versace and Hill) who had precious little patience for developing young players.

Williams' progress would be another preseason issue to be resolved.

There were others. Sam Mitchell didn't fit into Brown's mold. A power forward by nature but a small forward by stature, the 6-7 Mitchell would have to prove himself.

prove himself. So would Sean Green, another flashy dunker who had distinguished himself only by averaging more than 30 field goal attempts for every 48 minutes played.

This was a team with far too many uncertainties. Either these players had not lived up to their potential or had been vastly overrated. They needed help, and the 14th pick in a relatively thin draft didn't promise much.

"You can probably get help with the top eight picks," said Atlanta general manager Pete Babcock, "and maybe there are a couple after that you can feel good about, but you can't expect to get a big contributor right away."

The fifth or sixth pick, however, might just solve a handful of problems all by itself. At either of those spots, Walsh and Brown expected to be able to select the nation's best senior, a versatile 6-foot-7-inch swingman who they felt could step in and start at small forward immediately.

Indiana University's Calbert Cheaney also figured to sell more than a few tickets.

Walsh historically had frowned on the concept of bringing in players who had become celebrities as local collegians. In 1987, the Indianapolis populace wanted him to use the 11th pick on Hoosier hero Steve Alford. When he selected Miller instead, Walsh was vilified.

Walsh's logic was sound. Even though these players might sell a few tickets and generate good will in the short term, that would all backfire exponentially if the player turned out to be a bust. As popular a move as drafting Alford would've been, cutting him would've brought death threats and two cancellations for every ticket Alford had originally sold.

An assistant in '85-86, Walsh saw the reaction when the Pacers released Quinn Buckner, who clearly was finished. I.U. coach Bob Knight, zealously defending one of his prized former pupils, chastised pro basketball in general and the organization in particular.

Perhaps in no other market would the release of a 32-year-old backup guard averaging 3.7 points a game have created such animosity. The only way Walsh would move on such a player again was with no risk at all. It had to be a sure thing. Cheaney, they decided, was just that. Obtaining a pick to use on Cheaney would be the first priority.

It was clear who the first four players picked would be, if not the order: Michigan forward Chris Webber, Brigham Young center Shawn Bradley, Memphis State guard Anfernee Hardaway and Kentucky forward Jamal Mashburn.

To ensure the ability to select Cheaney, the Pacers felt they had to have the fifth pick, which belonged to Minnesota. For bait, Walsh would dangle Schrempf, plus the No. 14 pick, a juicy package. "The offer I made was sick," said Walsh, who thought it would be impossible to turn down. The Timberwolves thought otherwise, and offered a flat rejection.

Still, there was an alternative. Minnesota probably wouldn't draft Cheaney, but Washington surely would at No. 6.

The offer was made to the Bullets, who had sounder logic for turning it down: in Tom Gugliotta, they already had a younger version of Schrempf.

A week before the draft, they knew Cheaney was beyond their reach. "We just couldn't get it done," said Irvine. "I swear to God, if we offered Schrempf, Smits and Miller, no one would take them to trade up. It's amazing how much better these picks become the closer you get to the draft."

And so the Pacers confronted the reality that they would be picking from the middle of the pack once more.

They interviewed three point guards (Nick Van Exel of Cincinnati, James Robinson of Alabama and Lindsey Hunter of Jackson State), three shooting guards (Thomas Hill of Duke, Scott Burrell of Connecticut and Terry Dehere of Seton Hall), two small forwards (Chris Mills of Arizona and George Lynch of North Carolina) and two centers (Luther Wright of Seton Hall and Scott Haskin of Oregon State).

"I'm beginning to get excited about this draft at our pick," said Walsh. "Between the guys we interviewed and the potential of guys who could fall to us, we're going to have a pretty good selection."

He would have to face the wrath of a large portion of the populace, though. Another Indiana University senior, guard Greg Graham, was going to be a first-round pick, and local support for his selection was strong. Graham thought he had helped his cause by spending the summer as an intern under Pacers public relations director Dale Ratermann, but not enough to merit a long look at No. 14.

Just who would the Pacers take?

They really liked Van Exel's toughness and defensive ability, but his shot selection in college was poor, and his attitude was brought into question when he missed an interview with Charlotte. Mills was an excellent shooter who could play either big guard or small forward, but the Pacers already had Sealy and Williams and had given up on neither.

The decision was made to go big and perhaps find someone to either push Smits, or at the very least provide solid backup. Stipanovich, who has lived in Oregon since his retirement, had seen Haskin play several times and called to offer an enthusiastic endorsement.

A 6-11, 250-pound center, Haskin could shoot hooks with either hand, was a long-armed shot-blocker and physical defender with adequate athletic skills. The biggest question mark on his resume was a back injury that required surgery and forced him to sit out the 1990-91 season. He came back from it strong, though, producing two straight all-Pacific 10 Conference seasons. Going into draft night, the Pacers knew that Haskin was their man.

The first round went about as expected until something shocking happened. Jerry West fooled everyone by drafting exactly who he said he wanted.

West, the Lakers' general manager, is one of the best pre-draft smokescreeners in the business. If he says he's going big, everyone assumes he's going small. If he says he likes a guy, he probably hates him, and vice versa. So when word leaked out of Los Angeles in the days before the draft that West wanted to take North Carolina forward George Lynch, few took it seriously.

Lynch was projected much later in the first round, meaning West must really want Van Exel or Acie Earl or Chris Mills, the latter an L.A. native. When West actually took Lynch, then the L.A. Clippers followed at No. 13 by selecting Dehere, a couple of names the Pacers hadn't counted on had slipped to them.

Earl, widely rated ahead of Haskin, was there. So was Mills, a potent scorer. Walsh was unfazed.

Anticipating the fallout, Walsh did not make the announcement. He sent radio play-by-play man Mark Boyle to the podium to let the 3,000 fans gathered at Market Square Arena in on Walsh's little secret. When Boyle spoke Haskin's name, the arena erupted into violent boos. Chants of "Walsh must go," echoed through the building for several minutes before most of the angry throng departed.

Three picks later, Graham — the people's choice — went to Charlotte, then was involved in a three-team deal that sent him to Philadelphia. The Hornets wound up with Hersey Hawkins and Eddie Johnson. Seattle picked up Kendall Gill. The Sixers got Graham and Dana Barros.

The second round proved just as interesting, with Van Exel's name falling like a rock. The Pacers held the 39th pick and knew Van Exel wouldn't get past West at No. 37. They tried desperately to put together a package, but West wouldn't budge. The Lakers got a young point guard who would work his way into their starting lineup.

The Pacers wound up with Duke shooting guard Thomas Hill, who would not make the team. With the 51st pick, they took Great Britain's Spencer Dunkley, a 6-10 center who played for Delaware, who would not even entertain the possibility of coming to training camp. He headed straight to a professional league in Israel.

For all the anticipation and all the hype, the draft produced little.

The biggest news that night had little to do with the draft itself. Richardson, scheduled to become a restricted free agent July 1, agreed to a seven-year, $18.2 million contract. It was an astonishing deal for a player whose future with the team was uncertain, and who had come off an alarmingly poor season.

Walsh wanted to send two messages with the massive extension. He wanted the players to realize the franchise's commitment to Richardson was serious. And he wanted Richardson to feel it as well. Those messages would soon be lost, if they ever got through.

Brown sent one of his own to Schrempf in his post-draft comments addressing the team's needs.

Asked to expand on an earlier statement about the team needing "a legitimate three man (small forward)," Brown pressed ahead.

"The way we would like to play, I don't think you can play (Schrempf) exclusively at small forward," he said. "I thought we used him best when he came off the bench and we could use him at either forward spot.

"I think Detlef is a very, very difficult player to replace. He's an All-Star. He wants to win, and we'll use him in the best possible place for us to win. In order to put him on the bench, some of these other guys are really, really going to have to step forward."

Schrempf already had been offered for the fifth, sixth and seventh picks. Now, Brown was again talking of returning him to the bench, a role Schrempf had said he would not accept.

It promised to be a sweltering summer.

Much more quietly in the days that followed, Walsh completed two transactions that would have an impact no one could foresee.

Haywoode Workman, a journeyman point guard who was originally drafted by Atlanta in 1989 and had spent a full season with Washington in 1990-91, came to the Pacers in large part due to a strong recommendation from Blair. He had spent the past two seasons with Scavolini Pesaro of the Italian A-1 league.

At best, Workman was thought to be a capable backup, the type of player who would work hard in practice and be ready in case anything happened to Richardson or Fleming. Though he got a two-year guaranteed contract, the money ($350,000 the first year) was minimal.

The same was true for Antonio Davis. A second-round pick from Texas-El Paso in 1990, Davis headed straight for Greece then because he knew he wasn't ready for the NBA. After a second season overseas, this time in Italy, Davis flirted with the idea of joining the Pacers, but did not. This time, he would not hesitate. He, too, got a two-year guaranteed deal that seemed a bit pricey (totaling $1.2 million) for just another big body, a 12th-man candidate.

Both deals turned out to be the steals of the season, although at the time, Walsh's critics thought he had been taken.

4 Goodbye, Detlef

Detlef Schrempf would leave the Pacers as he came to them: under a cloud of uncertainty. The years in between, though, were an illuminating experience.

When Walsh shipped Herb Williams to Dallas for Schrempf prior to the February trading deadline in 1989, the deal was hardly met with universal approval.

Schrempf was very much an unknown commodity. The eighth pick in the 1985 draft, he had spent three and one half undistinguished seasons with the Mavericks. A finesse player who split time between shooting guard (behind Rolando Blackman) and small forward (behind Mark Aguirre) in Dallas, Schrempf's 15 minutes of fame came when he was runnerup to Larry Bird in the 1987 three-point shootout during All-Star weekend.

Versace was strongly opposed to the deal. The coach told Walsh he didn't want another European, the inference being Schrempf was a methodical caucasian with little creativity. When the staff assembled to cast lots on the deal, Versace showed his flair for theatrics. When his turn came to speak, he leaned back in his chair, looked around the room, and said, "C ... N ... P."

This produced nothing but befuddlement. What, exactly, did Versace mean by that?

"Can Not Play," came the reply.

Though a native of Leverkusen, Germany, Schrempf had developed his basketball skills in the United States, where he spent his final two years of high school in suburban Seattle and four years of college at Washington. What Versace also did not know, and could not know, was that the player the Pacers were obtaining was vastly different from the one the Mavericks had drafted.

Schrempf had hit the weightroom hard, bulking up to a chiseled 230 pounds. At 6-10, he had added power forward to the list of positions he could play comfortably. He retained his smooth ballhandling skills, enabling him to be one of those rare players who could muscle in for a defensive rebound, then drive the length of the floor to lead the fast break.

He could start, and he could finish. And he was coming from a team that had All-Stars in front of him to one that would give him every opportunity to succeed. Which he did, early and often.

When the deal was made, the Pacers had tied the franchise record with 12 straight losses. After Schrempf joined the team, Indiana won two at home, then accomplished the unthinkable, taking three of four on a West Coast road trip, with Schrempf making key plays in each of the victories.

This brought about a first, and quite possibly an only, in the Versace tenure. The coach admitted he was wrong. Schrempf was from Europe, but he wasn't a European player.

And the Pacers had a losing record, but they didn't play like losers with the newcomer. A team that was a dismal 11-41 before the deal went 17-13 thereafter.

From one of the franchise's most depressing seasons had come a bright ray of hope. Schrempf had not only given the team something to be proud of, he made Walsh look like a genius.

Though he was 25 at the time of the trade, generally a player's physical peak, Schrempf would only get better with time. His scoring average increased from 14.8 in his first half-season with the Pacers to 19.1 in 1992-93, which would be his last. His rebounding climbed from 7.2 to 9.5. His assists jumped from 2.9 to 6.0. He earned the league's sixth man award in 1991 and '92, then moved into the starting lineup at small forward and made the All-Star team, no mean feat for a player with this franchise.

In 18 NBA seasons, there have been just four All-Stars from the Indiana Pacers. Don Buse and Billy Knight both made it in 1977, then came a 13-year chasm until Miller broke through in 1990.

Schrempf's '92-93 season was one of the best in club history. He averaged 19.1 points, 9.5 rebounds and six assists. He shot 48 percent from the field and 80 percent from the line. He was, by all accounts, a great player in the making, the closest thing the league had seen to the next Larry Bird. This also made him the Pacer with the highest trade value, particularly so with a relatively low $1.5 million salary.

Still, he wasn't enough to attract the fifth or sixth picks in the 1993 draft. After failing to get through to Minnesota at No. 5 and Washington at No. 6, the Pacers also explored a deal with Sacramento, and again were turned down.

It was becoming clear Schrempf's looming free agency after the '93-94 season was mitigating his attractiveness to most teams. But there was one exception. Seattle had been interested for three years. Nothing would change that.

"A lot of rumors are coming up. That's the thing that's bothering me," said Schrempf in mid-August. "I might not fit in. I might get traded all over the league. It's a little upsetting. I don't know what to expect. It's a little weird that they really don't know yet. We'll wait and see what happens."

The Schrempf-for-McKey deal could not take place before September 30 because of a contract extension McKey had signed the year before. Though McKey was to earn $1.2 million in the coming season, his three-year, $8.4 million extension was signed when the Sonics were over the salary cap and the raise (to $2.6 million, more than doubling his previous salary) well exceeded the limit of 30 percent.

That turned McKey into a "poison pill" player. Any team that wanted to trade for McKey would need to have a slot that was within 15 percent of $2.6 million, the average of his extension, while the Sonics could only take back a player earning within 15 percent of McKey's current salary, which was less than half that.

The "poison pill" expired a year after the extension was signed, though, making a late September deal possible. The Sonics would have to throw in a player making around $250,000 to match Schrempf's $1.5 million, but that would be no problem. There were several candidates.

Walsh was publicly non-committal about the rumors. "This is a trade that's been talked about for three years," he said on August 16. "That's where it is: talked about, but not being done."

Seattle general manager Bob Whitsitt was similarly cool. "I just listen to those things flow out of your city every summer. I don't comment on them," he said of a report in the Indianapolis News that the trade was imminent. "To me, there's deals and there's no deals. We've made no deals. There's guys signed and guys unsigned. The stuff in between makes for great talk-radio and sports copy. We're happy with the progress of our team. We're under no demand to go out and make changes."

That wasn't quite the case. True, the Sonics were coming off a 55-win season in which they had pushed Phoenix to seven games before losing in the Western Conference Finals, but there was pressure on Whitsitt to push his team to the championship level. The trade for Kendall Gill was evidence of that.

Behind the scenes, Schrempf had gone to Walsh and asked, if he intended to make the trade, to please do it as quickly as possible. Otherwise, Schrempf planned to add a swimming pool to his home in Indianapolis, along with some other remodeling. He also wanted time to move his family properly, to get his wife and two young children settled without the urgency that comes with an in-season deal.

Schrempf's agent, Jeff Neal, was given permission by Walsh to meet with Whitsitt, who wanted some kind of assurance that the Sonics would be able to re-sign Schrempf the following summer. No deals were struck; Whitsitt and Neal just wanted to make sure they were thinking along similar financial lines, which they were.

As it stood at the time, the Sonics did not expect to make an attempt to keep Ricky Pierce, who would be a 35-year-old free agent after the 1993-94 season. That would open up a $2.2 million slot. Adding the standard 30 percent increase each year, that meant Seattle could offer either a five-year package that averaged $3.52 million or a six-year deal that averaged $3.85 million.

By all appearances, an agreement to make the trade was in the works. But one sticky detail remained to be worked out. Walsh had re-worked Schrempf's contract the previous summer, bringing forward compensation that originally was scheduled to be deferred. Five annual installments of $250,000 each remained.

Walsh and Whitsitt could not agree on who should pick up what portion of that particular tab, but that was only part of what killed the deal.

"Look: there's no trade. It's not going to happen," Walsh said. "The only way I'm going to trade Detlef is if it's a real good trade for us, and they're not presenting that. Derrick McKey is a good player, but Detlef is better." Walsh said he told Schrempf, "You're going to be here, you're going to like playing for Larry Brown, let's get this settled and move on."

Walsh's words, which rang with finality, would come back to haunt him two months later.

That left just one trade rumor unresolved.

Brown wanted John Williams, the talented but chronically overweight forward. After missing most of two seasons with an eating disorder, Williams, whose weight swelled to well over 300 pounds, was traded to the Clippers prior to the 1992-93 season.

A true lover of reclamation projects, Brown got through to the 6-8 forward, who became a productive reserve, averaging 6.6 points and 7.3 rebounds in 74 games.

Once a potentially great young player, the former LSU star had three strong seasons with the Bullets before losing control of his appetite. Brown held out hope that his career could be salvaged. He pushed Walsh to put together a deal for Williams. "He's a good player," Brown said, "and he's definitely worth the gamble, but it depends on what you have to give up."

There was one other factor to consider: some members of Clippers management apparently felt Brown had betrayed the franchise when he left so abruptly and were in no mood to deal with the Pacers at any level. Despite Brown's prodding, that one would not come to fruition.

Not that the summer would be without its moments.

On September 4 in Hazen, North Dakota, his bride's hometown, Brown was married to the former Shelly Galster, a striking, 26-year-old brunette who had been a successful real estate broker in Los Angeles.

Two weeks later, Haskin signed a six-year, $8 million contract. In seven seasons, Walsh had failed only once — with Dale Davis in 1991 — to have the team's first-round draft pick signed in time for training camp.

Walsh had high hopes for Haskin. "He's got a chance to be a very good player," he said. "He's aggressive, he's got talent and he's an athlete."

Haskin knew he was an unpopular selection, but he dealt with it in a mature manner. "I played basketball 2,500 miles from here," he said. "Just watch and see. Don't judge me before I'm out there."

After three days at the NBA's rookie orientation meetings in Dallas, Haskin would return to begin informal scrimmages with several of the Pacers at the team's off-season home, the National Institute for Fitness and Sport.

Essentially a huge health club surrounding a basketball court, NIFS, located near downtown on the campus of the unfortunately named Indiana University-Purdue University at Indianapolis (IUPUI), was a place for the players to gather, practice, lift weights and do assorted other conditioning exercises.

In the two weeks before training camp opened, it also would be the site of two ominous injuries.

Miller rolled his left ankle in a pickup game at NIFS on September 24, suffering a severe sprain. "They grade sprains as a class one, class two or class three," said Miller. "I hit a home run." He would miss all of the two-a-day practices and at least the first four exhibition games.

"Maybe this'll give us a chance to work more with some young kids," said Brown, looking for the silver lining. "We've got to find out if they can play."

A week later, Haskin sprained his left ankle, as well. It was thought to be a minor injury that would heal completely with time. The problem was, there wasn't much left before the grind of training camp.

* * *

If no one surrounding the Pacers organization knew quite what to expect of this team, they were offered some unwanted hints in the annual wave of preseason magazines. Six of the seven national preview magazines picked the Pacers to finish either fourth or fifth in the Central Division. One had them in sixth.

To some coaches, that would be motivational fodder. Not Brown.

"I think most people who write those things know basketball," he said. "I think it's more because of the improvement of the other teams around us. If you look at Orlando, Charlotte and Miami, those are no longer expansion teams. They're closer to being elite teams. I don't want to concern myself with (expectations) because I don't know what to expect. We should only be thinking about going to training camp and concentrating on making this the best team it can be. If we do that, we'll prove everybody wrong. If we don't, we'll prove them right."

On October 6, one night before the Pacers were to report to training camp, the NBA was rocked to its very foundation and the Eastern Conference race was thrown wide open.

Michael Jordan announced his retirement from basketball.

At the time, no one other than perhaps Jordan himself knew that meant the birth of a baseball career. The Chicago Bulls had won three straight crowns, but Jordan was the king. His retirement was a virtual abdication. No one considered the Bulls unbeatable any more. For all practical purposes, the league would spend the season with a lame duck champion in office, waiting to be replaced.

The basic line of logic was crystallized by Vern Fleming. "When you lose a player like Michael," he said, "the only thing you can do is get worse."

Fleming also suggested Jordan would be back after a year off. To him, that meant just one thing. "You better win now," he said, "while he's gone."

* * *

West Lafayette, Indiana, is a typical midwestern college town. When school is in, the place is powered by the energy of youth. When school is out, it's a ghost town.

When the Pacers convened at Purdue University, school was not in session. While this meant your choice of rooms at the team's hotel, it also meant nothing going on in the immediate vicinity.

For those who like nightlife, hell, any life, the annual training camp trek 70 miles up I-65 meant a painfully boring week. For the coaches, it meant an idyllic environment. They would have a captive audience because the most interesting thing happening in town, quite literally, was in Mackey Arena twice a day in early October.

Usually, camp is enlivened by spirited competition for jobs. Not so, this year. When camp opened, 13 players had guaranteed contracts. The only real question about the roster would be in determining which one would go on the (allegedly) injured list when the final cut to 12 was made.

Brown did have a full agenda, though. Physically, the primary search would be for a shooter to back up Miller and bring punch off the bench. Former Washington guard Ledell Eackles was brought in briefly but weighed more than 250 pounds and left camp after his first practice. On his way to the airport, Eackles asked the driver to stop at a fast food chain so he could order a whole chicken. The drive would take almost 90 minutes, after all. A man could starve.

This would be a month spent on re-shaping the team's mindset toward defense, on evaluating how much to expect from the younger players, on establishing leadership from the veterans.

"Our priorities have to change," Brown said. "We can't play every other night. We can't say we're going to rebound better and defend better, we have to do it. Detlef Schrempf and Reggie Miller can't talk about being leaders, they have to do it. There comes a time when you have to put up or shut up. If it doesn't work out with this group, then it's time for Plan B."

Which is?

"We make some changes."

Wasn't that Plan A entering the summer? "Donnie thought we really needed to shake the team up," said Brown. "We tried to get Calbert for obvious reasons, but it didn't work out. Then, the consensus was to let me see how the team is. Let me see how the players react under different circumstances. So we didn't make any changes. I'd like to find out about the players, to see if we can win with the group we have."

Win what? That was the question. Even Brown seemed to be bracing for a difficult year when, even before camp opened, he said, "I'm not trying to make a case for mediocrity, but we might not win a lot more games and still be a much better team."

This hardly had the feeling of a drive toward championship contention.

* * *

Step one, for Brown, was to find out if he could do for Richardson what he had done for Mark Jackson the previous season with the Clippers. Namely, rejuvenate a career.

"I recruited him (at UCLA). I've known him. He's going to be great," said Brown. "He knows me and knows what I'm about. I had a great experience with Mark and I think it's going to be the same type of situation with Pooh."

Aware Richardson had alienated not only Hill but many of his teammates the previous year, Brown had a well-conceived plan. He would ride Richardson so hard the other players would empathize with him. If Richardson survived the stress, he would have regained the team's confidence and proven himself to the coach.

"Donnie didn't know about Pooh," Brown said after the season. "He thought he could play but didn't get a chance to evaluate him last year because he was hurt and there were obvious problems with Bob and the team. But Pooh had a lot of the skills I thought were necessary to play the way I wanted him to play.

"I was tough on him in training camp. I was happy with the way he tried and I was thrilled with the way the team responded to my being so hard on him."

For a while, it was working.

"I couldn't do anything right in practice early on," Richardson said with a grin. "He was riding me hard, but I knew it wasn't personal. He just does it to help you be a better player."

His first season with the Pacers represented a giant step backward. Hill was a stoic, middle class midwesterner. Richardson was a funky kid from the projects of south Philadelphia. Their personalities meshed about as well as pickles and milk.

Richardson posted career lows in scoring (10.4) and steals (1.27). And, though he left the low-scoring Timberwolves for a team that should've represented a gold mine of assists, Richardson's average instead dropped, from 8.4 in 1991-92 to 7.7, 11th in the league.

The Pacers thought they were getting one of the NBA's rising stars at point guard. What they got instead was heartburn. Was Richardson another Sherman Douglas, a player capable of racking up impressive statistics with a bad team but unable to stand out on a team expected to win? Or was it something else?

"I was kind of backing off from my strengths, some of the things that made me a player," Richardson said. "I didn't know when, and when not.

"I was trying so hard to fit in, I tried too hard, instead of just going out there and doing what I know I can do and letting the game come to me."

When things went well, Richardson inevitably would say, "Coach is letting me be me." When they went poorly, he would say, "I can't be myself out there."

Just who was this me person? No one in the organization ever figured it out. Richardson had no close friends on the team and, though cordial with the media, he never really opened up. His comments were repetitive, superficial and generally self-serving. He said what he thought you wanted to hear, not just to the press, but to coaches and teammates.

Still, it was hard not to like him. Richardson had an outgoing personality and, to his credit, did not allow the circumstances to turn him into a bitter, surly sulker — at least on the outside.

Walsh wanted him to succeed. So did Brown. The rest would be up to Richardson and his teammates.

His success was deemed imperative to that of the team. Though his backups, Vern Fleming and Haywoode Workman, were veterans who could play without making major mistakes, neither was much of a creator, and both had extremely suspect outside shots.

* * *

For Miller, October was very much a lost month. Not only would he miss all but the last two exhibition games, he had to deal with a major snub. When the first 10 players for Dream Team II were announced, he was not among them.

Though no active shooting guard had amassed more points over the previous four seasons, Miller was passed over at the position in favor of Joe Dumars of Detroit, Dan Majerle of Phoenix and Steve Smith of Miami.

Miller and Mitch Richmond of Sacramento were the only players at that position who had averaged at least 20 points over the previous four seasons. In that span, Miller totaled 7,302 points (a 22.3 average), Richmond 6,350 points (22.7), and Portland's Clyde Drexler 6,349 (22.7).

Dumars (6,409 points, 20.4 average), Majerle (4,666, 14.9) and Smith (a 13.7 average in two NBA seasons) all lagged behind Miller, offensively.

"There's really nothing I can do about it," Miller said. "I'm not going to sit around and pout.

"When I was mentioned for the (original) Dream Team, it was quite an honor because of the company that was on that team. This team, you look at it. . . . They've got good players, but, hey. It makes it a little easier to go out and be motivated to work a little bit harder. It gives me a little bit more incentive to go out and do well."

Miller was among the finalists for the original Dream Team and, as such, appeared to be a virtual lock for the second NBA-dominated U.S. national team. Even with Walsh's presence on the USA Basketball selection committee, Miller was omitted.

"There are a couple of players I honestly didn't expect to be on the team — Dominique Wilkins, Mark Price and Dumars," said Walsh. "It's not because of their ability, but because of their age. When they made it, I knew Reggie was in trouble.

"I spoke up for Reggie very vociferously. What it came down to was not everybody agreed with me. The votes weren't there. As I told Reggie, there are two ways to go: you can sit around and feel like you were treated unjustly or you can go out and do something about it and show everyone."

Two roster spots remained open, to be filled later in the season. It was possible, then, that Miller could play his way onto the team. "He's got a chance," said Walsh.

"He's in a better position now than he was for the first Dream Team, and he was in the top 16 then."

Because success in international competition is often based on a team's ability to hit the three-pointer, Miller's shooting skills could be needed. Of the big guards, only Dumars was comparable.

"That's exactly what my point was when we talked about the team," said Walsh. "Reggie ranks with any shooter in the league but, beyond that, he's just as good, or a better, basketball player than some of the guys who are on the team. . . . I'm biased, but I think he's the best shooting guard in the league."

Miller tried to downplay the snub but could not completely conceal his anguish. "My teammates are telling me I got robbed," Miller said. "As long as, in their eyes, I should be on that team, then I'll look at it that way.

"You know me. I never complain. It adds fuel to the fire. My tank is already three-quarters full. Once this ankle gets well and I can get out there and compete, it's going to be full. That really added a lot of fuel."

With Miller out, Sealy stepped in and was the brightest spot of the exhibition season. He led the team in scoring (16.8) and shot 50.5 percent. He also impressed Brown with his defense.

Walsh had been telling Brown he felt one of the team's biggest physical needs was a shooter behind Miller, someone to come in and add punch to the second unit. Through the preseason, Sealy looked like that man.

* * *

The most compelling individual battle was waged between the Davises, Dale and Antonio. Unrelated by birth, their games were virtual twins.

Both were unusually gifted leapers for their size (Dale is 6-11, Antonio 6-10), excellent defenders and shot-blockers, and neither had an offensive move other than the thunderdunk.

When Dale Davis reported to camp out of shape, he didn't exactly impress Brown, who gave the challenger every opportunity to push the incumbent starter at power forward.

"I try not to look at it as a battle," said Antonio. "If a guy works hard and I work hard, we'll make each other better and we'll make the team better and that's what's important."

He certainly had gotten Dale's attention.

"A couple of times, he jumped over me," Dale said. "Usually, I've been the guy jumping over people. I haven't really had that done to me that often."

It was a new experience for Dale. He came to the team as the kid trying to win a job. Now that he had it, there was a mirror image coming after him.

He would stave off the challenge thanks to a strong preseason (12.8 points, 8.2 rebounds, 2.6 blocked shots), but Antonio had played his way into a far more significant role than originally anticipated.

* * *

There were happy campers, and then there was Smits, who must've thought he'd stepped into an alternate reality.

For five years, the 7-4 center had heard how he alone must lift the Pacers beyond mediocrity.

For five years, he was told he needed to get bigger and stronger to handle the rigors of the low post.

For five years, shooting pains in either knee, sometimes both, sidelined him for significant portions of training camp and the preseason and never really went away.

This year, however, things couldn't have been more different.

Brown wanted to take 25 pounds, and a ton of pressure, off the talented big man. "I think too many people focus on Rik," he said. "If all the other guys were so damn good, we wouldn't be 41-41. I didn't see the Bulls focusing on (Bill) Cartwright. I haven't seen many championship teams lately with dominant centers. . . . I truly believe his presence is going to make everybody better. But I don't want to put all that responsibility on any one guy. This isn't a one- or two-man game. We need everybody doing what they're asked to do."

Brown wanted the weight reduction for two reasons: to allow Smits to be more agile and to take stress off his troublesome knees.

"He'd be so much more athletic, it would be so much easier for him to get up and down the floor, and I don't think he'd put as much pressure on his knees," said Brown. "I don't think strength is a problem with him. Both him and LaSalle (Thompson), I think more than anything, need to lose a lot of weight.

"He had a lot of blocks and rebounds early in his career and he ran better when he was lighter. I think now he's matured enough where he's got the strength."

Smits' best season was his second, when he posted career-high averages of 15.5 points, 6.2 rebounds and 2.06 blocks — and, just as significantly, 29.3 minutes. In part because of a succession of knee and ankle injuries, Smits' production had dropped off.

Perhaps overly concerned with foul trouble that plagued him his first two seasons (in which he was disqualified 25 times and averaged 3.9 fouls per game), Smits stopped trying to block shots. Over the past three seasons, he averaged just 1.24, with a career-worst 0.93 in 1992-93.

Twice, he lost his starting job to Dreiling, who would do the things Smits would not, or could not: set solid screens, battle for rebounds and protect the lane.

Through it all, there were glimpses of what his future could hold. Against Ewing's Knicks in the '93 playoffs, Smits averaged 22.5 points and eight rebounds. "I've shown at times where I can be," said Smits. "I want to be there more consistently this year."

If Smits did not work out, there were more options than anticipated. Early on, in fact, Haskin looked like the steal of the draft.

"If the draft was today, we'd take him," said Brown during the first week of camp, "and we'd probably take him if we had the sixth or seventh or eighth pick. . . . He's more athletic than we anticipated and he's a real tough kid."

That would not last. The left ankle sprain that was thought to be minor never fully healed because Haskin was so intent on impressing the coaching staff he did not want to miss any practice. As a result, he lost mobility, agility, and confidence.

He would quickly drop to the end of the depth chart, never really to rise again. In fact, he joined Richardson as the Pacers who could do no right in Brown's eyes.

Brown had given Haskin a gift start for a game against his home-state team, Portland, in the fourth exhibition. Afterward, the rookie wondered if it was worth the trouble.

Describing Haskin's nervous play, Brown uttered a line that would be re-produced in weekly NBA notes columns across the country: "Thank God he has a mouthpiece to keep him from swallowing his tongue."

In the next game, Haskin had a respectable performance in a victory over New Jersey in Evansville, Indiana, but Brown gave only grudging praise.

"Scott was really active on the boards, which was nice to see because he's been a nervous wreck," said the coach. "He was hitting someone other than our guys tonight. He was more selective who to run into."

Haskin seemed to handle it well, never snapping back at Brown, just smiling and trying to do as instructed. He tried to convince himself the coach was doing this in his best interest.

"As long as Larry is yelling at me and making comments about me, I know he loves me," said Haskin. "As strange as it may sound, when a coach stops talking to you, you're either in the doghouse or on the way out."

There was other help on the bench. Thompson, whose place on the roster was secure only because he had two years remaining on his contract at $2 million apiece, surprised everyone by reporting in unusually good shape, although a summer in the weightroom had bulked up the man already big enough to earn the nickname "Tank" beyond Brown's approval. He, too, would need to shed some weight, but it looked certain that Thompson could contribute.

With either of the Davises able to swing over to play center, if necessary, the position had unusual depth and a complementary combination of talents. The big men would be called upon to anchor a team defense that had no choice but to improve drastically.

"With the talent we have, we can be a lot better than we have been," said Thompson. "People who have been around here and watched us for a number of years know we have underachieved. It's time to start achieving, and that all starts with the defense."

The past year's defensive statistics were the best of the last five years, and they were no better than mediocre. The Pacers surrendered 106.1 points per game, tied for 16th. Since 1988, they'd given up an average of 109.9 points, with an average ranking of 21st.

They didn't have the quick-handed defenders to apply active pressure, going for steals and overplaying to create turnovers that would lead to fast breaks. They would have to use passive pressure, instead, forcing opponents to use more time than they wanted to bring the ball upcourt, thereby leaving them little margin for error in running their offense.

"I'd like us to dictate the way the game is played, instead of sitting back and adjusting to whoever we're playing against," Brown said. "And we have to be a great rebounding team because that's a big part of your defense and it's an area we have to improve on. We need to be a team that changes ends well and does not give up cheap baskets.

"I don't know if we can go out and play 94 feet. I don't know if we can change defenses, but that's going to be our goal."

It was as much a matter of changing the team's mindset as much as its system, hence Brown spent an inordinate amount of practice time on defensive drills.

"I don't think I've ever coached a team that spent a lot of time, offensively," he said. "If you work hard, defensively, you're going to be unselfish, offensively. We've got to execute, offensively, but the whole personality of the club has to be on the defensive end."

In the interim, the team was running an offense that consisted mostly of the dreaded passing game. Though no one expected Brown to try and force it upon the team, that was precisely what was happening.

"I'd like to use it as a game tool because it's basketball," he said. "Everybody gets to touch (the ball), it's fun to play it, you can use more people because it's hard work, and it's a great defensive tool because to play against it really teaches you how to play.

"I don't know if we can do it. I don't know if the commitment to run it as strong enough right now. I want to make sure whatever we do, we do it well. This team should be able to run the passing game, run (set) plays, and run. I don't know. We'll have to wait and see."

Brown wouldn't have to wait long. By the end of the fourth exhibition game, it became clear the passing game would not work. The Pacers did not crack 100 points, shot 42 percent, and had nearly as many turnovers (78) as assists (80) while beating Dallas and Utah but losing to the Clippers and Portland.

"We don't have a lot of guys who break you down off the dribble," Brown said. "We don't have a lot of guys that are willing to set screens and get people free. We don't have a lot of guys, I think, who have a good understanding of just how to play. Our passing is just so bad. You get Reggie back on the court, and some of our older guys playing more minutes and it won't be as much of a problem. But we've got to run more stuff."

Injuries also were a problem. Fleming had a severely bruised knee that kept him out of five games. Smits missed three with bursitis in his hip. Dale Davis strained his right shoulder and sat out three games. And Miller would not return until just two exhibitions remained.

Historically a coach who likes to have his team sharp, in a position to start the season quickly, Brown was becoming distraught. Time was running out and he hadn't even seen the projected starting unit on the floor.

There was only one thing to do: work the team even harder.

When Miller finally returned to practice on October 27, his timing couldn't have been worse. Including mandatory weightlifting after practice, Brown worked the team four and one half hours, what would be the longest single session of the year.

"When I was with New Jersey (in 1981), we practiced 18 straight days in the exhibition season," Brown said. "We started out 3-11, but over the last 70-some games, we had the third-best record in the league (41-27) and we made the playoffs."

The starting lineup finally was intact when the Pacers played Charlotte in Carbondale, Illinois, on October 28. Miller scored 21 points in 24 minutes to celebrate his return. Though the night produced a 121-113 victory, Brown hardly was satisfied.

After the game, he kept the locker room closed for 20 minutes, during which time he let the team know they would return to two-a-day workouts in the week before the final exhibition game and the opening of the regular season. Fleming quickly dubbed it "hell week."

And it only would get hotter.

* * *

Though Schrempf had struggled in the passing game during the exhibition season, his relationship with Brown seemed to be going smoothly, with few exceptions.

Brown wanted Schrempf to be more of a perimeter threat. Schrempf's favorite scoring spot was the low post, specifically the left block, but the coach wanted to run more plays there for Smits and Dale Davis.

For Schrempf, who had spent the best seasons of his career as a power player, this meant a major adjustment. Brown felt Schrempf was hesitant to shoot the jumper because he either lacked confidence, or was concerned about missing.

"If you miss shots and the coach keeps playing you, people think the coach is a dumbass," Brown said. "He doesn't have anything to worry about."

The distractions of the past two summers seemed distant. In 1992, he wanted, and got, a salary increase, though he felt the need to ask for a trade in order to make Walsh take him seriously. This summer, he had survived the August rumors of the deal for McKey.

With the start of the season less than a week away, Schrempf had no reason to believe he would be anything other than a major player for Brown's Pacers.

"There's no doubt in my mind he can be a great small forward," Brown had said. "For us to be a better team, we need him to play that position as well as he can. He's going to have to adjust his game, but I think this can be his finest all-around year. I don't think he'll be asked to score as much, but his overall game may be better."

That would indeed be Schrempf's precise role. In Seattle.

On Monday, November 1, Walsh called Whitsitt and said, in essence, "Let's do it." The Pacers president wasn't completely certain it was the right move, but he was sure of one thing: a move had to be made.

In mid-October, the nature of free agency in the NBA had forever changed. Chris Dudley, a hard-working backup center — but hardly the type of player franchises typically fight over — had signed what appeared to be a seven-year, $11 million contract with Portland.

In practice, though, it was a one-year deal. The Trail Blazers wanted Dudley, but had only a $790,000 slot, vacated by Mario Elie, to offer. In order to attract Dudley, the Blazers wrote in a one-year opt-out clause that allowed him to become an unrestricted free agent.

This created a gaping loophole in the collective bargaining agreement. Because teams could exceed the salary cap to re-sign their own free agents, the Blazers would be able to negotiate with Dudley without restriction, after one season. He might be relatively underpaid for a year, but then he would collect.

The NBA felt this was a blatant attempt to circumvent the intent of the salary cap and voided the contract. The Blazers felt otherwise. The two sides went before a special master, as called for in the collective bargaining agreement. New York Judge Dickinson Debevoise ruled the contract valid.

The next step was to send the case to imperial arbiter Daniel Collins, who also considered similar contracts signed that summer by Craig Ehlo (with Atlanta) and Toni Kukoc (with Chicago). He, too, upheld the original deal.

Until then, the Pacers felt secure they would be the only franchise able to adequately compensate Schrempf when he became a free agent the following July. With the validation of the one-year opt-out deal, though, they would be competing not just with Seattle, but the rest of the league.

Suddenly, the prospect of losing Schrempf to another team with no compensation had become very real.

For Brown, who had just left the Clippers in large part due to an eerily similar set of circumstances with Manning, it brought on a new sense of urgency. The last thing he wanted to see done was nothing.

"It wasn't Derrick over Detlef, but what are you going to get for Detlef?" Brown would say later. "Are you going to get nothing, like with Danny? That was really on my mind."

McKey was, at 27, three years younger than Schrempf. And he had four more years under contract. He would earn $1.25 million in the coming season, and $2.6 million, $2.8 million and $3 million the following three seasons.

By NBA standards, then, he was a relative financial bargain, even if he was hurt. McKey pulled a hamstring in an intrasquad game on October 13 and had not practiced until the day of the trade. He still was far from 100 percent. Gerald Paddio, a journeyman shooting guard, came along primarily because his $250,000 salary was needed to balance the deal for cap purposes.

The timing may have been all wrong, but Walsh now felt this was the right move. After the second practice of the day, he called Schrempf down to his office. Several players, sensing something was about to happen, lingered in the locker room.

Within a half-hour, a visibly distressed Schrempf stalked into the locker room, gathered up his Pacer uniforms, warmups and shoes, slam-dunked them into the trash and left. He felt thoroughly betrayed by Walsh, who had told him just two months before that there would be no deal.

"I'm excited to be going back to Seattle — my phone's been ringing off the hook — and I'm excited about the team," Schrempf would say later, "but, at the same time, I'm also a little mad. A little upset. They could've done this a month ago and shown me a little respect. Or they could've not let me go through two practices today when they knew this morning that this was going to happen. It just shows you it's a business, and that there's no loyalty.

"They basically had this deal done in the summertime. They asked me how I felt and the only thing I said was that, if it was going to be done, do it right away to give me and my family time to settle in before the season starts."

Walsh presented the decision as a combination of business and basketball.

"To keep Detlef here, I had to feel real deep in my heart that we were going to have him here next year," Walsh said, "or else we stood a very difficult chance of losing him for nothing. It got to the point where I didn't think it would be wise to risk it because the percentages were starting to work against us."

For Schrempf, there was consolation in his new situation. He was regarded as the final piece to Seattle's championship puzzle and would enjoy local celebrity far beyond what he had experienced in Indianapolis.

Within days of his arrival in Seattle, his attitude was firmly upbeat.

"I hear it on the streets, I even heard it at the airport on the way in. We've got to go the Finals this year, nothing less. It's a big change for me, and I love it," Schrempf said. "Expecting to win a championship and expecting to make the playoffs - there's a big difference."

If Sonics coach George Karl originally had his way, Schrempf would've begun his career in Cleveland, and the coach might never have left.

When Karl was the Cavaliers coach in 1985, he hoped to orchestrate a trade that would bring Schrempf to the Cavaliers. Karl held the ninth pick and felt strongly that Dallas, at No. 8, would select Schrempf. Karl offered Golden State, which had the seventh pick, $1 million to trade draft positions. But Golden State feared, if it did so, Dallas would take the man the Warriors wanted all along, Chris Mullin.

The Cavs wound up drafting Charles Oakley, then made the mistake of trading him to Chicago for Keith Lee and Ennis Whatley. It was the beginning of the end for Karl, who had to wait eight years for his next shot at Schrempf.

"I've always been a big fan of his and more of his ability to be a player with a feel for the game," said Karl. "He's one of the few players in the league who I think make other people better and that is a big-time asset to bring. To add that to a championship caliber team, I think, is very, very important."

Still, it was a difficult move for Whitsitt to make.

"The first two deals (for Sam Perkins and Kendall Gill) were no-brainers," said Whitsitt. "The third one was a little bit more delicate. To trade a 6-10 guy like Derrick McKey who does so many things for you, there's only a few guys in this league that we would've considered doing that for. But for the talent, the personality, chemistry and work ethic, we got one of those guys. To take a very good player and get a great player back, this is something else. He even wants to be here."

For an Indiana team that already wondered what to expect from itself, the trade was a serious jolt.

"We've been in the 40-42 win category for a few years," said Walsh. "If you want to get out of that category, you have to take a shot. That's what we're doing, we're taking a shot with this trade."

The players who were left behind that day looked more like they'd been shot. The heads that weren't down were shaking, and a locker room normally alive with banter had taken on a funereal pall.

"I'm not commenting," said Miller.

"No comment," said Dale Davis.

Sealy?

"Nothing I can say, man."

Mitchell?

"Hell, no. I might be next."

Their reluctance to speak was understandable. To criticize the franchise for the trade would make their new teammate feel unwelcome. And, sometimes, the unsaid is understood much more clearly.

One who did talk was Antonio Davis. In his few short weeks with the Pacers, he had seen two friends shipped off in Schrempf and Sean Green, who earlier in camp was traded to Philadelphia for a second-round draft pick.

"I've seen this twice and I still don't understand it, that look in their eyes," he said. "It must really hurt. I guess you can't explain that feeling."

Like Schrempf, McKey was leaving a locker room full of friends behind. Like Schrempf, he had been traded away from the team he had grown up with, professionally.

He knew he couldn't replace Schrempf's statistics, but was convinced he could help his new team.

"I'm going to a situation where they want me to do well and I don't think I'll let anybody down," McKey told The Indianapolis News the night of the trade. "I'm not going to put up the numbers Detlef Schrempf put up, but I think everybody else will be better."

Fully aware the deal was met with universal disapproval in Indianapolis, McKey was prepared for the wrath of the fans and the scrutiny of a skeptical media.

"Hopefully, they can accept me for the person that I am, the player that I am," he said. "I understand he was a popular player there, but I didn't make the trade. I'm coming there to go to work and to play as well as I can. I'm not going there to please everybody."

Where Schrempf was primarily an offensive player, McKey's strength was defense. He had guarded all five positions during his tenure with the Sonics, from Tim Hardaway to Hakeem Olajuwon and dozens in between.

The main criticism of McKey had been directed toward his reluctant offense. It wasn't that he lacked the skills; he only periodically chose to make full use of them. His scoring average had declined four straight years to 13.4 in 1992-93.

"I never heard anybody say that he plays inconsistently, defensively," said Brown. "George (Karl) told me he was the best defensive wingman in the league.

"About the offense, I've always heard that. But if you look at their team, they've always had a lot of guys who score. Our team doesn't have as many guys who command the ball, so there should be more opportunities for him."

Complicating the transition, McKey missed his flight to Indianapolis the next morning and would not be able to practice with the team until Wednesday, two days before the season would open in Atlanta.

Brown had been particularly sensitive to Miller's reaction. He called the team co-captain to explain the trade and its meaning. Miller would have to step forward, but so would a lot of other players. McKey would have to be welcomed into the fold as quickly as possible for the good of team chemistry.

Miller took it to heart, but it was clear his feelings were, at best, mixed.

"We know this is a game we've been playing since we were kids," he said the day after. "Now that we're grownups, playing this game, when you get to this level, the business side kind of comes into effect. If anything, that's what this showed. Sometimes, we put that out of our minds because we're men playing kids' games and we forget about the business side.

"It was a business decision and it hurts. It hurts our team, but it was something that had to be done. We've got to move on. We can't hold our heads down. If we hold our heads down, we could be 15 games down by the end of December.

"You ask nine of 10 guys on the street, they're probably going to tell you it hurts the team, but they don't know the relationships that have bonded here. We have to accept Derrick McKey. He didn't make this trade. The fans need to give Derrick a fair chance. This is not Derrick McKey's fault. We've got to embrace him into our family and accept him."

Miller didn't realize it at the time but, with those statements, he had assumed team leadership. It would be the first positive effect the trade had on the team, and perhaps the most important.

5 Ominous Opening

A particularly brutal preseason had come to an end, and there was little mercy in sight.

Camp opened on October 7. When the players and coaches returned from the next-to-last exhibition game on October 29, they had spent 19 of those 23 days on the road. After they were beaten in the exhibition finale by Utah, they had a week off, but it would bring anything but rest.

Brown wanted it used for two-a-day practices.

Then came the sudden trade for McKey, who arrived late, and injured. Smits was uncertain for the early games because what was first thought to be a bruised hip had become bursitis. Instead of practicing, he was doing swimming pool therapy.

"He's training," said Brown, "to swim the English Channel." The coach wasn't amused.

A full month of practices and exhibition games had offered more questions than answers. The approach of the regular season normally is eagerly anticipated. This one felt more like something looming.

The schedule offered a slight break, although it was just a tease. Of the first 11 games, seven were at home. This promised little advantage for two reasons: the Pacers had lost all three of their exhibitions at Market Square Arena, and they simply weren't physically prepared to take advantage of the opportunity.

"Everything we did in training camp, you might as well throw it all out the window," Brown said after the season. "I didn't know how this team was going to play."

Or even who was going to play.

"It was," he said, "pretty frightening."

One thing Brown did know was that he had been pleased with Richardson's performance. That was counterbalanced by Smits' general ineffectiveness and sporadic availability.

"It was a pretty incredible situation," said Brown. "The only thing I did know was I liked the players and I liked the coaches, but it was pretty discouraging in terms of knowing what style we should play or how far along we were."

Having given up on the possibility of a fast start, Brown instead decided to use the first few weeks of the season as an extension of training camp. It wouldn't produce much in the way of results, but it would pay off, eventually.

The beginning of Brown's tenure had been marked by change, starting with the coaching staff and continuing through the roster. Nearly half the team wasn't here a year ago: McKey and Paddio came in the Schrempf deal, Haskin was a first-round pick and Antonio Davis and Workman were brought in from Europe. And two of the holdovers, Sealy and Dale Davis, would be thrust into roles far more prominent than at any time in their young careers. Most of the starting lineup would be the same, but that was about all.

Instead of relying on an offense that had been among the league's most prolific over the last four seasons, Brown had shifted the focus to the previously deficient defense.

"At times, it looks like we've made terrific progress," he said. "At others, I'm not so sure."

At least McKey had settled his first personal problem: what number to wear. In Seattle, he was No. 31, but that already belonged to Miller. His number at Alabama had been 30, but that one was hanging on the Market Square Arena wall, retired with McGinnis.

McKey chose No. 23, saying, "I'm Jordan in another form." In another universe, maybe.

Within two weeks, he had changed again, finally settling on No. 9. And all along, the Pacers had thought he wasn't a numbers guy.

* * *

This most uncertain of seasons opened, fittingly, on the road.

All that defense Brown had been preaching looked to be a forgotten lesson. Atlanta hit its first eight shots, scored on its first 12 possessions and kept the Pacers on their heels the rest of the night in a 116-110 victory.

Of the Hawks' first 30 baskets, 25 were either dunks or layups against an Indiana defense that did little to shed its reputation as squeezably soft.

Smits was healthy enough to start but didn't produce much in 27 minutes. McKey's debut (eight points and two rebounds in 26 minutes) left much to be desired. He obviously was laboring on the sore leg, and was out of shape.

Though Miller scored 19 points, he had six turnovers and admitted the healing process on his ankle was going slowly.

"I've got to play through this," he said. "I'm 75 to 80 percent. My drives aren't as smooth as I'd like them to be. I'm better as a slasher, and it's tough for me to make cuts with the ball right now."

Not that the trip was a total waste of expense money.

Sealy had the best night of his pro career with 27 points and 10 rebounds. Richardson had 16 points and 15 assists, the latter figure his most since joining the Pacers.

Sealy's performance reinforced his strong showing in the exhibitions. It was starting to look like he would at least be able to fill the need for scoring off the bench, and the wildly optimistic foresaw him doing some of the things Schrempf had done as sixth man.

* * *

Drafted by the Pacers in the middle of the first round in the glamour draft of 1992, that's precisely where Sealy's production settled that year. Of the 13 players picked ahead of him, 11 had double-figure scoring averages. Of the 13 players taken behind him, just two cracked double figures.

Though the numbers hardly portrayed him as a bust, they did little to alleviate his personal frustration. The 6-foot-7 swingman from St. John's expected much more from himself than 58 appearances and a 5.7 scoring average. He was more widely known for his line of designer ties than his production on the basketball court.

"Last year was terrible," Sealy said. "But when I went home, I still had friends who believed in me and that helped me get through the summer. I had people who wanted to help me work out so I'd improve, so I wouldn't be in that same situation this year.

"I came back stronger. I came back ready to play, and I think the coaches know it."

They did. Sealy couldn't have made a stronger first impression.

"I had Sean Elliott (in San Antonio) and he's very, very similar to Sean — and you know how good Sean's been in this league," said Brown. "Malik has a lot of the same attributes and he's much faster. He may not be as good with the ball yet and he doesn't shoot as well from the outside, but he's quicker."

Sealy hit the weightroom and added 10 pounds of muscle to his slender frame (up to 200). In the process, he bulked up in a more important area: confidence.

He acknowledged at least partial responsibility for his rookie drawbacks. He reported to camp in less than top shape, in part because he did not foresee a rapid end to his contract impasse. And he struggled to stay focused as Hill used his reserves erratically.

"There were doubts in their minds as to whether I could play or not," Sealy said, "and there were some doubts in my mind, sometimes."

Those days seemed long ago.

* * *

The home opener came the following night against Detroit, and it was in many ways a repeat performance.

The Pacers lost by six, this time 113-107, and followed the same painful pattern. Trying to change their image from soft to hard, they had yet to impose their new style upon the league's officials.

In the losses to Atlanta and Detroit, the Pacers were whistled for 74 fouls and outscored 70-47 from the free throw line.

"Right now, we're just going through a trial period of showing our new style of play," said Miller, who looked strong with 31 points. "It's going to take some time till all the officials understand this is our style of play. They're not used to this kind of Indiana team. They're used to the passive style. That's not us."

Miller was leading by example. He fouled out in each of the first two games. This, from a player who had fouled out two times in the previous three seasons and five times in his career.

Smits made his own sort of history. Removed from the starting lineup because he could not practice regularly, Smits picked up four fouls in the first two minutes of the second period, then two more early in the third. He wound up fouling out in six minutes, tying the second-quickest disqualification in NBA history.

Daily uncertainty over Smits' status was starting to wear on Brown. "If he doesn't practice, he isn't playing," Brown said. "I don't think anybody on our team knows how to play with him because he hasn't been out on the court. I hope he gets more athletic, but it's hard when you don't practice."

Thompson, who started in place of Smits, took much longer, 20 minutes, to foul out.

"Tradition-wise, the Pacers have been known as a soft team," said Dale Davis, who picked up three fouls in the first 100 seconds. "We're trying to come out and play aggressive, but at this point in time we're getting a lot of ticky-tacky fouls. I guess it's going to take some time, and we're going to have to earn that respect. If we don't have it yet, we will get it. I'll make sure of that."

Though they played much more aggressively than in Atlanta, the Pacers demonstrated a lack of familiarity with the nuances of the style mastered by the Pistons in the late 1980s and carried on by the current New York Knicks.

The next game was three days away in Orlando, the team that had benefited so much from losing the playoff tie-breaker to the Pacers just six months ago.

Bob Hill was an assistant now, to first-year Magic head coach Brian Hill, but, in many ways, he felt he had upgraded his status. Great things were expected from Orlando. Nothing was expected from Hill's former team.

There had been so much change, the Pacers hardly looked familiar.

"It's really a different team than I had," said Hill. "It's not going to be like I thought it was going to be. George (McCloud), Greg (Dreiling), Sean (Green) and Detlef (Schrempf), those guys are all gone. It's going to be different but, emotionally, I haven't thought about it other than as a game we need to win."

Hill had been Brown's assistant at Kansas and felt he understood his personality. As such, the Schrempf deal did not surprise him, though he hardly approved.

"I guess knowing Larry and knowing Detlef, and knowing he probably wasn't going to go back there next year, I wouldn't have been surprised if they'd done something at some point," Hill said. "I was thrown off by the timing of it. It kind of puts them behind the eight-ball. To coach Detlef is to trust him and give him some freedom. You had to leave him alone and let him play, trust him to make the right decisions. Larry's a little more rigid than I am, so I could see there was at least the potential for problems."

With a 104-98 victory, Orlando tied its best start ever at 3-0. The Pacers, on the other hand, had their worst start, at 0-3, since 1988.

And it was all made possible by the player the Magic earned by failing to make the playoffs. Anfernee Hardaway compensated for an otherwise poor night by hitting a late three-pointer to ice the victory.

Like the game in Detroit, the Pacers had blown it with a poor fourth quarter. On a night when their three key players would come up big — Miller scored 25 while Smits and McKey had 20 apiece — they would lose, nonetheless.

O'Neal had missed Orlando's shootaround with the flu, but showed up strong, scoring 37 points to generally overwhelm Smits.

"I think he's going to have a huge year," said Smits. "I'm surprised last year they didn't go more to him because, I wouldn't say he's unstoppable, but he's pretty close to that when he's near the basket."

A more immediate problem than how to stop O'Neal had arisen, though. McKey tweaked his hamstring injury in Orlando. Though he came back to play 35 minutes, his status for the coming games was very much in doubt.

"I want the leg to be better," said McKey, "but I don't know if it can get fully healed at this point in the season."

Richardson had been criticized by Brown after the Orlando loss for his passive play. In 28 minutes, he committed five turnovers and scored just two points.

He responded in a big way two nights later at New Jersey.

His overtime jumper with 17.4 seconds capped a 17-point night, put the Pacers up 106-103 and brought Brown off the bench in congratulation. His defensive work on New Jersey waterbug Kenny Anderson, who shot seven of 20, also drew the coach's attention.

"The last couple of games, Pooh had great opportunities to shoot the ball and didn't," said Brown. "And I really got on him about it. Tonight, he made the biggest shot of the game."

Trying to fit in, Richardson refused to be self-congratulatory about the big shot. He had wanted Miller, who led the team with 28 points, to have the opportunity.

"It was cool, but I really wanted Reg to be the guy who took the shot because he was basically carrying us," said Richardson. "But when he came off the pick, he didn't think he was open so he got it back to me."

The game also offered reinforcement that the defensive philosophy Brown had been preaching since the first day of training camp had merit. They trailed 86-76 midway through the fourth quarter before putting the clamps on the Nets, who scored just one bucket in a six-minute span late in the game.

Most importantly, it was the first victory for a team that was starting to wonder when it would come.

"It was starting to get scary," said Antonio Davis. "You get on that train and play so many games in a row, you can be 0-10 before you know it. It feels different. It feels better. A lot of guys are smiling."

With the next four at home, things were starting to look up, but this would be another lesson in lost opportunity.

In Jordan's absence, the Knicks had been dubbed the rightful heirs to the throne, at least in the Eastern Conference. It really came about by process of elimination: no one else looked like anything remotely resembling a champion.

Cleveland had talent, but needed time to adjust to Fratello. Orlando would be good, but was too young. Atlanta would merit watching, if only because of Wilkens' presence. Chicago was expected to slip into the land of the mediocre. The one team that appeared to have a chance was Charlotte, which not only had a boatload of young talent, but the experience of a first-round upset of Boston the year before.

Those were the only teams given a chance to contend with the Knicks, but not much of one.

So, when the lowly Pacers trailed the mighty Knicks by just three, 62-59, in the middle of the third quarter, it looked like a promising night. Patrick Ewing left the game early in the period with a strained neck, the result of a Smits elbow late in the first half, and John Starks was on the bench with four fouls. Those two were responsible for nearly half the New York offense.

In their place were journeyman Herb Williams and unproven second-year guard Hubert Davis. This was an upset being served on a silver platter.

But for one small detail: in order to beat the Knicks, you have to score against them, at least a little bit.

The Pacers fell apart to lose 103-84, and more streaks were kept alive. The Knicks were 5-0, equaling their franchise's fastest start ever. Indiana hadn't won yet at home.

Clearly, the Pacers were struggling in their transition from an offensive to a defensive team.

"We're still thinking we've got to outscore people," said Mitchell. "That's not it. Look at New York: they've got two scorers, and Starks isn't there every night. Everybody in the NBA can score.

"You've got to do the other things. We've got to make up our minds to play defense. It ain't about, 'Did my man score?' If a guy scores, he scores on all 12 guys."

Brown was a coach who harped on the little things: loose balls, long rebounds, hard picks, protecting the basket. Those are the plays that don't make ESPN SportsCenter's highlights, but they do show up in the standings. To Brown, a team unwilling to do the dirty work had a serious character flaw.

Consider the problems facing Brown in this young season:

His front line was getting manhandled.

His offense was a mess.

His defense was erratic.

His bench was unsure.

His newest starter faced an uncertain physical future unless he rested a lingering injury.

His home court had been anything but an advantage.

"I ain't even worrying about wins and losses," Brown said. "I'm worrying about us improving. This team needs to win some games and play well at home. They've worked so hard it's a big deal, confidence-wise, but I don't know if you can harp on the games.

"If you put so much emphasis on the games, then you put a lot of pressure on these guys. We've just got to get better. Nobody wants to lose but, if you lose and feel you're making progress, you can live with it."

Brown's problems would only grow in the next game.

In a 102-93 loss to Charlotte, the Pacers started with 12 relatively undamaged players and finished with seven. One writer suggested they re-paint the team bus white, with red crosses on the sides and flashing lights on the roof.

McKey re-aggravated the hamstring in the first half and played eight awkward minutes in the second before limping to the bench for the rest of the night.

After driving for a layup that put the Pacers ahead 73-69 early in the fourth, Miller crumpled to the floor when he re-sprained his left ankle.

His replacement, Fleming, was quickly sent to the bench with a bloody left elbow.

Then his replacement, Paddio, sprained his right ankle.

Antonio Davis added the final chapter to the night's voluminous medical log by spraining his right ankle after a lay-in late in the game.

Of the five, the two most serious injuries were to the most important players.

Miller had started 345 consecutive games, the longest active streak in the league. Not only was that in jeopardy, but he doubted he would regain full health at any time during the season.

"It's going to be with me all year," Miller said. "There's no way I'm going to get over this. The only way it can get better is if I take two months off, and that'll never happen.

"I've got to be out there on the floor. I've been able to play with pain throughout my career but I'm in the major leagues with this one. This ankle controls my game."

McKey had thought his leg was healing, but was reminded about the unpredictable nature of a hamstring pull.

For a team that had been among the league's healthiest in recent seasons, the Pacers were playing catch-up with the odds.

"I hope we're snakebit early so we can get it over with," Walsh said. "This is a tough way to begin a season."

At full strength, this was a team given little chance at anything more than a scramble for a low playoff berth. And the Pacers had spent most of Brown's first six weeks at anything but.

The coach was starting to wonder about the succession of injuries. Maybe it was more than bad luck. Maybe it was fate.

"Maybe this is one of those years," he said. "You could almost sense it in training camp, when every game we played there would be three or four guys out that we didn't expect. Then we make the trade, and the guy we get is hurt. We just have to keep plugging, get healthy and not get discouraged."

That would be hard. Houston was coming to MSA with a 7-0 record, the fourth unbeaten team the Pacers would face in the first seven games. And they would do so without McKey, who would be placed on the injured list, meaning an absence of at least five games.

Kenny Williams, who had done little to impress anyone in training camp, was activated.

At least Brown had one thing to smile about: Richardson's continued improvement. He was averaging 12 points and nine assists and shooting 51 percent. "Pooh's getting better and better and better," Brown said. "He's our most improved player by far."

With Miller sitting out his first start since the 1988-89 season, and also missing McKey, the Pacers played gamely until the fourth quarter, when the Rockets pulled away to win 99-83. Another opponent had matched its best start ever, courtesy of the Pacers.

Early in the fourth quarter, before things had gotten out of hand, a heckler offered a painful suggestion to the bench.

"Somebody yelled to me to put in somebody to make a shot," said Brown, "but I'd been thinking about that for 48 minutes."

Antonio Davis, who had sprained his right ankle the game before, this time sprained his left. Would this never cease?

Fleming and Sealy, who replaced Miller and McKey in the starting lineup, combined for 25 points on 12 of 29 shooting. Smits, whose offense was needed now more than ever, fouled out with nine points in 23 minutes. In his first game back, Williams produced a three of 17 shooting night.

"Whenever you're in a situation where things are going real bad, you have to be optimistic that it can't keep going this way," said Sealy. "We just have to try to hold the fort till the big guns get back."

The problem was, they were guarding the walls with slingshots against a league stocked with automatic weapons. Though they were 1-6, the Pacers didn't feel that far away from being able to compete. One quarter away, to be exact.

In the fourth quarters of their losses to New York, Charlotte and Houston, they had shot 35 percent and been outscored 89-54.

"When you get to the fourth quarter," said Thompson, "other teams can send their stars back in." The Pacers anxiously waited for theirs to return.

Richardson had done his part to absorb more offensive responsibility, but Smits had not. Hunted once again by the touch-foul police, the center had spent an inordinate amount of time on the bench. Already, he had fouled out three times.

Players who do not fit the league's physical stereotypes have their careers disproportionately affected by the officials. Little men like Muggsy Bogues and Spud Webb generally get favorable whistles because their lack of height makes them underdogs. That same mentality worked against a taller player like Smits, who, in his sixth season, was still getting remarkably little respect.

Part of it was Smits' own passive nature. Officials also tend to lean toward the aggressors, which usually meant whoever was going against Smits. But much of it was the fact that Smits developed a soft reputation early in his career and it still hampered him.

"It's the worst I've ever seen in my life," Brown said. "It's a joke. They let other big guys bang each other. With Rik, it's a foul. He's got a reputation that he fouls and doesn't get fouled, and that's the way it is."

Brown also wondered about the team's lack of veteran leadership. The older guys on the team, Fleming, Mitchell and Thompson, all had lesser on-court roles. None had achieved much in the way of professional success, either, so their words lacked credibility.

"We don't have natural leaders on this team," Brown said. "We have guys with good character, but not guys who make demands of one another. Our veterans are all great guys but I don't think we act professionally."

Brown did get one piece of good news, though. His wife learned she was pregnant. The baby would be due in late June.

Soon, his toddling team would take its first steps.

Boston brought a 6-2 record into consecutive games with the Pacers, the first at MSA, the second in the Hartford, Connecticut, Civic Center.

Devastated by the off-season death of Reggie Lewis, the Celtics weren't expected to contend but had started the season well.

With Miller out again, joined by Antonio Davis, Richardson again stepped forward and produced his best game of the season. He had 24 points and 11 assists, including an off-balance, shot-clock-beating turnaround jumper that ended a late Boston run and put the Pacers up 96-89 with 1:35 left.

Brown had been hard on him, but it was paying off.

"He knows what he's doing," Richardson said. "When you've got a guy who wins every place he's been, you've got to go with it. He knows what he wants, and I'm learning more every day."

So, too, was Dale Davis. In his third season, he was projected into a far more prominent role in the offense. Brown compared him to a young Buck Williams and forecast stardom. Not until recently, though, had Davis lived up to the billing. He had career highs of 21 points and 22 rebounds against Boston.

It was a discouraging loss for the Celtics. Robert Parish summed it up by saying, "A lot of no-names kicked our butt."

The bruise only got deeper in Hartford. In a 102-71 demolition job, the Pacers established a franchise record for the fewest points allowed, held Boston to its lowest output since the 1955-56 team lost 83-69 to Rochester and allowed the Celtics just eight points in the fourth quarter, the lowest in that franchise's history and tied for the second-lowest ever in the NBA.

It was a performance so good, it very nearly satisfied Brown.

"I'm kind of shocked," he said.

This defensive attitude looked like it was starting to catch on. After allowing each of their first six opponents to break 100, the Pacers held the next three to descending totals of 99, 94 and 71.

"The only way we're going to win," said Miller, "is to guard each others' backs."

Before the game, Bird acknowledged publicly, for the first time, that he had been contacted about the Pacers' coaching vacancy before Brown was hired. And he did it in his own inimitable style.

"I can imagine if I took that job and the first day, I walked in and they told me they were going to trade Detlef because they couldn't pay him," Bird said. "I'd just turn around and follow him out the door."

* * *

Bird had been given the title of assistant to the senior executive vice president with the Celtics, but no one was quite sure what that meant, including Bird. He basically did special assignment work, checking out a promising college player or offering input on a personnel decision.

In general, though, he seemed to be coping well with retirement.

"There's always adjustments," he said. "You play basketball for 27 years and then one day you get up in the morning, and you don't. It's OK. If I feel like working out, I do. If I don't, then to hell with it. . . . I had a hell of a run, and now it's over. Sometimes I made the big basket, sometimes I didn't. But one thing I can say is I had the opportunity. I got every inch of talent out of my body that I could, but now that it's over I don't worry about it. It's somebody else's chance to be a hero."

Bird's rivalry with Magic Johnson carried the NBA out of obscurity and into the mainstream in the early to mid-1980s, then Jordan's brilliance made the league an icon of pop culture.

For the first time since 1979, the league was operating with none of the three. Some saw that as a crisis. Not Bird.

"Just because me, Michael and Magic's all out of the league," he said, "that doesn't mean they're going to stop making great basketball players."

Jordan's sudden retirement was viewed skeptically by some who doubted he could stay away from the game. Others went so far as to say Jordan would be back for the playoffs. From personal experience, Bird thought otherwise.

"It's hard to predict what somebody else is going to do, but the more I'm out of it, the better I like it. . . . I feel a lot better, I've got more things on my mind than basketball. It's a different life," he said. "I'd say, if Michael wants to come back, he's probably about the only guy who could because he's a superior athlete and he's in good shape. But I'd say the more he stays out, the less chance there is he'd come back."

Bird was in Hartford to have his number retired there, along with other Celtics greats who had played in one of their homes away from home. His number also had been retired at Springs Valley High in West Baden, Indiana State and Boston Garden.

Were there any more such ceremonies left?

"Only in heaven," he said, "but that'll be a while."

* * *

When Philadelphia gambled the No. 2 pick in the draft on one of the world's few true 7-6ers, Shawn Bradley, one of the most stinging criticisms was that he might turn out to be no better than another notoriously tall former second pick. Smits.

On this night in late November, Bradley demonstrated a defensive presence that far exceeded the veteran. Though Bradley's stats showed three rebounds and three blocks in the fourth quarter, his effect went far beyond that. More than any other, he was responsible for Philadelphia's 108-97 victory at MSA.

"He's going to be a great player," said Brown. "Every time you drive to the basket, he's there. I don't think they made the pick thinking he'd have an immediate impact, but he's going to be a remarkable player.

"He's certainly more of a defensive force than our guy."

Smits scored 25 points, but 15 of those came in 19 minutes against journeyman Eric Leckner, who started. When Bradley was in the game, the Pacers started shooting jumpers and, when they did post up, inevitably shot fadeaways.

"We wanted to go inside," said Brown. "We were begging them to go inside."

They didn't.

It was, in many ways, a flashback to the old Pacers, who would get themselves mentally ready for a formidable opponent but would come out flat against a light-weight.

"These are the hardest games to play," said Miller. "I'd rather be playing the Knicks, or one of those kinds of teams."

That statement from one of the leaders ensured that the maturation process, for this team, would take longer than hoped.

The friendly portion of the schedule ended with a home game against the disheveled Los Angeles Lakers, who had tied a franchise record with eight straight road losses. That streak ended, though, on what amounted to a well-guarded desperation shot.

With Sealy hanging from his shooting arm, center Vlade Divac pushed in an off-balance 19-foot jumper with one second left to deliver a 102-100 victory for the Lakers.

"That last shot," said Richardson, shaking his head. "Malik not only flew by him, he actually grabbed his arm, but he still made the shot."

Doubling the frustration was the loss of what could've been an uplifting victory.

The Pacers rallied from an eight-point deficit with five minutes left to tie it three times, the last on Miller's baseline three-pointer with 13.7 seconds left. They had momentum and they had the biggest crowd of the season (16,313) whipped into a frenzy, but they didn't have the ball.

Divac, who made the Lakers' only two baskets in the final five minutes, sent the Pacers to their sixth home loss in seven tries.

Their next four, and 13 of 19, would be on the road.

"It's tough, but I think this team matures more on the road," said Miller. "We can't get a win at home and I can't figure it out. The fans have been very supportive."

A big problem had been the bench. With Sealy starting in place of McKey, Brown had lost his biggest reserve weapon.

Though Sealy averaged 13.4 points and 4.6 rebounds in those five starts — numbers that exceeded McKey's averages of 9.8 points and 4.0 rebounds — he would return without protest to the bench when McKey was activated for the start of the road trip.

Sealy's impact on the second unit had been immense. In his six games as a reserve, the Pacer bench outscored its counterparts 201-163. In his five games as a starter, the bench had been outscored 182-89 — an average deficit of 18.6 points per game. Only once in that span did any reserve reach double figures, when Fleming scored 10 against Boston.

"I wouldn't even worry about the lack of bench scoring, but the play was bad," Brown said. "I've got to re-evaluate the guys we've been playing and think about going with guys who haven't been getting out there as much, like Kenny and Scott."

Brown's patience had been tried against Philadelphia. It had been stretched against the Lakers. At halftime in Sacramento, it snapped.

A poor Kings team further weakened by the absences of Wayman Tisdale (sprained ankle) and Pete Chilcutt (who sprained an ankle in the first half), shot 55 percent in building a 68-46 first-half lead. The Pacers had looked thoroughly disinterested.

In the locker room at the break, Brown unleashed his frustrations. Poor execution was one thing. But not playing hard? Not playing with enthusiasm? That simply was intolerable.

"We didn't even talk about winning the game," he said "because, quite honestly, I was just hopeful we would compete."

The deficit grew to 74-50 before the Pacers asserted themselves. Over the final 20 minutes, they outscored Sacramento 55-29 to take a 105-103 victory that was secured by a pair of big plays from Dale Davis.

With the Kings down by a point in the closing seconds, Mitch Richmond ran Sealy into a screen, drawing Richardson on the switch. He beat the point guard to the baseline and appeared to be sailing in for the potential game-winning basket.

Davis came flying at Richmond from the weak side, forcing him to alter his shot in mid-air. The ball struck the bottom of the rim, wound up in Richardson's hands, and the Pacers had in their grasp what seemed out of reach.

Davis wasn't quite done yet. After Richardson made one of two free throws to put Indiana up by two, the Kings had one last chance with five seconds left. But the power forward deflected an inbounds pass to Lionel Simmons, causing precious seconds to dwindle. By the time Simmons regained control of the ball, the only shot he had left was a desperation 20-footer that wasn't close.

Even with that victory, the team finished November with a 4-8 record, with three road games in four nights to start December. This was no way to start a season.

6 Point, Counterpoint

For the Pacers, visits to either of two cities scarcely felt like road trips: Los Angeles and New York.

Half the team, it seemed, was from one or the other.

They opened December in the dank Los Angeles Sports Arena, easily the worst facility in the NBA. After adding up the dozens of tickets needed for family and friends of Los Angeles natives Miller and Haskin, not to mention Brown, former "UCLAn" Richardson and off-season resident Thompson, the Pacers were unusually well-represented in an otherwise sparse crowd of 8,737.

Miller played like he owned the place, scoring 35 and looking fully healed as the Pacers won their fourth straight road game with a 120-100 victory.

"We always play better on the road," said Miller. "We've got to win at home, sooner or later, make it a tough place for people to come into. But we've always been comfortable on the road. We like the odds. We love the underdog role."

Their good fortune soon came to an end.

A 103-87 loss in Salt Lake City to the Utah Jazz returned things to their more normal state of affairs.

The locker room was preoccupied by yet another potentially crushing injury. Sealy was not in uniform and would be sent home. The early diagnosis was a possible stress fracture in his right foot.

Richardson, too, was uncomfortable. He had been kicked in the right calf in Los Angeles the night before but thought it was just a bruise. He would try to play through the pain. This team, after all, had enough to worry about.

There had been another development in Los Angeles. Walsh and Brown met with Byron Scott, still an unsigned free agent after a decade with the Lakers. They also talked over the possibility of signing point guard Gary Grant, who was looking for work.

Had they known about Richardson's injury at the time, Grant might've taken the first priority. As it was, the possible loss of Sealy - who had been backing up both Miller and McKey - was too threatening to ignore.

Brown had been pushing Scott to Walsh for weeks. In fact, had Brown stayed with the Clippers, that team planned to bring the veteran cross-town.

The Pacers had a $650,000 salary slot to offer, the result of a settlement with the players association, which had filed suit claiming the league had under-reported the revenues that determine the salary cap in 1992. Every team was awarded a slot — $550,000, if it was used for the 1992-93 season, $650,000 the following year.

"One of the first things Donnie told me we needed was a two-man (shooting guard) behind Reggie, but I didn't know about that until I could evaluate the team," he said. "Now, with Malik's injury, that might precipitate doing something right away."

That would have serious ramifications at point guard. Not only would Grant not be pursued, but Sealy's injury virtually killed the possibility of a deal with Dallas for Derek Harper. He was the player who most interested the Mavs. If he was out, so was the trade.

Sealy returned to Indianapolis and, on December 3, was told there was no stress fracture, but rather a sprain. That would not dissuade Walsh's interest in Scott.

After the team returned home with another loss, 99-92 at Golden State, a deal with Scott's agent, Tom McGlocklin, would be struck. The point guard situation, in the meantime, was starting to degenerate. Richardson, still not yielding to the injury, looked awful in committing 11 turnovers against the Warriors. Fleming, struggling with a strained lower back and bursitis in his right shoulder, could offer little help.

* * *

When Scott walked through the jetway and into Indianapolis International Airport, he was entering a new world.

Out of the shadows of Magic Johnson, Kareem Abdul-Jabbar and James Worthy, he was relishing the chance to become a leadership figure on a developing team.

And he wasted no time filling the role.

One of the first things he said, while walking to baggage claim, was that he had been in the playoffs 10 straight years and he saw no reason for the streak to end here.

"This team's been to the playoffs a number of times but hasn't won," he said. "It's going to be my job to make sure we get there, and win."

The Pacers were 5-10 at the time. Having begun December with one Western Con-ference road trip, they would have another before the month was over. Scott's confidence sounded, at the very least, misplaced. The point guard position was heading toward disarray. Fleming had to be placed on the injured list, forcing the activation of Workman, who had been abysmal in the preseason. He would be the only backup to Richardson, who was struggling.

Room for Scott was made when Thompson, who had a sore left knee, was put on the list. Though Sealy would miss at least a week, the staff opted to keep him on the active roster.

Through the course of his first few months, Brown identified areas of glaring need: a shooter on the bench; veteran leadership; the professionalism that leads to consistency; respect throughout the league.

Those just happened to be Scott's strengths.

"It's uplifting for everybody," said Brown. "One of the things this team needs is a guy who has been in a winning situation, has had success, knows what it takes to win and what responsibilities veterans have. From anybody's standpoint, having him in the locker room is a plus."

He was greeted warmly by the players, particularly Miller, who looked at him as something of a mentor. Beyond that, Scott's presence on the bench would allow Miller to push himself harder without having to worry about becoming tired or fouling out.

"I still think he's a hell of a ballplayer," said Miller. "Whatever he has left in him, I hope he gives it to us. This is a guy who has won three NBA championships. You can't mess around with that. He's been to the mountaintop and back."

Coming to the Pacers represented a considerable climb down, but Scott relished the opportunity to serve as an elder statesman.

"It's a very easy adjustment," Scott said. "This is what I've been looking forward to. I've stated all along I would like to play in a backup role. I've had my days as a starter, all that glory. It's easier for me to kind of be in the background and play a different part — especially for a young team like this, who I feel has an opportunity to have a very special season."

There he was again, talking positively about the season's potential. Hadn't he been paying attention?

"This team is getting better and hopefully he can put us over the hump," said Miller. "He doesn't have to come in here and score 16-20 points a game. Right now, we need his leadership and his on-court attitude."

It didn't take Scott long to make his presence felt in practice. He quickly offered Miller some pointers about using his body to run defenders into screens, showing no hesitation to offer advice.

"He'll be able to help Reggie out a lot with the experience he has at that position," said Richardson. "He's made a lot of big shots in a lot of big games.

"Plus, it's like having another coach out there. A coach can tell you things but, sometimes, when you hear it from another player, it comes through more clearly."

One thing was certain. Scott had kept himself in shape. During the mandatory physical prior to signing his contract, Scott had to be asked to get off the treadmill. The test was over, but he wasn't tired.

He would be ready to play right away. He had to be.

* * *

Layups are nice, for some, but they didn't do much for Kenny Williams. His personal philosophy: I slam, therefore I am.

When sore ankles that developed early in training camp took the charge out of his most precious physical gift, electrifying leaping ability, Williams literally was grounded for an uncomfortably long period of time.

"I found myself laying the ball up a lot," Williams said. "That's not me. One time in practice, I went up and Pooh blocked my shot. I said, 'Hold on, this is not right.' "

In a 105-87 home rout of the Sacramento Kings, Williams' game took flight once again.

When McKey limped to the locker room with a pulled calf muscle early in the first quarter, Brown had little choice but to reach deep into the bench for Williams. McKey's regular backup, Sealy, was out for at least a week with a sprained right foot.

Williams played his way into Brown's heart with 16 points and six rebounds in 26 minutes. It wasn't the first time someone from deep on the bench had stepped in and produced, a trend that would continue throughout the season.

"I got off to a bad start in training camp," he said. "He hasn't seen the Kenny Williams that everybody else has seen here the last three years. I had to prove myself to Larry Brown. Now, maybe he's seeing that I can play, that it's not just a rumor."

If Williams was for real and Scott and Workman could provide quality time, the bench could turn from a liability into an asset.

Scott was rusty in his debut, but not shy. He hoisted 10 shots in 11 minutes, but made just three. One of them, though, was a shot-clock-beating jumper that put the Pacers ahead for good, 75-74. He hadn't lost his knack for the big one.

McKey's calf injury turned out not to be serious. "They say I tore a muscle everybody doesn't have," McKey said. "Now I don't have one, either."

With McKey, Richardson and Sealy all resting injuries, the Pacers had just nine healthy bodies for their December 8 practice. In the process, they discovered someone who played like a coach on the floor.

That's because there was a coach on the floor. Assistant Billy King suited up to give the Pacers enough bodies for a scrimmage. The 6-6 King played mostly point guard.

It wasn't the first time Brown had to ask an assistant coach to dress out. When he was with the Clippers, Brown had occasion to call on another former Duke player, Quin Snyder, to fill in. "And he wanted a 10-day contract," Brown said, smiling. "After today, Billy might want one, too. He was pretty good."

He was?

"He was all right," said Miller. "He had a pretty good practice, pretty consistent. He looked more like a player than a coach. After he got his third wind, he was OK. The first two were awful."

"He was coming down, calling plays, taking people to the hole," said Williams. "He did pretty good, but they did have an oxygen tank out there for him, and I saw him looking over at it every now and then."

King, 27, went to the Final Four twice while with Duke, earning a reputation as a defensive specialist. After spending one season as an ESPN analyst, he joined the Illinois State staff as an assistant. After four years there, he was given his break into the NBA as the last addition to Brown's staff.

So it wasn't like he didn't belong. He did, after all, get tryouts with Sacramento and Charlotte coming out of college.

His trial run with the Pacers, at the very least, gave the team a distraction from the season-long injury problems that had played havoc with Brown's plans.

The holiday season was upon the team and spirits were high. Scott already was having an effect in the locker room, and soon would on the court. Maybe this wouldn't be such a bad year, after all.

At the very least, the players seemed to like each other. That had to count for something.

When first the Pacers and Orlando Magic met in the third game of the season, O'Neal scored 37 points, blocked four shots, and hit 14 of 19 from the field. Smits fouled out, although he did last long enough to score 20 points.

Most coaches might've viewed that as a need to give Smits as much defensive help as possible, in the form of double-and triple-teams when O'Neal caught the ball in the low post. Not Brown.

For the second meeting, Brown left Smits on O'Neal by himself much of the time. Though the individual mismatch looked like Godzilla vs. Bambi, the Pacers learned something important about the Magic.

Like any young team with a dominating player, the rest of the players tended to throw the ball to Shaq and expect him to win the game all by himself. He certainly tried, scoring a career-high 49, but just one teammate, Hardaway with 18, scored in double figures.

Though Smits fouled out again, this time with just 11 points, eight Pacers scored between 10 and 23 in a 111-105 victory.

"If you look at games where one guy gets big numbers, normally it's a close game," said Brown. "You might have a real difficult time guarding a great player, but it allows you to play other people when they're so conscious of taking advantage of a guy having a great night."

Of O'Neal's 11 first-half baskets, nine were dunks. Smits only fouled O'Neal once, primarily because he couldn't keep him within reach. "He was kicking my ass in the first half," said Smits, who stuck closer to O'Neal in the second, and wound up fouling out with 8:28 remaining. "But I'll take him scoring 50 as long as we win any day. Well, not any day. The guys saved me."

Though O'Neal continued to score in the second half, he did not dunk again as Smits, Antonio Davis and Haskin managed to keep their bodies between his and the basket. O'Neal scored 14 of his 26 second-half points from the free throw line — where he scares no one.

Davis was particularly impressive, scoring eight of his 12 points in the fourth quarter while leaning on O'Neal as much as possible.

Richardson entered the game bothered by the sore calf and left with three more problems. He took an O'Neal elbow to the head and another to the nose before Scott Skiles opened a bloody gash on his right eyelid with an inadvertent finger in the fourth quarter. A season that had started with so much promise for Richardson was beginning to unravel.

When he had been activated from the injured list prior to the Sacramento game on December 7, Workman was third in a two-man rotation, wondering if he'd ever get a chance to play. When the Pacers faced New York on December 11, he was the only point guard left standing.

Fleming had been placed on the injured list prior to the Sacramento game. Richardson had been unable to practice for days and now could not play.

Coming out of the preseason, Workman was a major question mark. He struggled so badly that, if not for his two-year guaranteed contract, he might've been cut. As it was, he opened the season on the injured list with what was loosely described as a "foot problem."

Workman would joke about that one. He might've been the only player whose career ended on an injury that never happened. "I was wondering when I was going to come off (the injured list), or if I was going to come off," Workman said. "Pride took over for a while and kept me from getting frustrated. I just had to wait my turn. I came here to play. I want to show everybody I can play."

In his first two appearances off the list, Workman demonstrated the toughness and hustle that earned him the contract.

"In the preseason I was trying to do too much, going too fast," he said. "Now I've had a chance to see everything, so when I come in, it's a matter of slowing down, taking my time and being more in control of the situation. I don't think I was in the preseason."

* * *

Workman and Antonio Davis were among the 20 NBA players who had spent at least the last season in Europe, fertile ground in the league's burgeoning global farm system.

Their reasons for going to Europe vary, but most go with one thing in mind: taking a step toward the NBA.

They were established veterans like Kenny Walker of Washington, Greg Anderson of Detroit and Pete Myers of Chicago, who got lost in the NBA shuffle and needed the overseas experience to rebuild their resumes.

They were rookies not ready for the NBA when drafted, like Davis, P.J. Brown of New Jersey and Popeye Jones of Dallas.

And they were native Europeans, like Boston's Dino Radja and Chicago's Toni Kukoc, finding their way across the Atlantic in greater numbers.

It was much different than in years past, when Europe was a final resting place for has-beens or a long-term career option for never-weres.

"I think the one big advantage you get with a player who has been in Europe is he's had time to become a professional in his thinking," said Walsh. "In Europe, they're a lot harder on guys, especially Americans. Over here, we'll give a player some time. Over there, they have to produce right away.

"There's a lot of pressure on them, so they understand the business they're in when they come back."

Davis had been a revelation to the Pacers. A second-round pick out of Texas-El Paso in 1990, Davis knew he wasn't ready for the NBA. He headed to Greece, where he played for two years. Though he was a standout in the Pacers' 1992 summer rookie and free agent camp, he opted to go back to Europe for one more season, spending the previous year with Philips Milan of the Italian A1 League — generally regarded as the strongest competition on that continent.

"I needed Europe for a lot of different reasons," Davis said. "I started playing basketball kind of late (the 10th grade). I just needed to play, wherever I could, whenever I could. I didn't think I was ready. My confidence wasn't there."

The Pacers signed Davis anticipating little more than an active big body to fill one of the final roster spots. They had gotten much more.

"He's a lot better than we thought," said Walsh. "Some of it is that he played in Europe. More than that, it's just his attitude."

The most valuable experience Davis gained overseas was mental, not physical.

"The biggest thing is I'm more mature as a person," he said. "I know a little bit more about some (basketball) things than I did when I went over — some ways to score, how to guard bigger guys — but, really, it was how to be a professional . . .

"The biggest part of the game over there is being mentally prepared. You're away from home, adapting to being over there. You get lonely and there's nobody to talk to. You get to the point where you're just looking for ways to get you through to the next day."

Workman played with Atlanta and Washington from 1989-91. Uncertain of the Bullets' desire to re-sign him, he headed for Italy. A teammate on his Scavolini Pesaro team was Myers, who had inherited Jordan's spot at shooting guard in Chicago.

"It's a lot harder than what people think because of the pressure that's put on you," said Workman. "They only play once or twice a week, so every game is so important. If you lose it's the end of the world."

The concept of the European vacation, then, was a thing of the past.

"You've got to go over there to work," said Davis. "Some guys think they can go over there and half-ass it because there's only one or two games a week. But it's tough. It's more mentally tough than physically tough."

With its bigger bankrolls and glamorous profile, Europe remained an attraction for graybeards, like Bob McAdoo and Reggie Theus, looking to pad their retirement accounts. But those situations were becoming more the exception.

"If you're going over there for the money, it's a gold mine," said Workman. "But if you're going over there to play, you've got to go to some extreme places and put up with a lot."

The European experience used to extend careers; now it expanded them.

* * *

Point guard was becoming a problem, one of many.

Of equal concern to Brown was his growing uneasiness over Smits' play. Patrick Ewing followed O'Neal's 49-point game by going for 32 against Smits in a 98-91 Knicks victory that dropped the Pacers to an unlucky 7-11.

"I'm not worried about whether he scores or not," Brown said. "I want to see how we're playing, whether he's defending, or rebounding, or making his man work for points.

"He's struggling right now, but we've played against some pretty good people. A lot of guys have a hard time against Patrick (Ewing) and Shaquille (O'Neal). He's not alone there."

Smits played just 18 minutes, producing 10 points and two rebounds.

"I think there's another level to Rik," Brown said. "He can be an adequate defender and rebounder, but it can't be every third or fourth night. We can't win with one block, four rebounds and six fouls.

"I was hoping the loss of weight would make him more athletic, give him some more quickness. But you see balls bounce all around him and he doesn't make an attempt to get them. You see people drive down the lane right past him."

Brown was quickly losing faith in Smits, frequently benching the team's lone low-post scoring threat in the fourth quarter. Brown could not live with a center who showed no passion for either defense or rebounding.

"If we're going to be any good, it's not the offense that concerns me, it's the defense and the boards," said Brown. "He blocked shots earlier in his career and he's had periods where he's rebounded well. Those have to be priorities with him every night."

Coming up were three teams that posed much less of a threat to Smits. Washington had rotund Kevin Duckworth, Atlanta immobile Jon Koncak and New Jersey prolific underachiever Benoit Benjamin.

The home game against the Bullets also offered the Pacers their first personal look at the player they had tried so desperately to obtain, Cheaney.

He opened the season in the starting lineup — a move that surprised Cheaney, since he was coming off a hamstring pull and was not in top shape — but was relegated to the bench after four games. Coach Wes Unseld, concerned about Cheaney's ability to defend small forwards, used him almost exclusively as the backup to shooting guard Rex Chapman, while Don MacLean replaced Cheaney in the lineup.

In recent games, Cheaney had been used at both positions as a backup. "I think I'm going to be real good," he said. "It's a matter of wanting to be good, of staying after it and continuing to work on my game. The only way to be a great player in this league is to outsmart and outwork your opponent. There's no secret formula."

The Evansville native scored scored 11 in his first professional appearance in his home state but it was hardly enough for the Bullets, who dropped their eighth straight game, 106-87.

Workman, Miller and McKey combined for 22 assists and Smits had 22 points. The Pacers had won three in a row at home after starting the year 1-6.

For Workman, it was a particularly satisfying night. He had started 56 games for the Bullets in the 1990-91 season and was startled when they did not offer him a contract the following year.

"I wanted to shoot it every time," he said.

That job belonged to Miller, who was still trying to find out how he could best serve the team. He scored in bunches in November, but that didn't produce victories. In December, he began coveting assists, racking up 39 in seven games. His 10 against the Bullets was one short of a career high.

"For me to be successful in this league, I've got to do other things besides put the ball in the basket," Miller said. "I've got to be able to raise the level of play of the other guys around me, no matter who they are."

Said Brown: "He's a much better overall player than I imagined."

The next day brought promising news, mixed with the usual batch of negative. Richardson felt healthy enough to play after a week off, but the word on Thompson and Sealy was discouraging. Thompson's troublesome right knee would keep him out at least six more weeks. He had flown to Los Angeles to consult with Lakers physician Dr. Stephen Lombardo, who diagnosed chronic patellar tendinitis and recommended rest and rehab. The Pacers medical staff suggested Thompson undergo an arthroscopy. Thompson, a player who hates the thought of any operation, no matter how minor, chose Lombardo's method.

That did not sit well with management for one very important reason. If Thompson had gone for the scope, he might've returned more quickly. As it was, his projected return was dangerously close to the February 24 trading deadline.

Thompson and Sealy were two-thirds of the package being offered to Dallas for Derek Harper, Sean Rooks and Terry Davis, and both were facing lengthy absences. Whatever chance that deal might've had was virtually eliminated.

Under their usual cloud of uncertainty, the Pacers headed to Atlanta for yet another game against a torrid team. In November, they had been victims of franchise-record unbeaten starts by New York and Houston.

The Hawks hadn't started well, losing four of their first five, but they hadn't lost since, a franchise-record 14-game streak that had them sitting atop the Eastern Conference at 15-4.

Two franchises that had entered the season in essentially the same positions couldn't be farther apart.

Both hired high-profile head coaches who stress defense, both made fairly significant personnel changes, both were coming off mediocre seasons, both set the goal of getting past the first round of the playoffs for the first time in this decade, and neither had captured the attention of its local populace.

Over the previous four seasons, these teams represented the peak of mediocrity. The Pacers were 164-164, the Hawks 165-163. They were franchises trapped in the middle.

In that situation, a franchise has few options. It can break up its current roster for scrap and rebuild, but that can take years in the lottery. Not every team will have the luck of Orlando or Charlotte. Others, like Washington and Minnesota, had failed to draw the top pick and remained among the dregs of the league.

Does a mediocre team have to get worse before it can get better?

"It's one argument," said Atlanta general manager Pete Babcock. "But it's difficult to live with because it's contrary to what you're in business to do as far as maximizing talent, maximizing potential.

"Ask the Dallas Mavericks how difficult it is to live with. They ended up having to go that direction of being a bad team again, but, they've got Jimmy Jackson and Jamal Mashburn and, pretty soon, they'll be right back up there.

"But it wasn't a lot of fun going through what it took to get there. The fans get upset, the press gets upset."

Some were wondering just what it would take to bring the fans back to The Omni. Though the Hawks were unbeaten at home, their attendance average was just slightly more than 11,000, next-to-last in the league.

They wouldn't get that many for the Thursday night game with the Pacers. Just 10,551 were in attendance.

"Their fans ought to be shot," said Miller. "That's unbelievable. You win 14 in a row, you're in first place in the Central, and you draw like that. That's awful. That's a bad lack of fan support."

The Pacers certainly did their part.

Brown overestimated Dale Davis had "about 2,500 ticket requests."

If that had indeed been the case, the Hawks would've been eternally grateful.

Actually, Davis needed 55 tickets: 30 for a group from his high school, Stephens County, and 25 more for family and friends who made the two-hour trek from the old hometown, Toccoa, Georgia.

Clearly, the pressure to perform was on in a big way.

"I had to play good," he said. "I had no choice."

Davis didn't let his fan club down. He racked up 19 points, 18 rebounds and all but eliminated Atlanta's forays inside as the Pacers handed the Hawks their first loss in slightly more than a month, 99-81.

Three key Pacers won their individual duels. Derrick McKey shut down Dominique Wilkins in the second half, Davis outplayed Kevin Willis and Miller kept Stacey Augmon from getting into the flow.

Wilkins scored 23 points, but only six in the second half. McKey severely limited his shot selection, cutting off drives and forcing jumpers. A full one-third of Wilkins' shots were three-pointers, and he hit just one of the seven. "Derrick played Dominique," said Brown, "as well as you can play him."

Then there was Davis, who took Willis (three of 12) completely out of the game with relentless ferocity at both ends. Augmon, a poor shooter who relies on quick drives and transition buckets, was one for 11 against Miller.

The Pacers opened the fourth quarter with a 72-66 lead, but Davis shook free for two dunks, then drained a rare 15-foot baseline jumper to push the advantage into double digits. The Hawks cut it to 82-74 on a pair of Wilkins free throws, but McKey and Miller combined to produce the game's next 11 points, spreading the margin to 93-74 with 2:10 remaining.

"He (Davis) was tremendous," said Brown. "He seemed to get his hands on every rebound. Then, when he hit the baseline jumper, I knew he was on."

Not bad for a guy who missed the team bus to the game and didn't get a chance to warm up.

"If it ain't broke," said Davis, cracking a sly smile, "don't fix it."

Those words could apply to McKey, as well. The Pacers, and their public, were beginning to see what this long-armed, laid-back player could bring to the team.

The early skepticism about McKey was well-founded. It was kind of like being told a blind date has a great personality. That may be the case, but it's only natural to worry about what the date doesn't have. When a coach describes a player as one of those guys who does things that don't show up in the box score, that often means it's because the player lacks the skills for the things that do.

McKey, the blind date who arrived when the Pacers broke up with Schrempf, was looking very much like an exception.

What McKey does is harder to describe than what he does not. He isn't a big scorer. He doesn't control the glass. His next triple-double will be his first. His value, then, is difficult to quantify.

How do you measure defensive ability? The pass that precedes an assist? The hand on the loose ball that becomes a rebound for someone else? The defensive rotation that forces a play to break down? One place: the won-lost column.

The Pacers had won four of five, and McKey had made himself heard.

"He's getting better, physically," said Brown. "I coached Bobby Jones, who I thought was as fine a defender as there ever was, and this kid is right there. That's the nicest compliment I can give anybody."

Nowhere else is the Pacers' change in personality more marked than at small forward. Where Schrempf was a quintessential offensive player, McKey was the opposite.

"So many people compare him with Detlef," said Brown. "They're different. Detlef is great in his way. Derrick is great at what he does."

It's just that no one gives awards for the things McKey does.

"I don't come in (after the game) and look at the stats," he said. "As long as we win, that's all that really matters to me."

Victories, you can measure. Ultimately, their number would be the yardstick of McKey's influence.

In Atlanta, Richardson played eight ineffective minutes, his lower right leg wrapped so heavily it looked like he was wearing a hockey goalie's pad.

When he did not practice the next day, Brown's patience was all but gone. Fleming rejoined the team and appeared capable of playing. Richardson had scarcely practiced in two weeks and Brown was growing weary of the nightly uncertainty about the availability of his point guard.

"We can't go game to game, practice to practice not knowing whether he can go or not," said Brown. "It's not fair to him or to the team. He wouldn't be saying he was hurt if he wasn't. It's just a matter of how much (pain) he can play with."

The latter statement told much of the real story. There was much doubt in the locker room about the severity of Richardson's injury. The medical staff couldn't come up with an explanation for Richardson's absence, though they changed the original diagnosis from a bruised calf to a bone contusion. Whether he played or not was entirely up to Richardson, an empowerment few were comfortable with.

Though the team had four straight road games coming up, including three out West that led right up to Christmas, Richardson would be placed on the injured list and Fleming activated. It was a decision made far simpler by Workman's startling play.

In an attempt to probe deeply into his psyche, a television interviewer proposed asking the same question four or five times, hoping to elicit a variety of responses from the new starter at point guard.

The question: "What words would you use to describe yourself?"

The answer: "workman."

That's a wrap.

It didn't take Freud to analyze this guy. His name said it all. In six games since Workman had come off the injured list, the Pacers won five, including a 108-98 victory over the New Jersey Nets at home that brought their record to 10-11. They hadn't been this close to .500 since they were 0-1.

Workman tied his career high with 21 points and contributed eight assists and three steals against the Nets, outplaying All-Star Kenny Anderson, who missed 12 of 20 shots and committed four turnovers.

The performance prompted a quote from Brown that was rife with between-the-lines meaning.

"No matter how well Pooh was playing, he couldn't be playing any better than Haywoode is," said the coach, "especially considering our priority for defense."

Reality would set in, quickly, for Workman and the team.

Against Phoenix's Kevin Johnson, Workman had trouble getting the ball upcourt and was harrassed into eight turnovers. The Suns won 102-94. It was a bad start to the trip.

While Johnson initiated the defense, Charles Barkley took care of the offense. Limping on a sprained ankle, a strained groin and a sore back, Barkley nonetheless scored 27 points. The Pacers tried guarding him with Dale Davis in the first half, but he wound up in foul trouble. Derrick McKey took over in the second, but his length could not counteract Barkley's bulk.

Still, the Pacers trailed just 96-92 with 2:15 left before committing three straight turnovers — the last two by Workman, who threw errant passes inside — and the Suns capitalized to build a 102-92 lead.

"Haywoode's a backup," said Brown, re-trenching. "He's had to play major minutes against great players, so he's going to have nights like this."

The next stop would be Seattle, where a party thrown by his former teammates awaited McKey. So did Schrempf.

A popular player in the Sonics locker room, McKey was particularly close to Nate McMillan, his teammate for six years. The two Southerners — McKey from Meridian, Mississippi, McMillan from Raleigh, North Carolina — had come to the Sonics as first-round draft picks a year apart. As teammates for six years, they had been integral in Seattle's growth to its current status as a championship contender.

"He's a good guy," said McMillan. "A great guy."

On the court, though, he was as mysterious to the Sonics as the Pacers. A truly gifted offensive player, McKey could shoot over most small forwards, not to mention drive past or post up, but he was thoroughly disinterested in scoring.

"I was excited about seeing how he would play with us this year. I thought he would change his personality as far as his approach to the game because we needed him to do more this year," McMillan said. "I thought he would step up and play more aggressive, be more selfish with the ball because Ricky (Pierce) is getting a little older and Eddie (Johnson) was moved. But they were basically going on how the offense looked in training camp. And we didn't look like we had enough."

While Seattle presented the trade as simply a basketball move, the Pacers had tried to politicize it. Rumors were started about Schrempf privately telling teammates he wouldn't be back, and that he had intimated as much to Walsh and Brown.

When Schrempf heard the rumors, the bitterness he felt over the trade boiled up all over again.

"Don't put words in my mouth, saying I never would have signed with the Pacers again. I never said that. I never would say that. I wouldn't have bought a new house and put a swimming pool in. I wouldn't have done those things if I didn't expect to be there for a few years," he said.

What Schrempf did do was make it clear to Walsh that he would consider the club's treatment of him before making any decision when he became a free agent in July. Schrempf felt Walsh had dragged his feet in a requested renegotiation that wasn't settled until after the player went public, telling The Indianapolis News during the summer of 1992 that he wanted to be traded.

"I treat people the way they treat me," Schrempf said. "He (Walsh) left me on the hot seat for a whole summer, so maybe, for the hell of it, I'd do the same thing. But I also told him, realistically, who's going to pay me? The Pacers were the only team that could give me a big contract. They've got to do their thing and justify what they did, but don't put words in my mouth."

With a 91-88 victory over the Pacers, Schrempf's new team raised its record to 20-2, a perfect 12-0 at home.

The Pacers did not go down without a fight.

Seattle's Ricky Pierce was ejected for throwing a punch at Scott after the two traded shoves at the end of the third period. Pierce appeared to initiate the exchange with an elbow, then a shove that Scott responded to, but said he was defending himself.

"I regret I missed," said Pierce, whose punch grazed Scott's neck. "That's all I regret."

A close game came down to the final few possessions, a situation that inevitably doomed the Pacers.

The game was tied 85-all with 2:07 left. After Gary Payton made a free throw to put Seattle ahead, the Pacers committed a 24-second violation; their 23rd turnover of the night. They then nearly forced the same result from the Sonics. But on an inbounds play with just one second on the shot clock, Kendall Gill spun free from Scott for a dunk that made it 88-85 with 1:09 left.

After McKey missed one of two free throws, Gill struck again, driving into the lane, then pulling up quickly for a short jumper that made it 90-86 with 33.2 seconds showing.

When the Pacers came up empty on their next possession — McKey's drive missed, as did Dale Davis' follow — the verdict was sealed.

Consecutive close losses to Phoenix and Seattle, two of the NBA's top teams, had hardly dampened the team's spirit. If anything, the Pacers gained confidence in their ability to succeed at this new, more physical style.

There was one not-so-small problem, though. The better the defense became, the worse the offense played. This was a team, it seemed, incapable of playing both ends with similar intensity.

Turnovers were the biggest problem, particularly for Workman. His career high coming into the season was five. In six starts, he had met or exceeded that number five times while averaging 5.5.

They trailed Phoenix 96-92 with two minutes left, but committed three straight turn-overs to let the game get away.

They were tied at 85-all in Seattle, but didn't make another basket until the final seconds.

The pattern would recur in Portland.

The 108-96 loss was the third in four nights. Though they had competed well against three of the league's top teams (Seattle, Phoenix and Portland were a combined 54-18 at the time), the Pacers were consistently coming up short late in games.

"I think we've got a good team," said Miller, who did not score in the fourth quarter. "It's not good enough coming down to the wire and losing. That period is over now; new team, new era, new everything. We've got to win these kinds of games. We can play with all of these teams, but that's no consolation when you lose all three."

The common threads in the defeats were turnovers and poor fourth-quarter production. Their 20 turnovers against the Blazers brought the three-game total to 68. They also failed to score 20 points in the final period for the third straight time, producing just 18 and going nearly five minutes between field goals.

"We're right there — right there," said Scott. "We're going to have that breakthrough and, when it comes, it's going to come big. We've got a long way to go, but we're getting there, and we're getting there pretty quick."

They had spent 15 of the last 23 days on the road, enduring two Western trips in a brutal grind made more difficult by the inevitable depression of being away from loved ones during the holiday season. Still, they had survived. The record was 3-8 when that stretch began; teams of lesser character would've returned home in disarray. Their chartered jet delivered them back to Indianapolis at about 9 a.m. on Christmas Eve with a 10-14 record. Not exactly the stuff of celebration, but not bad, all things considered.

There would be little time to celebrate the holiday. After opening presents and wolfing down a quick Christmas dinner, the players headed right back to the airport. The schedule-maker had been particularly cruel. Not only were they leaving their families on Christmas day, but their destination was Cleveland. Not only was the locale distasteful, so was the opponent. The Cavaliers had won nine straight from the Pacers.

The streak would grow to 10 in a game that followed the established pattern.

Leading 100-96 with 2:43 left in overtime, the Pacers produced two turnovers, three missed shots and a free throw on their next six possessions to allow Cleveland to rally for a 107-103 victory on a snowy Sunday afternoon.

In a game that left neither team satisfied it got a fair shake from the officials, the Pacers felt downright robbed because of one call in particular.

Trailing 103-101 with 28 seconds left, Miller was called for putting a hand in Bobby Phills' face while trying to get through a screen, an offensive foul that, as it turned out, cost the Pacers their last chance at tying the game.

Brown had to be buffered by assistants Heard, Blair and King in a postgame verbal assault on the officiating crew of Eddie F. Rush, David Jones and Ron Olesiak, but would offer no comment about the calls afterward. He would be fined $3,000 by the NBA for the incident.

This business of getting no respect was new to Scott, who had come from a Lakers team loaded with players who would get the benefit of the officials' doubts.

"I've never been through anything like this, where everything goes against you every game," he said. "It's very frustrating. The only thing you can do is stay optimistic and tell yourself it's going to get better. We have a good team. It'd be different if we didn't have the talent and a good coaching staff. You could accept it. We're just not getting our due respect, the justice we deserve, and it's got to change."

Several other themes recurred.

Brown continued to harp on Miller's shot selection. Earlier in the year, he wanted Miller to attack the basket more frequently. Miller was trying, but instead of going up strong, Miller frequently would flop or flail his arms after a miss, attempting to draw a foul call. When the whistle did not come, it would only increase his frustation. Miller was becoming touchy on this particular subject. "I'm the one that's out there on the court," he said. "I've got to understand what's going to work for Reggie."

Kenny Williams continued his history of irresponsibility, legal and otherwise, when he was pulled over at 2:24 a.m., the morning after the loss in Cleveland, and hit with a smorgasbord of traffic charges: operating while intoxicated, disregarding a red light, speeding, driving without insurance or registration. He would eventually plead guilty, receiving a one-year suspended sentence, 80 hours of community service and a one-month license suspension.

This was just the latest sign that Williams simply would never grow up. He expected the club to take care of things for him, the way star high school players had things taken care of: grades, cars, girls, spending money. In his mind, he still was the hot prospect who deserved to be spoiled. To the Pacers, he was becoming little more than a prolific waste of talent and time.

The other lingering distraction was the trade rumor that would not die, and it was starting to get to Sealy. A season that had started with so much promise was devolving. He hungered for some kind of resolution. "The only thing that distracts me is other people constantly telling me about it," Sealy said. "In that respect, I wish it would happen either way. You can't control where you go in this league. You just have to make the most of whatever situation you're thrust into."

Workman was struggling, shooting 10 of 34 with 19 turnovers in the four-game losing streak, but would remain the starter, if only because Brown didn't want to make it look like he was singling out Workman for blame.

After three days off, Brown would have a plethora of possibilities in the blame department, for the Pacers returned from the needed respite completely flat. They had won four in a row at home and had generally been competitive on the road, avoiding embarrassing blowouts.

A 107-82 loss to San Antonio didn't exactly ring in the new year. The Pacers, instead, looked wrung out. The second-largest home crowd of the season, a solid 16,044, was rewarded with a thoroughly despicable effort and booed the team. They trailed by 33 late in the fourth quarter and, if not for a meaningless late run, would've suffered the worst home loss by margin in club history.

"It was just a horrible game. Horrible," said Fleming. "That was embarrassing. If I was a fan, I would've booed the effort we gave."

"There's no excuse for something like that, not at this stage of the season," said Miller, who produced a season-low eight points. "We deserved every boo we got, and then some. We should go out and practice right now."

So bad was the offense that it took a late splurge of gimmes to drive the shooting percentage all the way up to .343. For most of the night, it hovered, like the winter temperatures, in the mid-to high-20s.

"There are some obvious problems we have," said Brown. "We can't beat a person on a drive and we can't create plays to make easy shots for other people. That's really us in a nutshell."

In each of the five straight losses, they had failed to reach 100 points in regulation. The defense was improving, to be sure, but the lack of offense was dragging the team down.

It wasn't that David Robinson (21 points, six rebounds) dominated. There was no need. Dale Ellis scored 16 of his 21 in the third quarter and J.R. Reid came off the bench for 22.

"They destroyed us. It wasn't even close," said Miller. "The varsity played the jayvee."

Some junior varsity players might've considered that an insult.

7 New Year, New Life

The embarrassment of the San Antonio loss, the thundering of boos in their ears, did not fade quickly. There would not be another game for five days, time Brown used for needed practice, time he hoped would bring his ailing team back to full health.

Richardson's lingering absence had driven both Brown and Walsh to distraction. Walsh went so far as to phone Richardson's agent, Arn Tellem, to find out what was going on with his player. The message being sent was clear. The Pacers thought Richardson had missed far more time than his injury normally would require to heal.

Soon, they would learn how wrong they were.

The team had three straight days of practice. Though Sealy survived all three days intact, Richardson did not. He was sent for yet another examination. This time, the Magnetic Resonance Imaging showed what had been the problem all along. Richardson had a stress fracture in the right fibula. The MRI didn't pick up the fracture itself, but instead showed the calcification that indicates the bone's healing process. That did offer tangible evidence Richardson was on the way back, though he would miss another two weeks.

There would be other changes with the dawn of 1994. Fleming would replace Workman in the starting lineup. It was less a reflection on Workman than a return to the more natural order. Fleming had been Richardson's backup coming out of camp and, as such, should inherit the job now that he was healthy.

Sealy, who had missed all but the first game of December, would be back in uniform. Neither his minutes, nor his role, would be as prominent as before. Scott had taken over as the backup shooting guard. Sealy would compete with Williams and Mitchell for whatever time was left behind McKey at small forward. At least the problem would be too many healthy bodies, not too few.

For a night, anyway, the Pacers looked positively robust. Not only did they beat Cleveland for the first time in 11 tries, 104-99, but they did so with a variety of players coming up with big plays down the stretch. Only 10,012 showed up at

Market Square Arena, a troubling sign that the San Antonio game had cost the team some fans, at least in the short term.

Miller scored 21 of his 29 points in a 17-minute span in the second half, but none in the final five minutes as McKey, Dale Davis and Fleming combined for the team's final 10 points.

The primary weapon was McKey. He took Bobby Phills out of the game early by taking the 6-5 starter inside, then used his quickness to beat bigger defenders late in the game. His jumper with 2:09 left ended an eight-point Cleveland run and put the Pacers up 96-95, and his low-post bucket with 49.3 seconds left made it 100-97.

"It seemed like, from the beginning of the game, every time he touched the ball, something good happened," said Brown. "We'd like him to be more conscious of scoring, but that's just not his nature. We've just got to get it in his hands more."

McKey had his best all-around game to that point: 18 points, seven rebounds, six assists and a pair of blocked shots. He was comfortable in the go-to role down the stretch, a job he was not unfamiliar with in his years as a big-shot player for Seattle.

"We felt like we had an advantage tonight, especially when they had the smaller guys on me," McKey said. "Later, they had bigger guys on me but they weren't sending a double-team. I feel pretty good against anybody, one-on-one."

Fleming racked up 16 points and 12 assists and finished the Cavs off by making four of four free throws in the closing seconds when the visitors were forced to foul.

While contributing his normal intimidation on defense, Davis also made a pair of big free throws with 1:26 left to open a 98-95 lead. Poor foul shooting had been one of the factors that kept Davis off the floor late in close games in previous years. Hill was forever concerned that Davis and his 55 percent career mark from the line would make an easy target and encourage opponents to foul.

This night, he was five of five from the line, startling numbers that stood out among his 15 points, 13 rebounds and four blocks. "Dale continues to play," said Brown, "about as well as you can play."

Though he would get even better the next night, the team would not.

An isolated arena with a roof shaped like a potato chip, the Capital Centre in Landover, Maryland, was now known as the USAir Arena, another in the wave of airline-sponsored buildings like the Delta Center in Salt Lake City, and America West Arena in Phoenix. It would've made more sense, and been a little catchier, to call it the USAirena but, then again, nothing about this place made much sense.

Most of the league's unpopular venues are so for one of two reasons: the location of the arena, or the weather in that particular city. Some of the suburban buildings were built in desolate locations.

The Palace of Auburn Hills was a spectacular arena, but the Pistons' home was in the middle of nowhere, a solid 45 minutes from the main Detroit airport, more like 90 if you had the unfortunate luck of flying out in the morning and had to battle rush-hour traffic in a city that takes its driving seriously. Most teams stayed in the suburb of Troy, which offered more entertainment alternatives, but still fell some-what short of lively.

The Cavs played in Richfield Coliseum, located halfway between Cleveland and Akron. When it was built in 1974, the vision was that the tiny hamlet would become something of a suburban boom town. It never happened. There was just one hotel within striking distance of that arena, the Richfield Holiday Inn. Though it had a spunky bar, the rooms were hardly up to NBA standards. Teams like the Pacers would float from hotel to hotel in various suburbs, willing to drive the 30 minutes by bus in exchange for staying close to civilization.

The former Cap Centre was along the same lines, about halfway between Washing-ton and Baltimore, but a much worse building, dank and depressing with poor light-ing and perennially awful teams.

They were teams, though, that haunted the Pacers like sweaty nightmares, relentless in their pursuit, brutal in their methods. This was the Pacers' Amityville, where supernatural causes were the only way to explain the events that consistently tran-spired.

It happened once more. Cruising right along, with a 12-point lead in the fourth quarter, the Pacers came apart and lost 97-95 to a pathetic bunch of Bullets that hadn't won at home in more than a month and had lost 14 of 16 overall.

Dale Davis had a career-high 28 points and 12 rebounds, but few others left the court with honor.

The Pacers closed the third period with a 19-5 run to take a comfortable 81-69 advantage into the fourth. Perhaps it was too comfortable. While the visitors dozed, the Bullets awakened behind none other than Kevin Duckworth.

Benched for his altogether ineffective play, not to mention his 300-pound largesse, Duckworth roasted the Pacers for nine points in the fourth quarter, seven in a 22-4 run that put Washington ahead 91-85 with 5:45 remaining.

Davis blocked four of six Washington shots over five consecutive possessions to allow the visitors to reclaim the lead, 95-93, on Fleming's drive down the middle of the lane with 52.3 seconds left.

Duckworth tied it with a pair of free throws, then Fleming's eight-footer banked off too hard with 20 seconds left, giving Washington a chance for the final shot.

It also provided a microcosm of the problems that had beset the Pacers in crucial situations.

"We called a timeout," said Brown, "and all I talked about was how we weren't supposed to double the pick-and-roll."

Davis followed his instincts but ignored the coach's instructions. When he left Tom Gugliotta to double-team Michael Adams 25 feet from the basket, the opportunistic point guard passed to Gugliotta, who caught the ball at the three-point line and took a drive down the Pacer turnpike to scoop in the game-winner with 1.2 seconds left.

The Pacers' next stop was in that other suburban dungeon, the home of the Pistons. Smits figured to be the center of attention, from both sides. Coach Don Chaney admitted his team had been pursuing a deal for Smits. "I like him because he's a big guy," Chaney told the Detroit Free Press. "Billy (McKinney) talked to the Pacers on various occasions but they've vacillated on him. They like him one moment, the next moment they want to talk trade." Young power forward Terry Mills was the player the Pistons reportedly threw into the discussion. It was a deal that could've been done, under the cap. More significantly, it gave a clear indication of just how hot-and-cold management's opinion of Smits was running.

One player who could not be pried from the Pacers, on the other hand, was Dale Davis.

In his third season, he had emerged as one of the best at his position in the Eastern Conference, with his stock rising more quickly than even the most optimistic had expected.

And he was only getting better. In a seven-game span that included a 101-92 victory over the Pistons, Davis had averaged 17.1 points, 14.1 rebounds and 2.57 blocked shots.

"He's playing as well as anybody in the league, I would assume," said Brown. "He defends every night, he rebounds every night, he's become a double-figure scorer and he's blocking more shots. I would think, when the All-Star Game comes around, whoever the coaches are that select the team will take a look at him."

Davis' time as an All-Star would not arrive just yet; New Jersey's Derrick Coleman, Charlotte's Larry Johnson, Atlanta's Kevin Willis and Chicago's Horace Grant all had more impressive overall numbers.

"The Franchise," his nickname in the locker room, soon would be demanding a much bigger piece of this one. He signed a substandard contract during his rookie season of 1991 because the Pacers simply had nothing else to offer but a $430,000 slot. As the 14th pick, he had little leverage. Now, as a potential All-Star, his salary of $668,000 was absurdly low. It ranked him 10th on the team and was roughly half the league average.

Though his original contract spanned seven years, he had an option after three to become a restricted free agent. His price would be high, but it was one the franchise clearly would be happy to pay.

When he was drafted No. 14 overall out of Clemson in 1991, Davis was very much an unknown commodity. He drew comparisons to Buck Williams — a similarly hard-working, no-nonsense power forward — who also had severe problems at the free throw line early in his career.

McKey saw a similarity with one of his former Seattle teammates, Shawn Kemp. "Dale's still getting better and Shawn's still getting better," McKey said. "They play similar games, but the difference is, Shawn shows a lot more intensity on his face, with all his expressions, while Dale gets it done quietly."

His first two seasons were spent in relative silence, but that didn't sway the Pacers' first impression. A team that historically lacked big men who combined athleticism with a stern countenance needed Davis.

"From the moment I drafted him," said Walsh, "I felt strongly he was going to be a great player."

A holdout cost him the preseason and the first 18 games of the regular season, and he wound up with modest averages of 6.2 points and 6.4 rebounds.

In 1992-93, he moved into the starting lineup for all 82 games and his numbers improved slightly, to 8.9 points and 8.8 rebounds. He finished third in the league and set a franchise mark with a field goal percentage of .568; unfortunately, that was much better than his .529 mark from the free throw line.

When Schrempf was away just before the season began, Davis' role on the team changed dramatically. Though Schrempf had been a starter at small forward, he played significant minutes as a power forward, particularly in the fourth quarter.

One of the main reasons that deal was made was to clear more time for Davis. It was a gamble, but one that was paying off. Davis was leading the team in minutes (35.8).

"When we traded Detlef, we knew he was going to be more of a focal point on the team," said Walsh. "With Detlef here, he was just a rebounder. Without him, he's become much more."

Davis had taken up virtually all the rebounding slack left by the departure of Schrempf, the team leader at 9.6 the previous season. With the agile 6-11, 230-pounder leading the way, the Pacers were tied for fourth in the league in total rebound percentage, second on the offensive glass.

"He's playing," said Miller, "like a full-grown man."

That Davis could rebound, defend and block shots, the Pacers knew. What surprised the team was his offensive development. Though his favorite shot still was the dunk,

Davis had been able to toss in his share of jump hooks, earning play-calls from Brown when a low-post bucket was necessary.

In the first 29 games, he had 16 double-doubles, a sign of growing consistency. He also had four games of at least 18 rebounds.

He also was thought to be unusually durable. Though he had problems with chronic shoulder separations, Davis was of the old, tape-it-up school. He hated to miss time. Once while at Clemson, he suffered a separated shoulder in the first half, had it popped back in place and wrapped and returned to play the second half.

And so, when he fell hard to the floor after goaltending a Lindsey Hunter drive midway through the second quarter, few gave it a second glance. Even when he came out of the locker room with tape on his left wrist, it surely couldn't be serious. In the second half, after all, he went on to play 17 minutes and grab nine rebounds.

He was sent for precautionary X-rays after the team returned home the next day only as a matter of routine. No one thought he was hurt. There was more concern about Smits, who endured the double insult of not only having a dunk blocked by Olden Polynice, but of having the Piston center do so with such force it strained Smits' right shoulder.

Miller missed the game with the flu, but Scott stepped into the lineup and led the team with 21 points.

A season that already had been crippled by injuries was headed for life-support. The X-rays showed Davis had a fractured navicular bone in his left wrist. It would require surgery to implant a screw, meaning he would be out at least a month.

Davis would be the seventh player, and third starter, to spend time on the injured list, and the season was barely one-third gone.

"Maybe," said Brown, "it's just one of those years."

His team was 12-17 and, in one night, had lost both its starting big men. To replace Davis, who had been one of the season's brightest hopes, Brown reached deep into the bench and pulled out Mitchell. Until then, the 6-7 veteran had been of little use to Brown, playing spotty minutes. At the time of his battlefield commission, Mitchell was shooting 32 percent.

In the 10 previous games, Mitchell did not play at all four times. In his six appearances, he totaled 22 minutes, four points and three rebounds. When assistant coach Bill Blair approached Mitchell after practice on January 10 to inform him of his promotion, Mitchell had an understandable reaction. He broke out laughing.

Brown's emotions were running in quite the opposite direction. He wasn't a coach, he was a maintenance man, trying to keep a roster together with bailing wire and duct tape.

"One thing is, you find out about your players in a hurry. You see if they can compete at this level," he said. "We're asking guys who haven't been playing much not only to play, but to start. It's not so bad if you've got one guy like that, but we're going to have three or four."

For the time being, winning ugly was the only option the Pacers had. No one knew it at the time, but it was exactly the style that suited them.

Antonio Davis had been waiting for just this chance, and he made it count. Ignored by the Milwaukee defense, which frequently double-teamed off of him, Davis racked up 26 points, 12 rebounds and three blocks to inspire an 82-76 victory.

Davis had 22 of his points in the first half, including five dunks, before fatigue set in. "A little tired? It wasn't just a little," Davis said. "I don't know how many minutes I played (37) but, even when you're tired, you can't quit. You have to keep battling."

Fortunately for the Pacers, Miller was there to pick up where Davis left off. Miller scored 16 of his 20 after the break, including a pair of huge baskets in the fourth quarter when the game was taken away from the home team.

The Pacers shot 39.4 percent and had more turnovers (19) than assists (16), but won with their defense, which held Milwaukee to 36.1 percent shooting for the game, 31.5 percent in the second half.

And, quite naturally, they lost another player. Fleming pulled a hamstring and, though he played 36 minutes, was limping badly and clearly unable to play effectively. Richardson was due back after the home game against Denver the next night, just in time for Fleming to go back on the injured list.

While the Milwaukee victory was largely the result of two big nights from individuals, the 107-96 defeat of Denver was very much a team effort.

The two stand-ins, Mitchell and Workman, both played major roles.

Mitchell produced a season-high 11 points, including a buzzer-beating jumper that stretched the lead to 101-94 with 2:45 remaining. Workman had 10 points, seven assists and four steals while putting the clamps on his counterpart, Denver's Mahmoud Abdul-Rauf, who went five of 19 from the field.

Those two complemented healthy starters Miller (29 points) and McKey, who came within an assist of his first career triple-double, adding 15 points and 10 rebounds. Smits returned to the lineup with 14 points and three blocked shots.

"It takes a little bit from everybody to pick things up," said Scott, who contributed 15 points off the bench. "That's what winning is all about. When you win in situations like that, you're going to be all right."

McKey's performance was another positive sign. When the team needed more from him, he was willing to provide. Long known as a multi-faceted player, it seemed strange that McKey had failed, in seven seasons, to produce a single triple-double. "I figure if I haven't had one by now," he said, "there ain't no sense in worrying about it."

They had stretched the season's unlikeliest winning streak to three games and were 4-1 in 1994. Their next game was in Philadelphia against the struggling 76ers. What should've been the worst of times were starting to look pretty good.

It was turning into a big week for Antonio Davis. On Tuesday, he got his first career start and starred in Milwaukee. On Thursday, he was among the 16 players selected to participate in the league's first all-rookie game as part of the All-Star weekend in Minneapolis.

"This tells me," Davis said, "that I can play over here."

Davis was averaging 8.5 points and 6.1 rebounds in 22 minutes per game. Those numbers represented about 7.5 points, 5.1 rebounds and 21 minutes more than the club anticipated.

"I had no idea he'd be stepping in this quickly," said Brown. "Donnie felt that the last couple of years, he was close enough to making the team, But I never thought he'd be one of the better rookies in the league."

Another thoroughly upbeat turn of events was Richardson's return to practice. The fracture finally was healed, though he did report some soreness in the calf muscle. Still, he said, "I think I'm going to be cool."

Things would get downright frigid in Philadelphia.

Two answered prayers, two scoring plays each executed in less than one second, ended the Pacers' mini-streak and lifted the Sixers to a 104-102 overtime victory.

The Pacers rallied from a 16-point third-quarter deficit behind Scott, who scored the team's first nine points of the fourth quarter to cut it to 85-83.

"From there," said Miller, "it was like a horse game."

Miller beat Shawn Bradley on a baseline drive, flipping in a reverse layup to put the Pacers ahead 92-91 with 5.5 seconds left.

H.

Clarence Weatherspoon then outleapt Mitchell for a 40-foot inbounds lob from Jeff Hornacek, and dropped in the reserve dunk to return the lead to the 76ers with 4.7 to go. That one took eight-tenths of a second.

O.

Workman beat Hornacek to the left on a drive and was fouled by Tim Perry, who blocked the shot out of bounds at the buzzer as the Spectrum crowd of 13,535 celebrated, unaware of the whistle. Workman stepped to the line with a chance to win the game, but missed the first free throw. He made the second to force overtime.

R.

Down 102-100 with 20 seconds left, the Pacers couldn't get a good shot, but tied it anyway. Mitchell's jumper was blocked by Weatherspoon; the ball deflected to Workman, who tossed up an airball that was wide left. Enter McKey, who snaked inside for the tip-in to tie it with five-tenths of a second.

S.

Hornacek struck again. Inbounding from the same spot near midcourt, he lofted a feathery cross-court pass that Dana Barros caught in mid-air and immediately flicked into the basket from 16 feet away.

EEEEEeeeeeeeeeeeek.

"We find ways to lose," said Brown. "That's what's tough."

Even tougher would be coming home to play an Atlanta team on another streak, the memory of this one still stinging the psyche. Could the Pacers cope?

Said Scott: "We'll see tomorrow."

When they arrived at MSA for their pregame preparations, they saw Smits in street clothes. Recurring soreness in his right shoulder would keep him out of the game.

That left Brown three options: he could go with Thompson, whose creaky knees had limited his playing time, not to mention effectiveness; he could start Antonio Davis, but run the risk of stripping the bench of its primary physical presence; or, he could take a total shot in the dark and throw Haskin out there.

Though Haskin had been the subject of many of the coach's one-liners, not to mention a few four-letter words in practice, the first-round pick got the call.

He answered, providing season highs in minutes (20), points (eight) and blocked shots (four) and adding five rebounds as the Pacers continued in their role as the Hawks' streak-busters. This time, the visitors' seven-game ride came to an end, 94-91.

This season had been much more of a struggle than Haskin expected. He caught Brown's eye early in training camp but quickly fell out of favor. Promoted into the bench rotation in late November, Haskin played a combined 47 minutes in three straight road games, producing 12 points and 16 rebounds.

It appeared then he had turned the corner, but instead hit another wall. In the following 17 games, Haskin totaled 48 minutes and did not play at all eight times. His only chance was on the practice court.

"I don't know how those first four (shots) went in, but I was thrilled to see that. He's a space cadet right now. He's still finding himself," said Brown. "Everybody on the team was glad to see it because he comes to practice every day and battles."

Much the same could be said for the Pacers, who handled the stunning loss in Philadelphia better than the Sixers, who lost by 43 points to Cleveland that same night, handled the victory.

"To have the kind of character we showed after that loss is really something special," said Brown. "As a coach, these are the most meaningful games. We were so short-handed, and to beat a great team, that's a pretty special win."

Brown had reason to be upbeat. His team had won five of seven. Richardson had returned to play 13 acceptable minutes and finally looked ready to go again.

* * *

On January 17, the Los Angeles area was rocked by one of the worst earthquakes in recent years. The aftershocks were felt by a half-dozen Pacers who had homes, friends and family in the L.A. area.

Miller, Richardson, Scott, Thompson, McKey and Brown had southern California ties.

For Scott, an L.A. native who said he had experienced "40 or 50" quakes, "but nothing this major," it was only slightly out of the ordinary. His wife and children were in their Ladera Heights home.

"It rattled the house a little bit, knocked pictures off the wall and broke some collector's items we had been saving," he said. "It just shook up the house and scared the kids."

Other than his sister Cheryl's home near the USC campus, which was hit hard, Miller said his family suffered only minor damage.

"Everyone's doing fine," he said. "Just a few shaken items . . . cracks in the driveways and cracks in the walls. Cheryl was really scared because she lives alone."

Thompson's mountainside home in the Hollywood Hills survived because of a contractor's mistake. When the house was built, it was on a foundation equivalent to that normally laid for "a 40-story office building," he said.

"I think it just did a lot of shaking," said Thompson. "Glasses and dishes broke but the house is OK. My house isn't on stilts; it's on a rock, but anything that wasn't bolted down fell over."

McKey, whose children and their mother lived in L.A., and Richardson reported no problems.

"I didn't lose anything," said Richardson, who maintains a home in Encino. "Everything happened around me. Nothing was touched. I was lucky, for a change."

The family of Brown's wife, Shelly Galster, lived in Sherman Oaks.

"They're right near the epicenter," he said. "Furniture was down, glass was broken and doors were jammed. They're pretty well shook up, but they're OK."

They all would get a chance to personally inspect the damage the following week, when the team had a game in L.A. against the Lakers.

Miller's parents left L.A. the day before the quake and arrived in Indianapolis just in time to experience the city's worst snowstorm in a decade.

"All things considered," Miller said, "they'll definitely take the snow."

*　*　*

With that Monday's practice would come another shakeup.

Richardson was inadvertently kicked by Miller in the same spot on his lower right leg that had been injured. He limped out of practice, hoping a day of rest would be all that was needed. When he did not practice again on Tuesday, Brown had had enough. He was reluctant to place Fleming on the injured list because of Richardson's iffy status. Now, Fleming would be out at least four more games, and no one knew when Richardson would be back. The Pacers were down to their one and only point guard, Workman.

Fortunately, their next opponent, Miami, had dropped five in a row overall and had never won in Market Square Arena. The streaks grew to six and 10 with a startlingly uncontested 109-92 victory.

Miami coach Kevin Loughery showed his frustration early. When the Pacers jumped out to a 21-7 lead, he brought in a five-man unit from the bench. One problem: no point guard. That group committed five turnovers in less than four minutes and the Indiana lead was 30-13 by the quarter's end.

It was an unusually easy night for the Pacers, who had experienced few. It also brought their record to 16-18 heading into back-to-back weekend games against the Bulls, Friday in Chicago and Saturday at home.

For Miller, the highest-scoring guard in the Jordan-less Eastern Conference, it was the kind of opportunity he relished. Big games, on big nights, in a big city, against a big team. He was two free throws away from breaking his club record of 51 straight, and 34 points from becoming the first Indiana player to score 10,000 points in the NBA.

The All-Star game was just weeks away, and yet Miller already had prepared himself for a snub. "I still won't make it," he said. "But I am curious to see what they have to say this year."

Offense was an assumed part of Miller's game. What had impressed Brown the most was the co-captain's willingness to listen and adapt his game to the new style. "He really tries," Brown said. "He's improving on the defensive end, he's going to the board more, he's becoming more of an all-around player. When that happens, he won't be left off any of these all-star teams. What has hurt him is in the past, he had a reputation of being a one-dimensional player."

Miller chafed at that notion.

"I can only go out and be Reggie Miller," he said. "If someone's going to have a stigma against me, there's nothing I can do, nothing I can say. All I know is, when they play against me, I'm the first guy they try to stop. I must be doing something right."

* * *

There was Elvis, and there were the Jordanaires. Without the King, there was no show.

When Jordan retired, the immediate assumption was that the Bulls would, like the Jordanaires, fade quickly from the spotlight, destined to spend the rest of their lives as answers to trivia questions. As it has turned out, this was no backup band, and the Bulls hadn't missed a beat.

"They won three championships," said Miller. "With or without Michael, they know how to win. That's the bottom line."

While Jordan was busy chasing curve balls, the Bulls quietly worked their way back into a familiar position: near the top of the Eastern Conference.

No one had replaced Jordan's 30 points a game, but the Bulls had gotten significantly increased production from Scottie Pippen, B.J. Armstrong and Horace Grant. European import Toni Kukoc was a major addition, providing the team the sixth man it had lacked even in the championship years.

The free agent signings of Steve Kerr and Bill Wennington, which didn't exactly rock the NBA when transacted, turned out to be of immense significance. Kukoc,

Kerr and Wennington combined for 29 points, 10 rebounds and eight assists per game. As a result, the bench, a perennial problem in the Jordan era, led the league in the percentage of points, rebounds and assists contributed.

"I coached the world junior team so I got to see Kukoc a long time ago in 1988," said Brown. "He's a terrific backup player and they've made some good pickups, getting Steve Kerr and watching the way Wennington's played, plus they have that tradition.

"As great as Michael is, those guys got something out of winning championships. They developed a lot of pride in what they've done and they've also been together a long time."

Their defense, the element that elevated the team to championship level, was as contentious as ever and the offense — like virtually every other NBA team, less productive — remained efficient in its triple-post execution.

Without Jordan, the Bulls would never be the same.

That didn't mean they couldn't be good.

* * *

Time doesn't stand still on the road. There are moments when it just seems that way, and they were happening to the Pacers with frightening consistency.

A week after Barros pushed in a floating 17-footer within the final five-tenths of a second to give Philadelphia a 104-102 overtime victory, Kukoc banked in a three-pointer at the buzzer to give Chicago a 96-95 win that proved devastating to the Pacers.

When Miller drained a fallaway 22-footer from the left wing to put the Pacers up 95-93 with eight-tenths of a second remaining, it appeared this might be their long-awaited breakthrough game. Miller, celebrating the moment, took two bows, one to each side of the hostile Chicago Stadium crowd.

Kukoc then stole the show. Given ample room to catch Pippen's cross-court inbounds pass by McKey, who went underneath a screen instead of over the top, Kukoc flung up a shot that banked in off the glass, shattering the Pacers.

The Bulls, quite naturally, claimed Miller's theatrics somehow provided them with the emotional fodder necessary to win. The reality was they had been graced with pure good fortune.

"It was sweet revenge typifying a Reggie Miller antic of bowing before the end of a game," said Phil Jackson. "I don't know if he was bowing or showing his butt. But, it was a premature celebration, no doubt about that."

Miller, however, apologized to no one.

"Why would I regret it?" he said. "That's my personality. I've done worse."

Though they had generally played at their highest level of the season, and done so in the face of enormous adversity, the Pacers were clearly shaken by this one. In their last nine games, they had won six times. The three losses were the two-pointer at Washington, where they were done in by Gugliotta's closing drive, the overtime two-pointer in Philadelphia, and now this one-pointer.

Had they won those games, the team would be on a nine-game winning streak, 19-16 overall, and ready to make a move. Instead, they dropped to 16-19 and began doubting themselves all over again.

"This hurts, man," said Mitchell. "We played as hard and as well as we can. To lead from start to finish and lose like that, it's worse than the Philly game because it already had happened to us and we should've learned. It starts to make you wonder what we've got to do to win games against teams like this."

The emotional hangover from that defeat carried over into the rematch, won easily by the Bulls, 90-81. The first sellout crowd of the season was summarily unimpressed by a lifeless performance from the home team, and watched without response as Pippen returned Miller's gesture by bowing to the stands, this time after the final horn had sounded.

"When you win," said McKey, "you can do that."

Richardson's situation again was festering with Brown. Though he originally was expected back after the Miami game, Richardson sat out the doubleheader with the Bulls.

"I show up every day expecting him to play," said Brown. "The sad thing is, if he had told us about this situation earlier, we could've gotten someone in here (from the CBA) until Vern gets healthy. Haywoode's killing himself and it's just not fair. And it's not fair for Reggie or Byron. It's tough. Neither one of those guys are point guards. Most teams have two guards that can really handle the ball. When our point guard is out, we don't have natural guards to handle it and break people down and that really makes it very, very hard."

With Fleming due back from the injured list after one more game, at home against Milwaukee, Richardson was headed to the injured list once again, only this time, for reasons more personal than physical. In six weeks since December 9, Richardson had made two appearances totaling 21 minutes, missing 17 of 19 games.

"I don't want to walk in here when we're shorthanded and find out this guy's not going to play," said Brown. "I don't want him to hurt himself, but we can't come in every day and be wondering. I don't think it's fair to the team, so we've got to move on. He's worried about his leg, so we'll let him worry about his leg."

There was one home game left before the third Western road trip in two months, a three-game swing through L.A., Denver and Houston. The Pacers didn't give themselves much of a sendoff, losing to the Bucks 96-88. Little-used Jon Barry scored a career-high 23 points. About the only fan that left Market Square Arena happy was his father, the legendary Rick Barry, coach of the CBA Fort Wayne Fury, who had driven down for the game.

The Pacers loaded up their jet to head west, with their season in parts unknown.

The Lakers had lost five of six and were honoring Scott in his first game back to the Great Western Forum. Brown, sticking to his personal tradition, gave Scott a hometown start at the point and he produced 19 points. But the Pacers lost 103-99 with their old nemesis, Divac, producing the killing play.

With the Pacers down 94-92, Divac, who had beaten them earlier this season with a well-guarded 19-foot jumper, this time hit a 20-footer from the top of the key. Fouled on the play, he made the free throw to put the Lakers up 97-92 and ensure the Pacers' fourth straight loss.

The unlikely hero club expanded by one in Denver, where struggling rookie Rodney Rogers became the latest to record a career-high against the Pacers. The least productive of the current crop of lottery picks, Rogers hit a three-pointer with 1:23 left that wrapped up his 25-point night and killed an Indiana rally. Still, the comeback showed there were signs of life. Down 88-73 early in the fourth quarter, the Pacers erupted for a 30-13 run to take a 103-101 lead with 1:40 left. Rogers hit his three-pointer, then blocked a Mitchell jumper to save the game.

On a five-game losing streak, farther below .500 than they had been at any point in this season at 16-23, the Pacers headed to Houston, where they hadn't won since 1979, to play the NBA's best team, the 31-9 Rockets, their sixth game in nine nights.

* * *

Other than the shocking nature of the victory itself, a 119-108 rout in which the Pacers shot 61 percent, there was little remarkable about that January 29 game in the Summit. There were no great individual performances; seven players scored between 10 and 21 points, and no one had more than seven rebounds or eight assists.

The team defense didn't exactly produce numbers to write home about. Houston shot 51 percent and outrebounded the Pacers 35-32. Hakeem Olajuwon did his usual thing with 27 points, 12 rebounds and three blocks, so it wasn't like they shut down the game's key player.

And there was little drama to the evening. A 10-point run in the third quarter broke a tie and put Indiana ahead 71-61. Another 10-point run in the fourth made it 104-83.

"This wasn't an accident," said Olajuwon. "They just beat us. It was no fluke. They just outplayed us and showed they wanted to win more than us."

At the time, no one looked at it as a turning point. It was a victory, albeit an important one, that ended a dangerous five-game losing streak. It turned out to be something far more significant: a tangible return for a team that felt its hard work had gone largely unrewarded.

"When you look back on it now, it meant everything," Brown said after the season. "On that trip, we had a series of heartbreakers. You ask a team to do certain things and they don't get anything to show for it, eventually they're going to say, 'Screw it.' But we beat a quality team, at the end of a road trip, and that was monumental. We showed we could beat a good team away from home, under difficult circumstances, and that was a big boost for everyone."

Four months, 40 games, 14 starters, 12 lineup combinations and eight trips to the injured list after training camp opened, Brown's Pacers got the feeling this season finally was about to get started.

8 The Big Boom

If the Pacers had turned the corner, Brown's hands were uncertain at the wheel. In his head, he thought the most logical path might lead to the lottery, where the team could pick up a prime young talent and fortify for a run at the top next year. With the trading deadline upcoming, decisions also had to be made about current personnel. Could Smits be a winning center? Would Richardson be better off elsewhere? Should fairly widespread interest in Sealy be exploited?

"Till the end of February, Shelly and I used to talk all the time that the best thing that could happen would be to go into the lottery and get a good pick," Brown said after the season. "I could really evaluate our players, be real honest with Donnie about what we needed and go from there. I thought we were establishing some credibility defensively and we were playing hard and we were playing unselfishly.

"I knew it would be disappointing and people would look at this as a total bust because this team has always managed to make the playoffs. But, sometimes, it was my curse: if you go in and fix it too quickly, you still don't have those building blocks. I thought maybe this would be a blessing. We'll take a step back, get a real good draft, and then — boom — be ready to take off."

This boom team would explode more quickly, and with more force, than even Brown could have foreseen.

Not that he was without hope. Brown hadn't seen the best of this team. There had been too many injuries, too many lineup combinations, too little continuity, to make a sound judgement on the level the Pacers should be expected to reach. "Every time I think we're ready to make a run, we've had some kind of major injury," he said. "I don't know what kind of team we have yet."

He would find out soon enough. The Houston game concluded one stretch of six games in nine nights. February would start with another.

The Bullets, a team that tends to wreak havoc on the Pacers at the worst possible times, were easily turned back, 116-96. Though Cheaney had a big night with 22 points, Smits and Miller each scored 25 and the Pacers weren't seriously challenged after the first quarter. Duckworth, who had killed the Pacers the last time the teams met, went scoreless, thereby opening an opportunity for 7-foot-7, 330-pound Gheorge Muresan. The mountainous Romanian played well with 12 points and nine rebounds in 18 minutes. It would not be his last significant performance against this team.

Though Richardson was eligible to come off the injured list for the following night's game in Charlotte, his right leg was still gimpy. He followed Thompson's lead and headed to Los Angeles to get a second opinion from Lombardo. Brown seemed beyond concern over Richardson's perpetual uncertainty. "We expected him to be able," he said, "but he feels pain, he doesn't want to play, and it's something we're going to have to deal with. If he wants another opinion and it'll give him peace of mind, then that's good." The coach and the team would move on without Richardson.

While the rest of the league was immersed in a record-setting defensive season, the Hornets seemed either immune or unconcerned with the trend. Coach Allan Bristow's young team was overloaded with offensive weapons but remained one of the leakiest defensive teams in the league. When a team has all its scorers healthy, it can win with that mentality. When one or two go down, the lack of commitment to defense can be a fatal flaw.

Larry Johnson and Alonzo Mourning, the franchise's two centerpieces, both watched in street clothes as the Pacers dismantled the Hornets 124-112. Indiana built an astonishing 80-50 lead at the half, shooting 67 percent. The Hornets started tossing up threes by the bushel in the second half to cut the margin, but were outrebounded badly (48-28) and lost to the Pacers for the seventh time in eight games. Miller and Smits both came up big again, with 23 apiece, and were complemented by Scott's 21. The replacements for Mourning and Johnson, Mike Gminski and Kenny Gattison, combined for 11 points and seven rebounds.

The winning streak had reached three, with the next three games at Market Square, the longest stretch at home since mid-November.

When the Minnesota Timberwolves came to town, it offered the chance to survey the wreckage of what both teams had thought, in 1992, would be a monumental trade.

Walsh didn't want to part with Person but could not argue the volatile small forward's detrimental effect on team chemistry. Person thought of himself as a franchise player, a problem that stemmed from his days at Auburn in Charles Barkley's shadow. Person was a premier player for coach Sonny Smith, yet Barkley attracted all the attention. Person felt himself every bit as good as Barkley. When he won the rookie of the year award in 1987 — something Barkley had not done — Person was deluded into believing himself a superstar. The problem was, his talents were closer to

Albert King than Barkley, and his egocentric tendencies grew more disruptive with age.

In his final season with the Pacers, he kicked a ball deep into the Chicago Stadium seats, very nearly hitting the wife of Bulls coach Phil Jackson, and later assaulted an Indianapolis News beat reporter in the locker room after a practice. Clearly, he had gone too far, even for Walsh, who set about pursuing a trade.

He offered Person around and found Minnesota the most interested, although the Wolves weren't enamored with the original package: Person and Fleming for Richardson and Mitchell. General manager Bob Stein wanted Micheal Williams instead of Fleming. Walsh thought giving up two starters from a playoff team for two from an expansion club was too high a price to pay, especially when considering the Pacers could have had Richardson at no cost to personnel had they drafted him in 1989.

The deal percolated for a while, then cooled. When Jack McCloskey moved in to run the Minnesota front office, one of his first decisions was to pursue this trade. When it was made, the Pacers thought they had obtained their long-sought answer at point guard. Mitchell was more than a throw-in but just how much more, no one knew.

Person would bring a premier offensive threat to the Wolves, and Williams was a young talent with a bright future.

It turned out to be a deal that did not work out for either team. Person eventually played his way to the bench, where he stewed. The only thing he hated more than losing was not getting the chance to do anything about it. He began making waves about wanting out of Minnesota. "I don't think I can compete getting 13 minutes," he said. "I would just as soon sit on the bench. They might as well tie my hands behind my back, leave me on the side of the road and feed me to the f-----g crows."

Williams had performed solidly but did not grow beyond the level he had reached in his first season as a starter with the Pacers. He remained indecisive in the fourth quarter and, defensively, concentrated so much on getting the steal that he often was beaten off the dribble. By the end of the season, he would be sharing time at the point with the nondescript Chris Smith.

At least Williams was playing. Richardson either would not, or could not. The Pacers weren't sure which. His first year with the team offered nothing but trouble. Hill, who did not want Person traded, would never put his faith in Richardson. Little changed under Brown.

If not for Mitchell, the deal would've been a total bust for the Pacers, and his status was anything but certain before the injury to Dale Davis.

In the interim, Mitchell had established himself as much more than a locker room leader. He was a valuable player, as well. In his 13 starts, the Pacers had gone 7-6. Though the 6-7, 225-pounder gave up substantial amounts of height and weight every night, he had been productive, averaging 10 points and five rebounds.

Being thrust from the end of the bench to the starting lineup was a shock, but it gave Mitchell's game a needed jolt. Sitting wasn't easy for this proud veteran, who missed just three games his first four seasons, but sat out six of the Pacers' first 29 before getting the unexpected callup.

"It's tough, but you have to realize it's a long season and, sooner or later, you're going to get an opportunity to play," he said. "That's part of being a professional, being ready. You have to take advantage of any opportunity you get because it might be the last one for a while. To me, I've done my job - play defense, rebound, guard bigger power forwards every night. I think I've more than held my own. I would like to think I've earned a spot in the rotation, but you never know."

Davis was due back soon, perhaps within a week, and Mitchell knew his days as a starter were numbered. At least he would get this chance to show his former team they made a mistake in trading him away. Though he was traded after the 1991-92 season, Mitchell still was the Timberwolves' all-time leading rebounder and entered the season in the franchise's top five in 16 statistical categories.

Proud of the work the outmanned team did in its first two years under then-coach Bill Musselman, winning 22 and 29 games, Mitchell was discouraged by the Wolves' lack of progress since. Their victory totals dropped to 15 and 19 the next two seasons and, despite the presence of three lottery picks on the roster, Minnesota was ambling along at 14-28 this season.

"It's kind of sad," Mitchell said. "We had pride in the franchise and we felt like we had started something. People looked at us on paper and didn't think we were any good, but we played hard every night and gave them everything we had. The way things are now, I'm kind of glad I'm not a part of it. We had a lot of guys who put in a lot of hard work the first three years of the franchise but then they came in and said, "Thanks but no thanks, you guys can't play." They look at a guy and see his talent. Talent is great, but if you don't have the desire and the work ethic to make the most of it, you might as well not have any."

The Wolves had more talent, but showed less desire. As a result, they weren't getting anywhere. The Pacers, on the other hand, had less talent but more desire. How far that would get them, no one really knew, but it was enough to get them past the Wolves.

The 114-93 rout was the fourth straight double-digit victory, all of which were punctuated by an offense that suddenly was prolific. A team that averaged 98 points and shot 47 percent in the first 39 games had averaged 118 and shot 57 percent in the four-game streak.

It didn't take an electron microscope to determine the key elements. Miller, Smits and McKey all had gotten hot in unison, the three combining for 60 points and 65 percent shooting.

Three games remained before the All-Star break. The Pacers, at 20-23, were three games below .500. It was a moment waiting to be seized. "Of course," said Scott, "if you win those games, you don't really want to stop playing."

* * *

Much to his chagrin, Miller was proven right in his previous prophecy of All-Star omission. That the fans didn't vote him into the starting lineup was no surprise. That the coaches snubbed him turned out to be more than a slap in the face; it was a sock full of quarters to the side of his head.

Instead of Miller, the highest-scoring guard in the East, the coaches picked his out-of-control rival, New York's John Starks, as well as Atlanta's Mookie Blaylock, a pair with shooting percentages in the low-40s.

Starks' selection was particularly insulting. In 10 head-to-head matchups over the past one and one half seasons, Miller had owned Starks, averaging 26 points on 49 percent shooting. Starks' numbers were awful: 14.3 points, 39 percent shooting.

It was clear the league felt the Knicks should have two All-Stars, but Charles Oakley was a far more deserving complement to Patrick Ewing. Four teams — New York, New Jersey, Chicago and Atlanta — occupied nine roster spots. Three of those teams were in huge media markets. The other, Atlanta, had the best record in the conference.

The Pacers would be represented by Antonio Davis in the all-rookie game and the slam-dunk contest, but those were sideshows. For a main event, the city would have to settle for the 1994 NBA Draft.

The city was formally awarded the draft on February 7, but the National Basketball Players Association was threatening action that would spoil Indianapolis' party. The collective bargaining agreement would expire before the June 29 draft was scheduled. The union felt this meant there should be no draft. The league felt strongly otherwise. The dispute would linger on long past the draft, settling nothing.

With the presence of Purdue's Glenn Robinson, Indiana's Damon Bailey and North Carolina's Eric Montross (of Lawrence North High in suburban Indianapolis), local interest was bound to be high. The best-case scenario was a sellout of 20,000 in the Hoosier Dome.

Walsh's history of making controversial selections could catch up with him. In 1987, he was booed for selecting Miller instead of Indiana's Steve Alford. In 1993, he was savaged for passing on another I.U. player, Greg Graham, in favor of Oregon State center Scott Haskin.

But those picks were made in front of relatively small gatherings at Market Square Arena. Could Walsh imagine the reaction from 20,000 should he pass on, say, Bailey?

The club president looked down, shook his head, and simply said, "No."

* * *

Mr. Inside and Mr. Outside continued their mutually beneficial play in a routine 111-102 defeat of Charlotte that extended the winning streak to five games. Smits scored 24 and Miller 21; the two combined to hit 19 of 27 shots. The Hornets were again without Mourning and Johnson, and their defense was again without a clue.

The following day, Dale Davis was fitted with a protective brace that would allow him to return within the week. The only problem was finding someone to go on the injured list to make room for Davis' activation. For a team that had never run short of unhealthy bodies before, this was a most unusual situation.

Thompson was approached, but was hesitant to voluntarily take himself out of the picture. Though he wasn't playing much, he wanted to be a part of the turnaround. If he went on the injured list again, he feared he might not get the chance to come back.

The next night, the Pacers and Golden State Warriors were enmeshed in a tight game, and there was a timeout in the closing moments, when Thompson left the huddle and walked over to press row, a huge grin on his face.

"Man," he said, "this is some exciting shit, ain't it?"

That it was, a rare confluence of all the elements that can make just another professional basketball game in February something special. There were spectacular individual plays from start to finish, with the Pacers and Warriors exhibiting a postseason intensity that was whipped into a near-frenzy by a vibrant crowd.

In the end, the home team emerged with a 104-99 victory, the sixth in a row, the longest streak in three years and one shy of tying the franchise NBA record. It was so satisfying for Brown, the coach made the ultimate personal sacrifice in his team's honor. He called off the next day's practice.

Recovering from a first half that had the potential for a Golden State blowout, the Pacers produced the most consistently electrifying half of the season. No more than six points separated the teams. The score was tied nine times; the lead changed hands seven times in the final five minutes.

Larry Brown became the Pacers' fourth head coach in six years when he signed a five-year $6.3 million contract in 1992. It is Brown's eighth head coaching job and the fifth NBA team he has been employed by. He has frequently said his ultimate career goal is to wind up in a high school gym, teaching and influencing teenagers.

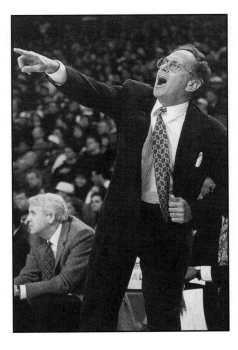

The center position was often a question mark with **Rik Smits'** wildly inconsistent play. Hampered by early injuries, Smits' sixth season eventually proved to be his best. He lost weight, gained strength and endurance, and became more of a stabilizing force for the Pacers.

Dale Davis (right) — nicknamed the "The Franchise" — and rookie **Antonio Davis** (below) are unrelated by birth, but their games bear a strong resemblance to one another. Both are unusually gifted leapers for their size, are excellent defenders and shot-blockers, and both Davises have a penchant for the thunderdunk.

The franchise's all-time leading scorer, **Reggie Miller** was snubbed by coaches and fans when he was omitted from the All-Star game. Miller's streak of snubs finally ended when he was named, along with Shaq, to one of the final two roster spots on Dream Team II.

"I don't know of many guys who are more of a winner than he is," said Brown of **Reggie Miller.** "He wants to do everything right, and he's completely unselfish... he'll do whatever it takes to win. That's infectious when your best player has that mentality."

Byron Scott's leadership and on-court attitude were a welcome addition to the Pacers. He relished the opportunity to serve as "elder statesman" on the team, making his presence felt in practice and offering pointers even to Reggie Miller, who welcomed Scott's advice.

Derrick McKey was fully aware that his arrival in Indianapolis, in a trade for the popular Detlef Schrempf, was met with universal disapproval. While Schrempf was primarily an offensive player, McKey's strength was defense, and Brown continued to harp on McKey to become more offensive-minded throughout the season.

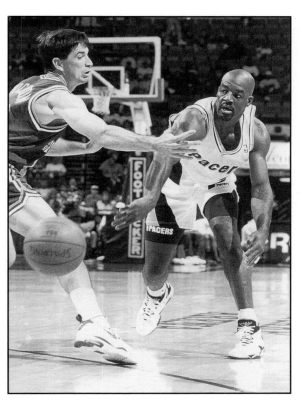

The name says it all — "Work Man." After a stint in Italy, **Haywoode Workman** was a major question mark in the preseason and opened the season with a loosely described "foot problem." Workman quickly demonstrated toughness and hustle when finally activated.

Sam Mitchell goes up against Hornet All-Star Larry Johnson. The veteran Mitchell provided valuable locker room leadership to the Pacers.

A personal favorite of Brown, **Mark Jackson** will play for the Pacers in the 1994-95 season coming from a trade involving Pooh Richardson and others. The 13th point guard employed by Walsh, Jackson is expected to solve the Pacers' perpetual point-guard problems.

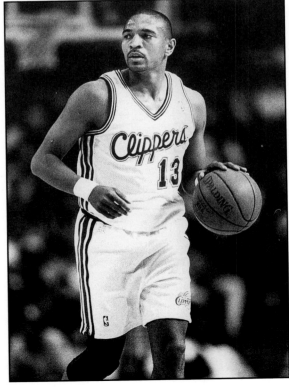

A crowd average in number (12,003) was anything but in effect. It left the players curious just how raucous their arena could become if sold out consistently.

"That," said Miller, "was the loudest regular-season crowd I've ever heard."

Smits had 28 points, 13 rebounds and four assists, easily his most complete performance of the season.

* * *

Smits had been through this before.

If not for stretches like these, no one would expect him to be anything more than a younger, more agile version of Randy Breuer. But they came every year, binges of brilliance, 20-point games piled one after another, giving rise to hopes he had finally broken through to a higher level. They had been as predictable, and as fleetingly frustrating, as Indian summer.

Was there reason to believe, this time, Smits' sun would continue to shine? His teammates thought so.

"I think he's starting to understand," said Scott, "that as he goes, we go."

For years, the Pacers wondered what direction he would lead them. He was continually hampered by some nagging injury, be it an ankle, a knee, an elbow or a shoulder. He was wildly inconsistent, averaging 20-plus points for three weeks, then half that for a month to follow. When he did not score, his rebounding and defensive deficiencies became more glaring.

And, in the process, he became a 7-4 target, an easy object of derision for fans bitter over the team's inability to be no better than mediocre. Those days now seemed a distant past for Smits, who lost weight, gained strength and endurance, and became a stabilizing force in the middle of last season.

"I feel a lot more confident and comfortable on the court," said Smits, whose sixth season would prove to be his most productive. "That comes from being injury-free and having the confidence of the coaches and teammates."

For Smits, it was a season of change, including the birth of his daughter, Jasmine, the previous September. A popular theory was that fatherhood brought out the best in Smits, but he wasn't so sure. "I don't really notice any difference," he said. "I get less sleep, I know that. There have been a lot of changes this year — the coaching, the family, feeling healthy — I don't know what to attribute it to."

After his second year (15.5 points, 6.2 rebounds, 2.06 blocked shots), Smits appeared on the verge of stardom, and was given advice that seemed to make sense, but turned out to be counterproductive. A skinny 245-pounder, Smits was told to gain weight.

He had height, agility, and a soft touch around the basket. What he lacked was the bulk to bang. His frame did not bear the extra mass well, hence recurring problems in both knees, primarily the left, that stunted the growth of his career.

The low point was reached in the 1991-92 season when Smits, struggling with sore knees, was benched in favor of journeyman Greg Dreiling. In the first-round play-off loss to Boston, Smits totaled 28 minutes off the bench in a three-game sweep.

After an erratic season in '92-93, again hampered by knee and elbow problems, Smits broke through in the playoffs, averaging 22.5 points and eight rebounds in a four-game loss to Ewing and the Knicks.

Through it all, Smits never complained and kept his composure. An even-tempered, approachable man with a quick smile, Smits developed a reputation as a player who either didn't have emotions, or hid them extremely well.

Until this year.

When new coach Larry Brown walked into Mackey Arena for his first day of training camp with the Pacers last October, he took one look at Smits and countermanded the previous orders. He wanted Smits, who reported weighing nearly 280, to lose 25 pounds, to get closer to his original playing weight.

Brown also wanted less of something else on the big center: pressure. For years, the Pacers pinned their hopes on a Smits breakthrough, then looked his way when the team failed. "I think too many people focus on Rik," Brown said before the season began. "If all the other guys were so damned good, we wouldn't have been 41-41."

Less was turning into more for Smits. The Golden State game was the seventh in a row in which he scored at least 19 points. In that span, he averaged 22.9 points and 7.4 rebounds.

Part of Smits' emotional development had to be attributed to Brown. Where previous coaches would not criticize Smits for fear of damaging what they incorrectly perceived as a fragile psyche, Brown treated Smits like everyone else.

"He's different than any coach I've ever had, but I respect him," said Smits. "It doesn't matter if you're the top scorer, the leading rebounder or the oldest guy there, he yells at everybody equally. He's either trying to motivate you or trying to help you."

On his best nights, Smits was right behind the group of megacenters, Ewing, Olajuwon, O'Neal and David Robinson. On his worst, he looked like a glorified Chuck Nevitt. Lately, the Pacers had seen far more of the good than the bad.

Still, he remained something of a night-to-night mystery in that Brown never knew quite what to expect. The peaks and valleys that marked his early years, however, showed signs of leveling off.

"He has more skills, more moves around the basket," said Bill Walton, hired by the Pacers to tutor Smits in the summer of 1990. "He sees the game better and understands the control of the game. He has developed into a very nice player. He has the capability of becoming a really, really good player, even a great player. But everybody has the same capabilities. What separates the great ones is how hard they work, how bad they want it, how much they're willing to sacrifice."

Central to Smits' development had been the support of the Davises, Dale and Antonio. The two muscular big men did everything Smits did not — block shots, rebound, defend — to serve vital complementary roles. When Smits struggled, Brown could use the Davises side by side, an intimidating, if offensively punchless, tandem.

Among the most vocal critic of the big center's inconsistency in previous seasons, Miller now was quick to praise Smits.

"Everybody here wanted a big-time center and we've finally arrived and gotten one," said Miller. "I'm excited. He's excited. I've never seen Rik so animated, so fiery, rebounding, intimidating, he's doing it all. It's a new Rik. I don't know what's gotten into him."

Fleming had seen every step, forward, backward and sideways, of Smits' career. In the veteran point guard's opinion, the difference was confidence.

"He looks relaxed," said Fleming, "You can see it in his face. In the past, he'd been a little timid, a little nervous. He's just a lot more confident in himself."

In Smits' mind, the confidence came from an increasing understanding of the game. Double-teams used to force passes that looked like something from the arm of Bobby Douglass or Joe Kapp. He wasn't Sonny Jurgensen yet — more like Sonny Sixkiller — but he was working on it.

"If I don't have the shot, I can still pass it out and create something. I'm feeling pretty confident in that," Smits said. "When I draw a double-team, throw it out and it gets passed all the way around the perimeter before somebody hits an open three-pointer, I love that. To me, that's one of the most beautiful plays in basketball."

Smits first touched a basketball as a 15-year-old (one who stood over 6-9) at a party in his hometown of Eindhoven, Holland. Two years later, he arrived in the United States to play for tiny Marist College in Poughkeepsie, New York. Two years later he was the ECAC player of the year. Two years later he was the No. 2 player taken in the NBA draft, behind only Danny Manning. Now, he was a six-year starter on a climb toward stardom. His basketball career had sprouted much as he had.

As a tall, skinny teen whose main interest was rebuilding and riding motorcycles, Smits had to deal with the cruel jokes of youth. In Eindhoven, he was constantly taunted about his size and, like many big men, became apologetic about being bigger than everybody else. When he discovered basketball, though, he finally was exposed to an environment in which his height was an advantage and joined a club team at 15. As a member of the Dutch junior national team the following year, he got his first glimpse of NCAA Division I in an exhibition game against Hofstra.

LSU coach Dale Brown visited the Netherlands, liked Smits and advised him to start at a junior college. He applied to Wharton J.C. in Texas, and still is waiting for a reply. Then-Marist coach Mike Perry heard about the budding Dutchman through the grapevine and offered him a scholarship sight-unseen. That was all Smits needed.

In the U.S., Smits could walk the streets without being ridiculed. In fact, he was admired for his size, something that just didn't happen in his native country. He quickly became Americanized.

He maintains a home in upstate Walton, New York, where he keeps a stable of muscle cars he has rebuilt and customized. He also has a collection of old Cadillacs, "anything with tail fins," he said. He participates in auto shows during the summer as his great escape from basketball. He spent much of his time on the team plane studying manuals so that he eventually could become certified as an auto mechanic.

He returns to Holland usually once a year, and sponsors the Rik Smits Cup, a tournament in Eindhoven to encourage school-age players. Despite his NBA celebrity, Smits' success has not translated into more visibility for basketball in Holland.

"They show very few NBA games on television over there," he said. "And a bunch of (club) teams went out of business because they couldn't get any sponsors.

"In other parts of Europe, it's really caught on, but in Holland, it's actually gotten worse."

The reason? A major difference in culture. There are no school-sponsored teams in Holland.

"People (in America) are much more sport-oriented. When you go to school, you have all the sports. It isn't that way in Holland," he said. "You'd have a two-hour gym class and that's it. If you want to play, you have to join a club team."

When he came to the U.S., he spoke the language and knew the rudiments of the game, but found out he still had much to learn, like how to talk to his teammates, for example.

"I spoke English quite a bit, but I had to learn all the slang," he said. "In basketball, you learn that pretty quickly."

He also was a quick study in practical jokes. When a reporter approached him for a reaction on being runnerup to the Spurs' Robinson as NBA player of the week, Smits thought it was a put-on.

"Nah, you're kidding me," he said, shaking his head before accepting the sincerity of the information. "Really? That's pretty cool. Maybe I can get it next week."

There was little chance of that.

In the last game before the break, Smits looked like a rookie, scoring three points and fouling out in 25 minutes against Miami's Rony Seikaly, who plays with a chip on his shoulder against the Dutchman. Smits and Seikaly were part of the same draft class. A product of the highly successful, high-profile Syracuse program, Seikaly felt he should have been the first center taken in 1988. That Smits went No. 2 overall and Seikaly wasn't taken until the ninth pick by the Heat motivated him every time the teams met.

Smits wasn't the only player to struggle. His backup, Antonio Davis, also had problems with Seikaly and fouled out in just 16 minutes. Miller couldn't find his shot in a five-of-15 night.

The small forwards, though, came up big. McKey and Williams combined for 55 points to carry the Pacers to a 102-98 victory in Miami, sending them into the All-Star break with a seven-game winning streak, tied for the longest since the franchise joined the NBA. They also had climbed all the way back to .500, at 23-23, for the first time all season.

"We've got a long way to go," said Brown. "We're at .500, and it seems like that's what you start the season at. But I'm proud of the way we've been playing, proud of the effort. I'm sorry there's an All-Star break right now."

The players weren't. The season had been a physical grind. They needed the time to recharge. Nothing would change in three days.

"When we come back," Miller said, "we're still going to have seven straight wins."

They also would have close to a full roster. Dale Davis returned for the game in Miami, but only because of a deal the team had struck with Thompson. In exchange for going on the injured list, Thompson asked permission to head to his Los Angeles home, he thought, for the duration. His request, grudgingly, was granted.

For this team, under these circumstances, to be .500 at the break was an achievement. For this franchise, the All-Star break annually has been time to go back to the drawing board. Major trades had been pondered, some set in motion. Lineup and philosophy changes had been required.

The previous year, the team staggered into the break at 23-28. A seven-game losing streak was snapped only by a home victory over Sacramento before the break, sending Hill deep into the Michigan woods for a spiritual and mental cleansing. The end result of his journey to the hinterlands was the need to scrap the passing game.

This was, in fact, the Pacers' best record at the break since the 1989-90 team was 25-23, and that team had lost 14 of its previous 20 after a 19-9 start.

To be sure, .500 wasn't exactly unfamiliar territory for the Pacers. Over the last four and one half seasons, they were a dead-even 187-187. In the past, the teams were more dead. This one was more even.

They hadn't had their first unit together in more than two months. None of the other lineups had lasted longer than the current group's 13 games. Yet, the team had put together a major winning streak at a most improbable time, giving much more than hope to the season's second half. The Pacers now had a purpose, with several significant goals within reach, especially if they continued their historical pattern as a second-half team. Over the previous three seasons, they had won 60 percent of their games after the break.

The East had three formidable teams — New York, Chicago and Atlanta. Fourth-place Orlando also was separating from the pack. After that, there were five teams — Cleveland, Indiana, Miami, New Jersey and Charlotte — separated by just two and one half games.

They'd never won more than 44 games or finished higher than sixth in the East. They'd never won an NBA playoff series. Suddenly, all of those once distant goals seemed within reach.

The record wasn't much different than usual, but it was the only thing that felt the same about this team.

* * *

On the NBA road, there are only a few stops that elicit giddy anticipation from even the jaded. Miami, with the topless goddesses of South Beach and the bottomless glasses of Coconut Grove, was one. The Heat had an unusual homecourt advantage; teams from the frozen North would come in, work on their tans and get zapped by either the sun during the day or the fun at night.

San Antonio didn't have a beach, but it had everything else, especially for fans of Mexican food and, of course, margaritas. Most of the major downtown hotels fed into Riverwalk, a chain of bars, restaurants and shops that spanned both banks of a canal system that snaked through the city. There also was an expansive downtown mall, River Center. Access to a shopping mall with movie theaters was one of the prime requisites of road hotel selection. Nothing cuts through the dead time like a stroll through the mall and a matinee. Malls offered these easy-to-spot celebrities shopping of another sort, a veritable variety store of opportunities to meet women.

There was one area where the city had taken a giant step backward: the cavernous abomination known as the Alamodome. Built for football in a city without a team, the huge building was partitioned for use by the Spurs, with a huge curtain serving as one wall. A team that used to play in one of the league's loudest buildings, the HemisFair, was now in a sterile environment. Sure, there were posh luxury suites, a fancy scoreboard and high-tech special effects. Somehow, though, the homecourt advantage that once was prohibitive now seemed lost.

In this monument to the failings of progress, the NBA's two hottest teams would meet in the first game after the break. The Spurs, a team willing to tolerate Dennis Rodman's numerous indiscretions thanks to coach John Lucas, had won nine in a row.

They were the hotter team, and would stay so.

Robinson was helped along to a 34-point night by being sent to the free throw line 17 times (making 12). Smits, on the other hand, attempted none. That disparity, as much as anything else, explained the Spurs' 109-100 victory.

Robinson got unexpected help from secondary players. Reid hurt the Pacers again, bringing 20 points off the bench. Against the rest of the league, he averaged nine. In two games against Indiana, he totaled 42. Vinny Del Negro, who was too slow to play point guard but was the best the Spurs could offer, torched Workman for 20 points.

Indiana got 37 points out of shooting guards Miller and Scott, but precious little elsewhere. McKey suffered through a six of 17 shooting night, but that was notable in that it represented what would stick as his season high for attempts. A rematch with his old team, Seattle, was less than a week away. It looked like he was tuning up.

There was a welcome sight that night, though. Antonio Davis broke through the fabled rookie wall with 15 rebounds and nine points to rejoin the ranks of the living. Heading into the break, his game had all but vanished.

The experience of the all-rookie game, and the time away from the team, was valuable. He had seven points and five rebounds in the battle of the network rookies, then finished fourth in the dunk contest.

His selection as a replacement for the dunk competition demonstrated the NBA's less than scientific approach to those sideshows. When Rod Thorn had been in Indianapolis to make the All-Star game announcement, he had just learned that the Lakers' Doug Christie would have to pull out of the competition. On an elevator with Walsh after the press conference, Thorn asked Walsh if Davis could dunk, since he'd be there, anyway, for the rookie game. The league might as well save expenses, if possible. Walsh, naturally and correctly, gave his explosive young player the needed endorsement.

Another situation would soon have to be addressed. Richardson was practicing again and was anxious to be activated. Brown, understandably leery, would take a wait-and-see approach. Richardson had made just two appearances totaling 21 minutes in the last two months. He needed to get in shape. That could take a while.

In Dallas, the Pacers would take their habit of playing shorthanded to a new level. They would play without their head coach.

Brown felt chest pains before the game, a real scare for the 53-year-old. His father had died of a heart attack when Brown was seven, and he was sensitive to the possibility of an inherited problem. The Mavericks' team physician, Dr. J.R. Zamorano, administered an electrocardiogram before the game began and, though it showed no need for concern, Brown was advised to watch the game on television from the locker room.

His team's performance may have taken his mind off his chest pains, if only to divert it to the indigestion caused by an ugly 84-73 non-loss.

The team's pulse didn't register until midway through the third quarter of a game that matched the lowest combined point total in Mavericks history. Thoroughly putrid in the first half, the Pacers led by just two (37-35) even though Dallas shot 31.6 percent. The Mavericks missed their first 11 shots of the second quarter, managing a single free throw in nearly seven minutes, but the Pacers could do no better than a 25-18 lead.

Bad quickly got worse. With the Pacers committing seven turnovers in the first five and one half minutes of the third period, the Mavs strung together an 11-point run to take a 46-42 lead.

For Blair, who filled in, it was a nightmare revisited. "I was thinking, 'Jiminy Christmas, we've got to make some shots'," Blair said. "Why were they shooting like this for me?"

Blair sent in the second unit, and the tide finally turned. The Pacers outscored Dallas 17-5 the rest of the period to build a 59-51 lead that would not again change hands.

The Mavs cut it to four twice in the fourth quarter, but the game was effectively put out of reach when Miller drained a three-pointer to make it 76-66 with 1:30 remaining.

Dale Davis returned to the starting lineup with 16 rebounds and a pair of blocked shots. He also did not hesitate to step in as the enforcer when fellow bruise brother Antonio Davis was pulled down from behind by Popeye Jones, prompting an altercation.

It was a fitting scene in a painful night for all involved. Playing a hapless team like the Mavs, who were, for the second year in a row, threatening to produce the worst record in league history — this loss dropped them to 6-44 — puts an unusual pressure on an opponent.

"We were supposed to win, and if we lose, that's bad," said Fleming, a savior off the bench with 19 points in 21 minutes. "That's what gets you playing that way."

Upon the team's return from the road trip, Brown headed to Methodist Hospital for more extensive testing under the supervision of Dr. King Yee. He was cleared to return to the bench. Something of a workout fanatic, it turned out Brown had strained chest muscles. There was no problem with his heart, but he would have to stay out of the weightroom for a few days.

His heart would have to be strong to withstand the moment his team faced. Schrempf's Sonics were coming to town for a Sunday afternoon game that would be played before the season's third sellout. It was another opportunity to establish the Pacers not only within the league, but in the eyes of their skeptical fans.

Many of them came to pay tribute to Schrempf. They got something quite different: the most demonstrative performance of the season from McKey.

In the closing moments of the 101-95 victory, Brown took McKey out to allow an ovation from the crowd. He also earned a significant tribute from Miller, who bowed — this one given, not taken.

Showing the depth of his skills, McKey racked up 27 points, nine rebounds and five assists while befuddling Schrempf with aggressive defense. He even got involved in a little trash-talking with his former teammates.

He would leave that on the floor. His comments after the game were typically low-McKey. "They already know what I can do, so I don't have to send any messages. They've gone on, I've gone on. We're trying to establish something here and we've played pretty good lately."

While the Pacers won for the ninth time in 10 games to move above the .500 mark at 25-24, the Sonics lost their third straight. After a superhuman 30-5 start, they had gone 6-8 and showed signs of mortality. In 36 minutes, Schrempf produced just six points on two of 10 shooting. "That was as tentative," said Sonics coach George Karl, "as I've ever seen Detlef Schrempf play."

McKey's performance looked a little more familiar to Karl, but struck the Pacers as far more intense than usual. He scored 15 in the first quarter — normally a full night's work — to get the Pacers started, then came back after getting six stitches in the webbing between two fingers on his right hand to hit six fourth-quarter free throws.

"It was a Derrick McKey game," said Karl. "He quietly kills you."

Actually, this was about as noisy as McKey would get. Normally reserved about dunking — he prefers to drop the ball through the bucket, rather than slamming — he had two authoritative dunks in his first-quarter rampage. His work on Schrempf was equally frenetic. In his face all over the floor, McKey gave his adversary little room to maneuver.

"I'm proud for Derrick because I know a lot of people came to see Detlef," said Brown. "Now, maybe they can recognize Derrick's a pretty darned good player, as well."

True enough, but McKey had failed to convert the truly skeptical, who wondered how many games it would take for him to compile his next 27 points.

The next game brought home another prodigal son. Quinn Buckner, one of Bob Knight's favorite players, was in his first year as the Dallas head coach and he already was in danger of losing his job.

Buckner had been stuck in a nightmare, much of his own doing. He was too tight. He had too many rules. He was too authoritarian. He quarreled with his players. His job, despite a five-year contract, was in jeopardy.

None of which took Buckner by surprise.

"When you bring about change, you bring with it a certain amount of controversy," Buckner said. "We were changing things and I accepted it. As long as you're consistent about doing the right things, it will work out. As they found out, it's not about me. It's never been about me. It's about us."

With that realization, the Mavericks had given strong indications they were turning the corner. In their previous 11 games, they'd gone 5-6. It wasn't exactly playoff fever, but at least the chill had been broken.

Though the Pacers outlasted the young team 107-101, the Mavs got Brown's attention. "(Roy) Tarpley is waiting in the wings, and they're obviously going to get another great pick to go along with Jimmy (Jackson) and (Jamal) Mashburn," he said. "I think they're going to start to give people problems."

The one place a developing team typically struggles is at center. In Dreiling, Donald Hodge and Lorenzo Williams, the Mavs simply had no one capable of dealing with Smits, who had 27 points, 11 rebounds and a career-high eight assists.

It was another struggle, but it produced the 10th win in 11 games and third in a row. The Pacers were hotter than they'd been in years. And they were going to Disney World.

With Hardaway and O'Neal the centerpieces, ably surrounded by talents like Nick Anderson, Dennis Scott and Scott Skiles, Orlando had jelled quickly, leading club management to seriously consider a risky move that would mean championship contention this year, but uncertainty after that.

The Clippers finally were serious about dealing Manning. With the trading deadline just two days away, Orlando was one of several teams in what amounted to a sweepstakes. There were a couple of mitigating factors, though. Manning would be an unrestricted free agent after the season, so he was a player his new team could only rent. He held the option to buy. And Scott, O'Neal's best buddy on the team, was included in the offer for Manning.

Following Isiah Thomas' lead in meddling with team personnel decisions, O'Neal essentially threatened team management with his wrath if his friend were dealt. "We don't need Danny Manning," O'Neal said. "We don't need another superstar. The egos just won't match. I think things are fine just the way they are. I've asked, and someone has assured me that it's not going to happen. I'd be disappointed if someone looked me in the face, said nothing is going to happen, and then it happens."

The Pacers had a few rumors of their own to deal with. Discussions with Sacramento were serious. Lionel Simmons, a talented but moody small forward, and Randy Brown, a throw-in backup guard, were offered to the Pacers in exchange for Antonio Davis, Sealy and Mitchell. Brown, craving a scorer behind McKey, wanted to do the deal. Walsh, who correctly perceived that the loss of Davis and Mitchell would stretch the front line perilously thin, was less interested.

"The bottom line is, I didn't want to give Antonio up," said Walsh. "The one advantage I knew we had was the two Davises. Other teams didn't have anything like that."

Sealy, who had slipped behind Kenny Williams in the battle for minutes behind McKey, appeared the player most likely to be traded. In addition to the Sacramento talks, his name had come up in proposals involving Chicago (for Scott Williams), the L.A. Lakers (for Anthony Peeler) and Cleveland (for Terrell Brandon).

Discussions with the Clippers opened an important line of communication. Brown wanted to find a way to trade Richardson to L.A. for Mark Jackson.

The only trade the Pacers would make was involuntary: Miller for Anthony Bowie.

That lopsided transaction went down in the first quarter of the Pacers' 103-99 loss to the Magic. It was consummated not by general managers but by officials, who ejected both players after Bowie and Miller exchanged elbows. Bowie then horse-collared Miller and threw him to the floor. Both players were ejected — costing the Pacers their leading scorer and the Magic a fringe reserve — and would be fined $5,000 by the league. "I don't think," Brown said, "it was a very fair trade."

Though they had done a decent job containing O'Neal (28 points), the Pacers lacked the weapons to keep Orlando from extending its winning streak to five games, tying the young franchise's record.

O'Neal went down hard after banging knees with McKey late in the first half. A fairly commonplace occurrence, this one took on enormous dimensions because it involved O'Neal, the league's new marketing centerpiece. The Orlando Arena faithful watched in stunned silence, as though someone had just shot Mickey right between the ears, as O'Neal was painstakingly attended to on the baseline. He left under his own power but would not return until the early minutes of the third quarter, this time with pads on both knees.

In the meantime, another young center's career was threatened. Haskin crumpled to the floor after attempting a quick pivot late in the first quarter. His season was over. He had badly torn the anterior cruciate ligament in his right knee and would require major surgery. Not only was he lost for this season, but Haskin was not expected back until February of 1995, at the earliest.

Walsh's caution proved prescient. Had Antonio Davis and Mitchell been traded to Sacramento, Haskin's injury would've left the team with only the creaky-kneed Thompson to back up Smits and Dale Davis.

Still, Brown wasn't happy that the deadline passed quietly.

"I'm real disappointed because I thought there were some real opportunities," he said. "I had hoped some of our players who weren't playing a lot could go somewhere to get a better chance to play. I don't like having guys sit on the bench and not have the opportunity to play."

After a full week of practices, Richardson finally was activated for the February 25 game against Detroit. For the first time all season, the Pacers had three point guards on the roster. This was a new problem for Brown. Suddenly, he had a choice.

For two games, a 110-90 rout of Detroit and a revenge victory over the Bulls, 96-86 — snapping a nine-game losing streak in Chicago Stadium — Workman, Fleming and Richardson divided the minutes. But this three-headed point guard concept would not last. Brown had a longstanding tradition: starters could not lose their job because of an injury. Richardson would be worked back into the lineup, as quickly as possible.

Things were going suspiciously well. They had been 11-2 in February, the best month in club history. Their only losses were on the road to superior teams and one of those happened under the mitigating circumstance of Miller's controversial early ejection. And now, they were healthier than they'd been all year.

It was like the standard line in old Westerns: Things were quiet. Too quiet.

9 Marching in Place

The playoff race in the East was beginning to take shape. Atlanta, New York and Chicago would have to suffer monumental collapses to avoid having homecourt advantage in at least the first round. Orlando was in solid position, but hardly uncatchable.

That left a group of five teams battling for the final four spots: Indiana, Cleveland, New Jersey, Miami and Charlotte. Normally, an 11-2 month would send a team leapfrogging up the standings but, in the Pacers' case, all it did was keep them in the hunt. The Nets, Cavs and Heat combined to go 28-12 in February. The Hornets, missing Johnson and Mourning, were dropping out of the picture.

The Pacers' schedule was unusually difficult in March. Of the 16 opponents, 12 were above .500 entering the month. Nine of the games would be against teams battling for position in the East. There were six sets of back-to-backs.

"March is a brutal month," said Brown, the coach of the month for February. "Not only do we play a lot of games, we play a lot of the better teams. If you look now at what schedule lies ahead, we've got to play even better than we did in February. We've got to play our best basketball, and we can't take for granted we're going to be in the playoffs.

"You get really good at the end of the season, you could go a lot of places — you could go way up or way down. Our biggest concern is not to worry about the standings, just make sure we continue to improve. I don't want anybody to concede anything. It's stupid for us to think we're definitely in the playoffs and it's stupid for us to think we don't have a chance to get a homecourt (advantage in the first round). That's the way I'd like to approach it."

One thing Brown did feel strongly about: to give his team its best shot at not only rising in the East, but advancing in the playoffs, Richardson would have to be hustled back into the lineup. The Pacers, he believed, could not afford to go into the postseason with anything less than their most talented point guard.

Things started promisingly, as Smits racked up his fifth consecutive double-double with 24 points and 13 rebounds to lead a 106-94 home victory over a Portland team that had won six in a row.

So frustrated were the Blazers that, during a 10-point third-quarter run that put Indiana ahead for good, radio analyst Mike Rice was ejected by official Steve Javie for his overzealous gesturing during a timeout. One of the league's bright young officiating stars, Javie nevertheless has a hair-trigger reputation. He was standing across the court from Rice, who was gesturing animatedly while broadcasting. Javie and Rice locked eyes and exchanged words from 45 feet, prompting the official to walk over and toss Rice from the game over the protests of the Pacers' public relations staff.

Javie was fortunate the Blazers employed a two-man radio crew. Otherwise, he would've had some serious explaining to do to the listeners back in Portland. For a member of the working media to be ejected was unprecedented in the modern era of the game. It also represented a first for Rice. In 11 years as a college head coach at Duquesne and Youngstown State, Rice said he never was ejected.

That sideshow was witnessed by a disturbingly small crowd of 10,585. For years, the rap on the Indianapolis market was that the fans would only show up on a weekend, and only then if the opponent had a marquee name. This generally guaranteed sellouts when Larry Bird, Magic Johnson and Michael Jordan came to town, but now those three were gone. Shaquille O'Neal didn't sell out MSA. Neither did Alonzo Mourning, Patrick Ewing or Hakeem Olajuwon.

Market size was another problem. Indianapolis' metro population was roughly 1.5 million but, unlike many other small markets where the NBA team was a huge success, there was a great deal of competition for the sports fan's dollar. In Sacramento, there was no powerhouse college team, so the Kings would sell out every night, regardless of the team's lack of quality. In Portland, the Blazers likewise had a captive audience and could charge whatever price they wanted for tickets. In those cities, as well as San Antonio, Orlando and Charlotte, the NBA team was the only game in town.

Not so in Indianapolis. Less than an hour to the south, in Bloomington, Bobby Knight's Hoosiers drew legions of fans from across the state. About 90 minutes to the northwest, there was Purdue, another big draw. In Indianapolis, you either went one way or the other; if you were a Hoosier, you hated the Boilermakers, and vice versa. The best-case scenario for the Pacers was that, if successful, they could cut across all the provincial boundaries and attract a regional following. At the moment, though, they remained trapped in the crossfire between Hoosiers and Boilers.

For a franchise that had never showed a profit, this was a troubling trend. The Blazers weren't exactly a bunch of no-names, and they were hot. So were the Pacers. Still, the fans remained cold to the team.

Those who doubted whether professional basketball ever could flourish in this small, conservative, largely caucasian market, were being supported by mounting evidence.

In their eight-game home winning streak, the Pacers had averaged just 12,918 and their overall attendance (12,518) ranked 25th in the NBA. They were one of just three teams to improve on the court, but decline at the gate.

"Since I got here, I was hopeful if we played a style the fans appreciate and gave effort, the fans would come," said Brown. "I think we are playing with effort, and I think we are fun to watch. Unfortunately, they haven't come. We can't worry about that. The most important thing is we've got to earn the respect of the people here by continuing to get better."

The 13,725 who did show for a Friday night game against New Jersey were rewarded. The Pacers racked up 14 impolite blocked shots and threw down 11 Richter-scale dunks to spank the Nets 126-110. They had won four straight, and 14 of 16. At 30-25, they were five games above .500 for the first time since 1981.

That they did it without their two primary scorers was significant. Smits, the offensive centerpiece in recent weeks, left after the first quarter with back spasms. Miller had a quiet 15-point night.

Instead, the Pacers produced their highest point total of the year on the broad shoulders of the Davises — Antonio had six blocks and four dunks, Dale had three blocks, 12 points and kept the Nets' Derrick Coleman on the bench with foul trouble — and a widely distributed offense that had eight scorers in double figures. McKey, who had gone back into his offensive shell since the 27-point game against Seattle (averaging 9.8 in the five games in between) came in this night with 24.

New Jersey coach Chuck Daly, whose team had won eight of 11 coming in, said the Pacers were "probably playing the best basketball out of anybody in the East."

The Pacers weren't about to argue.

"We're really enjoying the way we're playing right now," said Scott, who had 16 points in 20 minutes. "We're at the point now where we fear losing. We've been there, and we don't want to go back. That doesn't mean we should be comfortable or satisfied. It's just that now, we know what we can do."

They would quickly be reminded of what they could not do: win close games.

Brown's old pupil, Manning, wound up in Atlanta. The Hawks had made what appeared to be a steal of a deal, sending their aging free agent, Dominique Wilkins, to the Clippers for the far younger Manning, likewise a free agent after the season. It was a trade that made sense from both the business and the basketball sides of the operation. If the team was going to invest $5 million a year in a free agent, the money would be better spent on a 27-year-old like Manning than the 34-year-old Wilkins. Though Manning wasn't a spectacular scorer like Wilkins, he was a more complete player and, just as significantly, a complementary player. Wilkins tended to dominate the ball. Manning would not. On a team loaded with scorers, that was a significant trait to acquire.

Atlanta's fans tended to view the deal with emotion, rather than intellect. Wilkins had spent 15 years as a basketball icon in the state, going back to his days at the University of Georgia. He was the Hawks' resident superstar. Many viewed the deal as a cold-hearted franchise showing no loyalty to a valued member of the family. Any fan of modern professional sports who still believed that loyalty existed, in either direction, showed hopeless naivete.

In their hot streak, the Pacers actually may have played too well for their own good, piling up a series of easy victories, with double-digit margins the norm. In Atlanta, one of several upcoming games Brown had targeted as playoff-level, nothing would come easily.

A 12-point halftime lead didn't last long in a game that, like so many early in the season, would come down to the final few possessions. With the game tied 88-all, Dale Davis suffered another judgement lapse, going for a steal on an inbounds pass to Manning, leaving a clear path to the basket. Manning took advantage of a wide-open lane to drive for the game-winner.

There were 7.3 seconds left, giving the Pacers a chance to tie. What they got instead was a lesson in what they should've done on the previous possession. When Scott went hard to the basket, he was met by four Hawks and hammered to the floor. Manning swatted away the shot, there was no call, and Atlanta had the victory. It was a classic example of officials allowing the players to determine the outcome of a game.

It was the sixth time the Pacers had played a game decided by two points or less. They had yet to win one. Manning joined the Lakers' Vlade Divac, Washington's Tom Gugliotta, Philadelphia's Dana Barros and Chicago's Toni Kukoc as members of the fraternity of players who had beaten the Pacers with last-second shots.

Though they recovered to win in Milwaukee, 105-94, the Pacers continued to show signs that disturbed Brown. Against the Bucks, a team going nowhere, they committed a season-worst 27 turnovers and very nearly beat themselves. The Pacers averaged 18 per game, second-worst in the league. That would have to be improved, come playoff time.

"We just can't go into every game turning the ball over," said Brown. "We're making progress, but we're making it hard on ourselves. But this also shows our character because, when the game was on the line, we played well at both ends of the court."

The Pacers trailed 80-79 after Jon Barry's three-pointer with 8:18 remaining, but Miller answered quickly with a trey of his own to start the Pacers on a 17-6 run that put the game away. Milwaukee didn't help itself by missing seven of nine free throws and committing seven turnovers in the fourth quarter.

"We want to be winners," said Dale Davis, "but we can't go about winning like this."

Something had to be done to snap the team awake. The treacherous schedule ahead easily could undo the good that had been done in February. Richardson had played well against the Bucks, with 12 points and six assists in 24 minutes. While he was on the floor, the Pacers outscored the Bucks 65-37 and committed nine turnovers. When he was not, the Bucks held a 57-40 advantage and forced 18 turnovers.

It was time to return him to the starting lineup.

"Before I got hurt, I was into my game real heavy, playing real well," Richardson said. "I think now, I'm ready to pick up where I left off."

With Richardson in the lineup for the first time in three months and Smits still working the kinks out of his sore lower back, the Pacers played like a team without continuity in New Jersey, losing to the Nets 87-73, their lowest point total of the year.

Brown's chief concerns about Richardson — indecision in transition and a tendency to dominate the ball in the halfcourt sets — hardly were alleviated. He had four points, five assists and four turnovers in 27 minutes and looked particularly rusty on the run, continually waiting too long to pass and then making poor decisions.

"Every break," said Brown, "was an adventure."

Still, Miller was hot, scoring 26 through three quarters to keep the game close. The Pacers trailed 64-60 entering the fourth quarter, then proceeded to score 13 points to trip over the doorstep of opportunity. Dale Davis, who had two points, was the only starter to score in the final period.

The player who proved to undo the Pacers was notoriously lethargic center Benoit Benjamin, who outscored Smits 25-4. It was becoming hard to find the right way to identify the Pacers. They had won 15 of 19, but also lost two of three. In this one, they looked much more the latter with more turnovers (21) than assists (19).

Though they came back to win at home the next night, the 104-97 victory over Milwaukee settled little. Richardson did not commit a turnover and had 10 assists, but missed 10 of 15 shots. The offense once again came unglued in the fourth quarter, allowing the Bucks to make it more interesting than it should've been.

The basic strength of the team, its defense, had remained intact. The Pacers had held four straight teams and six of seven to less than 100 points. In their 15-of-20-game binge, they'd done so 13 times.

When they headed to New York for the March 15 game, it marked the beginning of a stretch of eight games in 12 days — four sets of back-to-backs — against teams that had a combined winning percentage of .653: the Knicks twice, Cleveland twice, Atlanta, Chicago, Phoenix and Utah. Those teams had five of the top eight records in the league. The worst of the lot, Cleveland, was also the hottest with 11 wins in 13 games.

"If you want to be the best," said Scott, "you have to beat the best."

Though the Pacers, too, were hot with 16 wins in 20 games, all four of their losses had come to teams above .500; they had fattened up on lottery teams, and now would come a far greater measure of where they stood against other contenders.

"We'll find out what kind of progress we've really made," said Brown. "I think we made progress when we beat Seattle, and we made progress when we beat Houston. I don't see these teams being any tougher, but I really believe we're going to have to play our best basketball. This will be a great, great gauge to see how far along we are and where we really stack up when it comes time to perform at a really high level."

The two Knicks games would lack the Miller-John Starks byplay that had been central to the rivalry. Starks had knee surgery Monday and would be out the rest of the regular season, a fact that disappointed Miller on several levels. "He blew out his knee? Damn," Miller said. "That's the whole point of going to New York, messing with him."

Not only did Miller miss a chance to exact revenge against the player who had been picked over him for the All-Star Game, he drew a difficult assignment in backup Hubert Davis.

"Hubert has always been a little bit more fundamentally sound, probably a better shooter, and a little bit more under control than John has been," Miller said. "It makes it a lot tougher for me, personally."

It seemed like so much Starks-baiting at the time, but Miller turned out to be correct, intended or not. Davis hit a pair of huge shots in the closing minutes as the Knicks overcame an Indiana rally to win 88-82. Davis hit a three-pointer to give the Knicks the lead for good, 77-76, with 4:39 left, then bounced in a tough left-handed drive to spread the margin to a prohibitive 84-78 with a minute remaining.

Though Miller had 22 points, he was one of four Pacer starters not to hit a field goal in the redundantly troublesome fourth quarter. They had come back from a 70-57 deficit to take a 73-72 lead on Scott's jumper with 6:10 left, but Indiana would get just two Smits baskets in the next five minutes against a defense that demonstrated why it is the NBA's best. It was the seventh win in a row for the Knicks, who had not allowed an opponent to break 90 in that stretch, a club record.

Richardson again struggled, missing eight of 10 shots. Though he played just 21 minutes, he twice asked to come out, early in the first and third quarters. Any plans Brown had about returning to the three-headed point guard were shelved when Workman went down with a strained right hamstring in the third quarter. Aggravating Brown's frustration was that the player Walsh had not acquired, Derek Harper, abused the Pacer point guards with 17 points, 12 assists, seven rebounds and five steals.

McKey also was limping on a strained calf muscle. With two key players down, the Pacers headed home for a game the next night against the league's best offensive team, Phoenix, and the Suns were on a four-game winning streak.

Naturally, the Pacers used those factors to their advantage and won 109-98, tying the franchise NBA record of 11 in a row at home. It also was played in front of the fourth sellout in the last 13 home games.

"It's strange," said Dale Davis, who had 13 points and 14 rebounds while limiting Charles Barkley to six of 15 shooting and two boards. "It's been happening like that all year. It seems the more guys we play, the better we get."

Williams stepped in for McKey and was brilliant. As the 15th player to get a start, the human pogo stick had 18 points, 11 rebounds and a career-high seven assists to help add fuel to an offense that had been running on fumes.

Barkley was impressed by the Pacers in general and Dale Davis in particular.

"They're a team on the rise," he said. "They've got a great young nucleus. Those guys are very aggressive. Both Davises are terrific, and McKey has been a great addition for them. I like their team a lot. They've just got to get some experience. I wouldn't want to play them in a five-game series.

"Chuck and Detlef, neither one of them was ever going to be a great defender. But Derrick McKey is a terrific defender. And Dale Davis is the perfect power forward. If you want to build your team the right way, if you can get a guy who just wants to play defense and rebound, he's the prototype."

Before the game, Miller was asked by a reporter if he thought the team might've lost its edge. He looked up, a quizzical look on his face, and shook off the question, obviously chafing at the mere thought. After he had scored 34 points, he pulled the reporter aside and said, "Does that answer your question?"

All things considered, the answer should've been no. The simmering Brown-Richardson conflict, which both had been able to keep beneath the surface, boiled over in the second quarter. Angry that Richardson had allowed Danny Ainge easy postups on consecutive possessions, Brown pulled Richardson from the game. Richardson, his furrowed brows visible throughout the arena, stalked to the bench and engaged in a lively verbal exchange with the coach.

"I got angry with him," said Brown, "and he got angry back."

After the next day's practice, both sides were in full damage-control. Brown said he was "thrilled with our point guard play," even though Richardson had shot 26 percent in four games since returning to the lineup and failed to take command of the offense.

Richardson said the exchange with Brown was a master stroke by the coach that prompted him to play better.

"I know, deep down, he likes me," Richardson said, "but sometimes it's hard. The thing is, he's motivating me. I see his point. He wanted me to be more aggressive defensively, to be more physical because he knows that's the way I like to play. Whatever buttons he pushed must've been the right ones. The guy's amazing. He really knows how to get to me."

Richardson would have to return to form, and quickly, to keep his job. In the next four games, he would face Atlanta's Blaylock, Utah's John Stockton and Cleveland's Mark Price twice.

"My job is to get the most out of him and I have been hard on him," said Brown. "We can't win without Pooh taking our game to another level and he understands that. What players perceive a point guard should do and what a coach perceives a point guard should do cannot be different, because that's such an important position. Before Pooh had his injury, that was pretty clear to him. Since he's come back, it's been a struggle."

It would continue in an 81-78 loss to the Hawks that ended the home winning streak at 11. Though the Pacers had set a club record by holding seven straight opponents to less than 100 points, they had won just three of those games. In the four losses, the offense had produced a paltry 80.3 points.

Down 79-78, the Pacers had three opportunities to take the lead and failed on each. Richardson missed a desperation jumper taken to avoid a shot-clock violation, then McKey failed to finish a drive. When Dale Davis tied up Jon Koncak on the rebound, winning the ensuing jump ball, it set up the decisive possession with 20.7 seconds left. Miller, whose only second-half baskets had come from beyond the three-point line, drove into a crowd of Hawks on the right baseline and tossed up a

13-footer that went 10. Manning wound up with the loose rebound and sailed in for a dunk with 2.9 seconds left.

When Workman's three-pointer at the buzzer missed, Pacers coach Larry Brown demonstratively objected to the lack of a whistle on Miller's drive. "I would never criticize those guys because it was a well-officiated game," said Brown, "but that's not fair. That's just not fair." The Hawks claimed Miller initiated contact by leaning into Blaylock. Manning came over to help and bumped Blaylock from behind, adding to the confusion. "I don't see how they can't call that," said Miller. "But that wasn't the game."

He was right. The Pacers missed 14 free throws and were badly outrebounded, 50-34. In the fourth quarter, the Pacers were five of 17 from the field, extending the trend. In the last four losses, they'd averaged 16.5 points in the final quarter.

"Our defense has been keeping us in games," said Miller, "but our offense is going to have to come around."

Mitchell provided a needed lift the next night against Utah, scoring a season-high 14 points in a 107-103 victory. If the Pacers somehow managed to reach the NBA Finals, they liked their chances of winning it all against whoever came out of the West. They had won nine of their last 10 against the West, beating six of the conference's top seven: Seattle, Houston, Phoenix, Portland, Golden State and now the Jazz.

This was not a victory that solved any problems, though. The fourth quarter continued to be a riddle. The Pacers went without a field goal for the final 6:16, allowing Utah to rally from an 18-point deficit to a 97-all tie on Karl Malone's turnaround jumper with 3:17 left.

The Pacers won it at the line, with Mitchell hitting half their 10 free throws thereafter, including four straight after Malone's bucket, to quell the visitors' momentum. Mitchell also produced one of the game's biggest defensive plays. With the Jazz down 106-103, Mitchell hounded Jeff Hornacek into an off-balance airball on a three-point try, then drew a foul and iced the game at the line.

It was a big night for Mitchell, who had stepped forward when Davis was injured. In his 18 fill-in starts, the Pacers had gone 11-7. But his minutes had become very sporadic. The 23 he got against Utah represented his most since Davis returned to the lineup.

This game contributed mightily to Richardson's impending downfall. Stockton, the one point guard whose name is spoken in reverence by Brown, racked up 19 points and 11 assists while Richardson paled in comparison. His shooting woes continued (two of eight) and he was not the type of player capable of compensating for a bad offensive night with defense and hustle plays.

The Pacers' final trip to the Richfield Coliseum would be Richardson's final game as a starter, and his tenure ended in ignominy.

Playing without four starters, with a front line that had a cumulative height disadvantage of 13 inches, and with a bench forced to employ some players who had been so deep they needed decompression before checking in, the Cavaliers humiliated the Pacers.

In their 93-61 loss, a flashback to the lurid past when they would dream of one day being mediocre, the Pacers established a club all-time record low and tied the third-lowest offensive output in the NBA since the shot clock was implemented nearly four decades before.

In league history, nine players had scored more in a single game.

All this from a night that had offered the Pacers a chance to move into a tie with the Cavs for third in the Central Division and sixth in the East. In the last nine games, the Pacers had gone 4-5. In the losses, they had averaged 76.4 points and 20 turnovers while shooting just under 40 percent. It was almost as though they were a better team when faced with adversity. All this good health, it seemed, was killing them.

"We're definitely not as hungry as we were," said Dale Davis. "When guys were out before, we had guys stepping up. Since everybody came back, we don't approach the games with the same mentality. In the position we're in, this just can't happen, and it'll surprise the hell out of me if it happens again."

Things were so bad, the Pacers couldn't even beat a hasty retreat. On a night when everything else went wrong, even their bus failed them; it got stuck on the ramp and needed a tow to make the climb out of the bowels of the coliseum. During the 45-minute wait for help to arrive, several players approached Brown and told the coach what he already knew. Richardson just wasn't getting it done.

They felt he had hurt the team by staying out longer than necessary when he was injured. Now that he finally was back, it was too late. He had lost his teammates' confidence, a mortal wound for a point guard.

In seven starts, he had made 28 percent of his shots, averaged 6.4 points and 5.1 assists. Even at his worst, Workman could exceed that. More significantly, the team's offense had fallen apart under Richardson. They had posted four of the season's five lowest point totals, including this record-setter, in the last two weeks. Workman would return to the lineup the next night, but the team's troubles were far from over.

In the rematch with Cleveland, the offense was only marginally better than the night before. Though the Pacers hung on to win 78-77, their last four baskets came on offensive rebounds.

Strangely, Brown chose to use Richardson in the final minutes, something the coach had been reluctant to do when he was starting, and it nearly cost the Pacers. Using far too little of the shot clock, Richardson drove and was fouled with 17 seconds left. He stepped to the line with the Pacers trailing 75-74. Even if he made both, the Cavs still would have plenty of time to set up a game-winner.

Richardson missed both, but Antonio Davis jumped over Danny Ferry for an off-balance tip-in to push the Pacers into the lead. Price then scored to put the Cavs up with 10.6 seconds left. Again the offense failed, with Miller tossing up an airball from the right baseline, but Dale Davis threw Gerald Wilkins aside with his left hand and put back the miss with eight-tenths of a second left. Fouled on the play, Davis missed the free throw — it was hard to tell if it was intentional, all things considered — leaving the Cavs one last chance with a half-second left.

When Price fumbled away the inbounds pass, the Pacers had survived. Barely.

The Pacers held the Cavs to 27 points in the first half, tying Cleveland's record low. At one point, the visitors missed 15 straight shots over a nine-and-one-half-minute span as the Pacers built a 46-27 lead early in the third quarter. That margin was all but gone by the end of the period, setting up the contentious fourth quarter.

Earlier in the season, Brown had been hesitant to pull a struggling Workman from the lineup because it would make it look like the point guard was to blame for all the team's problems. Sensitive to the circumstances surrounding Richardson's benching, Brown went out of his way to distribute responsibility for the slump.

"Pooh isn't the problem," he said. "We have a lot of guys who have not stepped up during this period. Derrick's got to shoot the ball 15 times and Reggie's got to shoot it 15, 18, 20 times. Dale's got to get back to the level of play before his injury, and so does Pooh. I don't think anybody should assume we're going to make the playoffs. Otherwise, we'll be one-and-done, or we'll be in the lottery."

For the first time in five years, Miller failed to score in double digits for two straight games, totaling eight in the doubleheader with the Cavs. In 58 minutes, he took just 15 shots. "It's nothing the defense is doing," Miller said. "I'm letting the offense come to me too much. I need to be more aggressive and go get my shot. I've been stinking it up the last two games. I haven't done my part. I'm man enough to admit that."

Others also had slacked off. After a torrid February, Smits' production dropped to an average of 12.6 points on 45.4 percent shooting in March. McKey had yet to consistently elevate his offensive game. He was attempting just nine shots per game. Brown wanted more. That difference of opinion, too, soon would come to a head.

Brown had prepared the team for the difficult stretch of schedule by telling them to look at it as a playoff preview. By that measure, they were due for quick elimination. They faced a tough weekend with a Friday home game against New York - their last chance to avoid a sweep by the Knicks, the one team they couldn't seem to beat - before heading to Chicago Saturday night.

Brown's distrust of Richardson was never more obvious than in the 85-82 loss to the Knicks. Richardson's driving layup capped a 17-2 Pacer run that tied the game at 79-all with 45.6 seconds left. In that span, the Knicks missed all seven of their field goals and committed six turnovers to blow a 15-point lead. But Brown promptly removed Richardson in favor of Scott, leaving the team with no point guard on the floor.

"I'm not sure what that was all about. I'm sure Byron was in there for offensive reasons and they didn't make a change," said Derek Harper. "We knew coming out of the huddle what we were going to do. The middle was open all night on the high pick-and-roll. Byron got hung up on the screen and it opened like a big door for me."

Harper walked right through for an uncontested layup — yet another fatal end-of-game defensive breakdown — that was the decisive play. For the eighth time, the Pacers had lost by three points or less.

"Again at the end, when it comes winning time, we made some bad mistakes," said Brown. "We can't let a guy, for a winning basket, lay the ball in the hole. Everybody on the team has to understand that because we've been burned by it."

There was no shortage of culprits, including the men frequently referred to as zebras, even though they wear grey jerseys, long pants, black sneakers and no stripes. At home, the Pacers were outscored 31-14 at the free throw line. The Knicks, in fact, made just 27 field goals, tying the fewest ever for an Indiana opponent.

"Rik gets two fouls in the first two seconds of the game, he's a big part of our offense, and they shoot 43 free throws," said Brown. "We got a lot of shots up, but we didn't make many (40 percent), and they spent the whole game on the line. We don't have the reputation of a great defensive team, so when we make the play, they're fouls but when they make plays, they're clean blocks."

Had the Pacers gotten even marginal offensive games from their primary frontcourt scorers, the game might've been different. But Smits and McKey combined for 12 points on four-of-18 shooting. That left Miller to go solo against the league's toughest defense. Though he wound up with 18 points, Miller's performance did not please Brown, who wasn't happy with a well-defended jumper that missed with 22 seconds left. As it turned out, that was the Pacers' last chance to either tie or take the lead.

"Reggie just buries himself," Brown said. "He stands under the goal, waiting for people to get him open. That's the problem. We can't find him. And when we do find him out on the floor, he either shoots a jump shot or a runner. You're easy to guard if you just shoot jump shots."

Every time the Pacers faced the Knicks, it seemed, some type of streak was on the line. This time, New York won its 12th straight and moved into the top spot in the East. The Pacers dropped into an eighth-place tie with New Jersey. As it stood, the Pacers would open the playoffs in New York against a team that swept them during the regular season. In other words, this season was looking very much like more of the same.

Just a week before, the Pacers were looking up in the standings, their eyes on sixth place in the East, and beyond. Instead of moving up, they moved down. Another bitter defeat, this one a 90-88 decision in Chicago, left them alone in eighth, feeling the hot breath of the resurgent Charlotte Hornets on their necks.

The Hornets had won eight of 11 since Mourning returned from a lengthy absence, and they had acquired Frank Brickowski, a Brown favorite from their days together in San Antonio, to provide needed depth up front. The Pacers had dropped seven of 12, allowing Charlotte to make up three games in the standings.

The offensive slump was reaching epic proportions. In those 12 games, the Pacers had averaged 87.9 points. In the last four, that figure dropped to a wispy 77.3. Miller, McKey and Smits had fallen into concurrent slumps. The Pacers had gone six games without a single 20-point scorer.

"If your three leading scorers aren't scoring, you're going to have trouble, and that's where we are," Walsh said. "But I'm not panicked by it. We knew this would be a tough stretch of games and playing these kinds of teams one after another after another has taken something out of our team."

Doubly frustrating was that, trailing 89-88 in the closing minutes, the Pacers came up with a defensive stop, leaving the Bulls nothing better than a three-pointer from B.J. Armstrong that missed with 20 seconds left. The long rebound, though, was tracked down in the corner by Horace Grant, who passed to Steve Kerr, who was fouled with 16 seconds left. Kerr made one of two, leaving the visitors an opportunity, but McKey's weak drive down the lane — he attempted to finish with a finger-roll, instead of going in with authority — was swatted away by Scott Williams as time expired.

Richardson was back in the lineup, but only because Workman was sitting out a one-game suspension, the result of a skirmish with New York's Greg Anthony. Oddly enough, it was one of Richardson's better performances: 10 points, seven assists, zero turnovers. It also would be one of his last in an Indiana uniform.

Thus ended the schedule's most difficult stretch, eight straight games, in 12 nights, against upper-echelon teams. Though the Pacers could say they survived, with three victories, they had done little to assuage doubts about their ability to win close games against quality teams. They wouldn't have many more opportunities. Of the final 15 games, 10 would be against sub-.500 teams.

Nothing cures a sick offense more quickly than a visit from a Western Conference team. Having gone nearly two weeks without a 20-point scorer, the Pacers had two in a 126-93 rout of the Clippers, who played like a team at the end of a long road trip. Smits scored 27 and Miller 22.

Workman stepped back into the lineup with an oustanding game, 16 points, nine assists and eight of 11 shooting, all done against one of Brown's personal favorites, Mark Jackson. "I think our team has responded to him," Brown said. "He stepped forward when Pooh was injured. He gives such an honest effort every night and the guys appreciate that. I've been hard on him, but he takes it and tries to get better. I think, if you ask everybody on the team, to a man, they'd want to see him succeed. In my mind, he has earned the right to play. It certainly wasn't given to him. He comes in and busts his ass every night. What's not to like about that?"

A quintessential overachiever, Workman was brought back from Europe as an insurance policy at point guard, a third body to have around in case something happened to Richardson and Fleming. Instead, he had achieved a point guard's ultimate goal: the team reflected his personality. Like Workman, the Pacers weren't a particularly gifted team but they did have the willingness to outwork just about anyone. "I've come in here and I think I've made a difference, helped the team," Workman said. "I've got to do things to better myself. I've got to dive into crowds. I've got to start a fight, something to get the team going. I'm a team player, and whatever it takes for the team to win, I'm going to do."

Any lingering doubts about who should be running the team were quickly laid to rest. Early in the second quarter of the last game of the month, in Boston, Richardson's career with the Pacers came to an end. Guarding point guard Sherman Douglas in the backcourt, Richardson ran blindly, full-speed, into a screen set by 6-7, 205-pound Xavier McDaniel. He tried to stay in the game but could not. His right shoulder had been separated.

The injury did little to dampen the night for Brown, who picked up his 700th career win as a professional coach with a difficult 103-99 defeat of the Celtics. The NBA only recognized 471. For whatever reason, the league combined ABA and NBA stats for players, but not coaches, cutting 229 victories out of Brown's official total. By the end of the season, that would change, as the league announced plans to include ABA victories in its ranking of all-time winningest coaches.

The Celtics had won three straight overtime games, and this one looked like it could well be the fourth. The game was tied at 98-all with 44.5 seconds left. Workman, who had the Pacers' only two baskets of the final four minutes, drove through a surprisingly open lane and scored to put the Pacers ahead. After Douglas missed the second of two free throws, Workman stepped to the line with 15 seconds left, the Pacers up 100-99, and a chance to ensure no worse than a tie.

He had been in much the same situation in the fateful Philadelphia game in January, when he missed a free throw that could've won it in regulation. This time, though, he missed both. Could this really be happening again?

Fortunately for Workman, the answer was no. Antonio Davis leaned into the lane to swat the rebound out to Workman, who was fouled again. This time, he made both.

It looked like March was going to go out like a lamb until the final week. The Pacers righted themselves with the two victories, and had two personal milestones to celebrate. One was Brown's 700th victory.

The other? Miller's streak of snubs was snapped when he was named, along with none other than Shaquille O'Neal, to the final two roster spots for Dream Team II.

10 Dream On

The day before USA Basketball was to make its announcement, the rumor of Miller's impending selection was the buzz of the locker room. His teammates gave Miller their blanket support. At least one wondered, though, if his elevated status would alter the nature of his relationship with Brown.

"If he makes it, that means he has arrived," said Fleming. "So, will Larry leave him alone now?"

Dream on.

Training camp would be in Chicago, not Monte Carlo. The games would take place in Toronto, not Barcelona. It wasn't even the Olympics, but instead the World Championships.

Like any sequel, Dream Team II would suffer from comparison to the original, but that didn't lessen the honor for Miller, even if he did get snubbed, in a way, in the process. When asked by USA Basketball officials what number he preferred, Miller was told that Nos. 4 and 13 were all that remained. Miller gladly took 13, his usual number in reverse. When they sent him the jersey, it bore No. 10. "If Shaquille comes out with No. 13," Miller said, "you know what happened."

Miller was genuinely surprised by his selection. Golden State's Don Nelson was the Team USA coach, and he was pushing one of his players, Latrell Sprewell, for the final guard spot. He wanted a better defender, someone more capable of creating plays. He also was said to favor his former player, Mitch Richmond, over Miller. The selection committee overruled Nelson, though. The U.S. had suffered too many upset losses in the past because its team was overloaded with athletes but woefully short on shooters. When the zones packed in, Miller would be there.

One of four players in NBA history to make at least 800 career three-pointers, Miller's long-range shooting skills would be magnified in international competition, with a three-point line a full yard closer to the basket than the NBA's 23-feet, 9-inches.

Miller wouldn't have the same problem on Dream Team II that he was having with the slumbering Pacers. In the World Championships, he would have plenty of help. In Indianapolis, it had not yet arrived, at least not consistently.

McKey's deference was the most consistently frustrating problem to face Brown. The gifted forward had a low-post offensive arsenal rivaled only by Smits. And yet, when McKey posted up, a pass was more often produced than a shot. Open jumpers were food for some but garnish for McKey, who was giving up far more opportunities than he was taking.

Unselfishness is one thing, but this was becoming quite another. In the last 10 games of March — he missed one with the strained calf — McKey averaged 9.4 points with an assist to turnover ratio that was disturbingly even, 31 to 31. The team's offensive funk coincided. Opposing defenses were basically daring McKey to shoot while focusing on Miller, who averaged less than 13 points in that span.

"We've got to get him to shoot the ball," said Brown. "We need the three man to take shots. It puts a lot of pressure on a lot of people. He does do a lot of other things to help the team but you look around and see we don't have a lot of offensive weapons. He's got to step up and do that."

When they obtained McKey from Seattle for Schrempf just prior to the start of the season, the Pacers knew they were sacrificing offense for defense. Still, the belief was that McKey would play a bigger scoring role than he did with the multi-faceted Sonics. "They had so many more options in Seattle and they created more scoring opportunities by causing turnovers," said Brown. "We don't have that. Instead of being the third or fourth option like he was in Seattle, he's a big option for us."

It was an option that was infrequently exercised. McKey was on pace for the lowest scoring average since the 8.5 of his rookie season of 1987-88, and he was nearly two full points below his career mark of 13.9. Though his assists were well up, over four per game, so were his turnovers.

McKey's lack of offensive aggression once led Seattle coach George Karl to kneel at his locker before a crucial game and pray for more scoring. Brown wouldn't let it get to him in quite the same way. "It's not going to drive me crazy," Brown said. "Derrick's still young and we've got to work on some things. I love the unselfishness and the things he does. But he's got to look at our team and who's on the floor and realize he's got to be a little more assertive — at least shoot the ball."

It was a seemingly unthinkable dilemma in the NBA, asking a player to be more selfish but, with McKey, it simply came with the territory. In the player's mind, it was a boundary that should not be crossed. The more Brown pushed him to shoot, the less he was so inclined. McKey was the one player on this team who could buck the system and be granted a free pass. How would it look, after all, for there to be a public feud between Brown and McKey, the player the coach had pushed Walsh to acquire?

Brown, instead, took it the other way. He might complain about McKey's passiveness, but he would be careful to balance it with a compliment about his total game. After the season, Brown went so far as to say, "If I was a player on this team, he would be my best friend. It's just what he stands for, the way he treats people, the way he carries himself, the way he plays."

None of it seemed to motivate McKey. It wasn't that Brown was asking him to become Michael Jordan or Scottie Pippen. He just wanted his small forward to accept the offensive responsiblity that comes with the position. On his aggressive nights, they were a far better team. When he scored 14 or more points (his career average), the Pacers were, at that point, 16-4. The alarming fact was that, in the team's 69 games, McKey had scored below his career average 43 times. In game 70, he would add sub-par performance No. 44.

Against a slumping Miami team that had lost six in a row and was without center Rony Seikaly, the Pacers came out flat and stayed that way, losing 101-91. That allowed the Heat to replace them in sixth in the East.

Dale Davis had 20 points, 15 rebounds and four blocks and Byron Scott hit his first nine shots and finished with 20. On any other night, those would've been superb complementary performances. The problem was, there wasn't anything to complement. Miller, Smits and McKey combined for 31 points on 29 percent shooting. McKey, the player Brown was trying so hard to reach, didn't hit a shot until the third quarter.

Brown was sticking to his theme that these games against quality teams were a simulation of what to expect in the playoffs. In that case, they were in deep trouble. They hadn't beaten a .500 or better team on the road in six tries since February 26 at Chicago and, overall, had lost eight of their last 11 to teams in playoff position.

"If the season ended today, with the way we're playing right now, if we went up against a Chicago or New York," said Davis, "I don't think we'd stand a chance."

"The missing element is we haven't come like it's a playoff game," said Scott. "We start off like these are regular games that have no extra meaning. That's unacceptable. I wouldn't want us to start the playoffs today, the way we've been playing. We've got two or three weeks left in the season. We've got to realize what's at stake and take it more seriously. If we do, I think we'll be OK."

Fortunately, they had four weeks to get their problems ironed out. But the only thing that got ironed the next night was Fleming.

Fleming learned the hard way just what kind of impact Shaquille O'Neal can have. The lithe 6-5 guard was cruising in for a layup early in the second quarter against the Magic. O'Neal, chasing from behind, went for the block and missed, falling squarely on Fleming in the process. "I didn't feel anything," Fleming said. "I think I was in shock. Then I saw teeth everywhere." The veteran had his upper dental plate crushed, with several teeth driven into his lower lip. He also suffered a six-inch gash above his right knee that required more than a dozen stitches to close. The latter injury was less gruesome but far more serious, since it prevented Fleming from bending his knee. With Richardson already out, the team was left without a backup for Workman.

The good news was that Workman was playing at his highest level of the season. He had a career-high 15 assists in the 128-113 defeat of the Magic. In the last four games, he had averaged 12 points, shot 56 percent, and totaled 33 assists against just nine turnovers.

The Pacers split the season series with the Magic. If they could catch Cleveland and finish fifth in the East, they would meet Orlando in the first round. Brown viewed that as something of a mixed blessing. Though the Pacers drew their biggest crowd in more than two years, 16,653, many were there to cheer O'Neal and wore Magic garb. "I'd be thrilled if we could get that far up," said Brown. "I don't know if I'd be thrilled to play them. I'm pretty sure it'd be a full house, but I'm not sure they'd be rooting for us."

Workman, who was returned to the lineup when Brown opted to bench Richardson, thought this might be his last big opportunity. "He put me in the lineup," said Workman, "so I figured if I was going to mess up, I'm going to mess up trying."

Still, he would need some relief.

It would come from veteran Lester Conner, another of Brown's L.A. reclamation projects. He had played 31 games for the Clippers in 1992-93 and was a valued reserve in the playoffs. He had no intention of returning to the NBA this year, though. He had made the first tour with Magic Johnson's barnstorming all-star team, then headed to the CBA to keep in shape for the second tour, when Brown called again.

Conner had an upbeat personality that would go over well in the locker room. He would occasionally commandeer a reporter's notebook or tape recorder to enliven an interview of a teammate. He also had a way with women, making tabloid headlines by dating Victoria Rowell, one of the stars of the popular soap opera, "The Young and the Restless."

There was something in his past Conner would just as soon keep buried. As a defensive specialist at Oregon State, more than a decade before, he had earned the unfortunate nickname, "Lester the molester." In the early 1980s, that was cute. Now, it was politically incorrect. "My mom really hated that," he said, "me being her angelic son."

Brown originally wanted to bring in two point guards, also considering Mike Iuzzolino, Steve Henson, Adonis Jordan and Corey Williams. But the Pacers only had room on the injured list for one of their two damaged point guards. Teams can not have more than three players disabled at a time, and Haskin and Thompson already were on the list.

When the team convened for practice on April 5, there was another serious shortage of bodies. Thompson, in from L.A. to attend to personal business, practiced with the team for the first time since being placed on the injured list with sore knees two months before. Smits sat out with the flu and Miller left early, with permission to fly to New York. USA Basketball called, needing his presence to participate in the preparation of promotional material. This offered versatile assistant coach Billy King one more chance to work out at point guard, and underscored how desperately help was needed at that position.

Conner would provide help, but would it be enough? At least he got to spend some time with Thompson, his close friend and former roommate in L.A., where the two highly eligible bachelors enjoyed an active social life. One writer asked Thompson, jokingly, if they needed a revolving door for the house. Thompson explained that wasn't necessary, but they did have a secret exit through one of the closets.

Thompson had no intention of staying. He figured, when Conner's 10-day contract expired, Fleming would return. Richardson would be back in two weeks. There simply was no place for him. Or so he thought. "I just came back," he said, "because I kind of missed the guys."

What Thompson did not know was that Walsh felt strongly about the need for as many big bodies as possible being in shape for the playoffs. He never used his return-trip ticket to L.A. Thompson was activated the next day as both Fleming and Richardson were placed on the injured list.

The Pacers' face was ever-changing.

Smits sat out an impressive 105-89 rout of the Pistons, allowing Antonio Davis to do his usual thing as the fill-in center: 18 points, seven rebounds, two blocks. Conner, who knew no plays, nonetheless got in for 11 minutes.

The game marked the final MSA appearance for an Indiana legend, Isiah Thomas. He didn't play particularly well with 10 points and six assists, though he did throw in one nifty left-handed hook for posterity. His retirement, though not yet announced, was a foregone conclusion. The moment was obviously lost on the local fans. When Thomas was removed with 5:19 remaining, there was no standing ovation, no tribute. Applause was sparse.

"He's such a great player, and he's been so good for this league," said Brown, who was obviously sorry to see Thomas go. "It's nice to go out when you have all your abilities, but this guy can still really play."

The admiration was mutual. Thomas was duly impressed by these new Pacers. "I have been playing against Indiana for the past 12 to 13 years and I have to say that this is the hardest-working Indiana Pacer team I've seen play," Thomas said. "Not the best team, but the hardest-working team, both offensively and defensively. If they keep playing as hard as they are right now, they're going to do well in the playoffs."

In three appearances in relief of Smits, Davis had averaged 19.3 points, nine rebounds and 2.67 blocked shots. But those games were against Milwaukee, Atlanta and Detroit, not exactly teams who offered formidable centers. In Charlotte the next night, he would get a start against his first premium center, Alonzo Mourning.

That matchup, though, would take a backseat to the main event: Brown vs. McKey.

The game itself was bad enough. With a chance to clinch the season series and reduce the magic number for clinching a playoff berth from five to two in one night, the Pacers instead suffered through another ignominious road blowout, this time 129-90. It was their worst deficit since 1987, but also their second loss by 30 or more points in their last four road games. They hadn't beaten a quality team on the road since the 96-86 win over the Bulls on February 26.

In the middle of it all, McKey decided he had heard enough about his hesitant shooting from Brown. During a timeout, he snapped at Brown to "get out of my face," among other things. The outburst took the coach by surprise, particularly since most everyone on the bench was chiding McKey to take the open shots he had become obsessed with passing up.

The two would renew the exchange after the game, and again in a lengthy team meeting the next day.

"I got on him about shooting the ball, and half the guys on the bench were yelling the same thing," Brown said later. "He jumped all over me. I said, 'Hey, I'm not going to stop telling you to do that. It's my job. I've got a responsibility to coach you. I also have a responsibility to bring out the best in you.' But I never had a problem with Derrick. I addressed that to him. I told him that sometimes, you can think you're the most unselfish player in the world, but it can be selfish not to shoot the ball because it puts the pressure on somebody else."

Brown was not the type of coach to punish McKey. He encouraged honesty from his players, though he preferred it to be delivered in a less vehement manner.

"I didn't care what anybody on this team said to me because they cared," he said. "I didn't want to let anything fester. If something came up, I wanted to address it."

He also could not come up with a reasonable explanation for his team's road lethargy, particularly in games against quality opponents. The last three trips had produced the monumental collapse in Cleveland, a worse-than-it-looked 10-point loss in Miami, and this abomination.

"We were beat from the first minute to the last in every way and I don't understand why," he said. "I know they played great and shot the ball well (a franchise-record 64.6 percent), but this was a big game for us and I knew it would be a big game for them and that's the thing that's discouraging. It's my job to get us ready to play and explain what the circumstances are, how important the game. I tried to do all those things. I haven't seen it in a long time, where we do understand that these are just like playoff games. That's the saddest thing because, if we do get in, it's going to be quick."

This on the heels of the promising home victories over Orlando and Detroit. "How can we be so great one night," said Antonio Davis, "then come back and be so lousy the next?"

They would avoid that pattern the next night in Chicago. They would follow one lousy game with another, this time, at home. They gift-wrapped a 100-94 victory for the Bulls by, once again, demonstrating a remarkable knack for falling apart late in the game.

The Pacers committed four turnovers, and five on their last seven possessions, to help the Bulls outscore them 12-2 in the final two minutes to take the game away.

"When it came down to winning time, like in so many games this year, we don't get it done," said a disconsolate Brown. "We absolutely just do not get it done."

After spending most of the night slowly climbing out of a 13-point hole dug in the second quarter, the Pacers found themselves with a 92-88 lead, and the ball, with less than two minutes left.

And then?

Dale Davis, who was thoroughly dominated by Horace Grant (outscored 19-4, outrebounded 14-6), was stripped by Scottie Pippen. B.J. Armstrong hit a pair of free throws to cut it to two, then Smits and Workman mishandled the inbounds pass and gave it right back. Grant tied it with a jump hook.

Antonio Davis proceeded to throw a simple pass through Workman's feet and out of bounds. Pippen worked open for a three-pointer and for a 95-92 Chicago lead with 42 seconds left.

Then came the clincher, a play on which the Pacers managed to commit two turnovers when one would've been quite enough. On yet another blown inbounds play, Workman did not cleanly receive the pass from McKey. The ball went through his hands, deflected by Armstrong, and touched Bulls coach Phil Jackson out of bounds — one violation. Workman then caught the ball out of bounds — another violation. Armstrong hit two more free throws to conclude the decisive nine-point run, although the Pacers did have one more turnover to get out of their systems.

Since their 14-2 run from late January through early March, the Pacers had staggered to a 9-10 record to lose their momentum, not to mention confidence. Eight games remained in the regular season, and six of the opponents were lottery teams. The schedule offered the Pacers a chance to get healthy, but only if their symptoms were properly diagnosed. That was Brown's job.

The numbers pointed to an offense that wasn't doing its part. In the past 19 games, they had averaged just 94.3 points. Miller, McKey and Smits all had dramatic drops in production.

Here, Brown gambled with a little reverse psychology. To belabor the obvious offensive problems would put an inordinate amount of pressure on a phase of the game that already was buckling. Instead, Brown gathered the team and told them that their problems were generated at the defensive end. To Brown, it boiled down to the things it does not take world-class talent to do: setting good screens, battling for loose balls, chasing long rebounds and jealously guarding the basket.

What he got, as a result, was a far more productive offense.

Smits had come back with a promising 25-point night in the loss to Chicago and did that one better with a season-high 32 points in a 121-108 defeat of Boston that gave the Pacers their first-ever series sweep of the Celtics.

In what was shaping up as a roller-coaster of a playoff race, the victory vaulted the Pacers from eighth to sixth in the East, two games behind Cleveland but just a half-game up on eighth-place Miami.

With Smits at his peak in February, so was the team. Bothered by back spasms that lingered for weeks, then the flu, Smits' production faded in March and early April. So did the team.

Smits was now showing signs of revitalization, which was very good news, indeed. When Smits scored at least 20, the Pacers had gone 15-5.

"The thing we have to do," said Dale Davis, "is keep going to him."

Smits scored 23 of his points in the second and fourth quarters, fouling out Boston starter Robert Parish and his backup, rookie Acie Earl, in the process. For Smits, who had fouled out a league-high 10 times, it was an unusual turn of events.

"We've always tried to throw it to him," said Brown. "Maybe we are running a few more things toward him, but I think he's been more aggressive. He knows we need him to be more assertive."

So did Miller and McKey, who both perked up, Miller with 22 points and McKey with 19, his biggest output in nearly a month. The team's three top scorers combined for 73, their best night of the season.

A team reliant on role players — Workman, Scott, Antonio Davis, Williams and Mitchell — could only go so far. For the Pacers to achieve their ultimate goal of playoff success, Miller, McKey and Smits had to step forward.

Miller and Smits could be relied on for some degree of consistency. The mystery man was McKey. "I don't think you're ever going to change him," said Brown, "so you might as well deal with what you've got."

What the Pacers had, logistically, was a road trip that combined bad cities, bad teams and bad timing. They would be gone eight days on a journey through Philadelphia, Minnesota, Detroit and Washington. It wouldn't be glamorous, but it offered the team a chance for something far more important, and elusive: success on the road.

One of the veterans who had been preaching the gospel to the younger players showed them the way in Philadelphia. Scott, sensing the opportunity, scored 21 points to spark a 115-87 victory over the 76ers. There would be no repeat of the unnecessary dramatics that had marked past visits to the Spectrum, an odious building nicknamed 'the rectum' by some members of the traveling party.

Philadelphia stayed close until Byron Scott took over, scoring eight points in a 13-3 run that expanded the Pacer lead to 52-38 late in the second quarter, and the deficit would not shrink into single digits thereafter. The Sixers' lone challenge was again answered by Scott. After the home team cut the gap to 79-67 late in the third, Scott had nine points in a 22-4 run that turned most of the fourth quarter into garbage time.

Dominant across the front line, the Pacers racked up a season-high 59 rebounds - 12 for Dale Davis, 11 for Smits — and also had 39 assists, another season-best, led by Workman's 13.

It was going to be Conner's last night with the team. His 10-day contract was about to expire. After he produced a solid game — seven points, four assists and three rebounds in 23 minutes — Conner was all set to return to the Rapid City Thrillers of the CBA, where he would continue to prepare for the Magic Johnson tour.

Aware Conner was expressing a lack of motivation to continue on, the Pacers were prepared to sign 5-7 Greg Grant, a former Sixer, to a 10-day contract.

What Conner didn't count on were emotional postgame appeals from several of the Pacers, including his former off-season roommate, Thompson, and former CBA teammate, Mitchell. After hours of deliberation, Conner called Brown in the middle of the night and said he would sign through the remainder of the season.

Fleming worked out before the Philadelphia game and the results weren't good. Swelling returned to the knee, which he still could not bend. Instead of returning within the week, as was hoped, he could miss the rest of the regular season.

Conner established an unofficial club record for the shortest retirement. Scott Skiles, embittered over the team's incessant losing, left the Pacers when the team was in New York in 1989 with the stated intention of retiring. On his flight to Indianapolis, he ran into Walsh, who talked him into returning to the team a day later.

Conner obliterated that mark. He could only stay away for a few hours. It turned out to be one of the most profitable decisions of the season.

It preceded a reminder of one that turned out to be generally unprofitable, the ill-fated Minnesota trade. The Pacers headed to Minneapolis to face the wretched Wolves and see how their former teammates were faring.

In the locker room before the game, Person was happy to see reminders of his more pleasant past. But the smile on Person's face betrayed the frustration that twisted his guts a little more with each loss. The Pacers, the team he called home, had moved on without him and left no forwarding address. "It's definitely been tough," Person said, "going from one high in your career to definitely a low point."

Indiana's 130-112 victory over Minnesota was the third straight blowout in a mini-streak that had inflated the team's record to 42-35. Against the Wolves, they racked up a 31-12 lead in the first six and one half minutes and coasted the rest of the way, establishing season highs for points in a quarter (44 in the first), total points and assists (40).

Smits, who quickly claimed jersey No. 45 when Person was traded away two years before, continued his scoring binge with 30. The other corners of the offensive triangle were sharp, Miller with 24 and the suddenly lively McKey with 19.

Person got up just four shots in 24 minutes, scoring a paltry two points. Micheal Williams played fewer minutes than Chris Smith. Richardson was nowhere to be found. At least Mitchell played creditably, eight points and three rebounds in 14 minutes. This wasn't the way the trade was supposed to work.

When Person left the Pacers, he was the franchise's leading NBA scorer. He had since been passed not only by Miller, but his close friend Fleming. He envisioned himself an Indiana icon. But now he had to accept that his jersey would never hang from the rafters of Market Square Arena. His memory was fading, like his career.

The milestones would belong to others, mostly Miller.

As he warmed up in the Palace for the game against Detroit on April 17, Miller was approached by assistant trainer Kevin Johnson, a thoroughly upbeat beer-barrel of a man who had the rare ability to give as good as he got in the inevitable verbal exchanges that would take place on the team plane, in the team bus or in the locker room.

Miller and Johnson were the Abbott and Costello, the George and Gracie, the Mutt and Jeff inevitably in the middle of every duel of insults. Johnson, who stood 5-6, was regularly reminded of the night he allowed Steve Alford to score 56 points against him in a high school game. Johnson would take one look at Miller and either make a Mr. Potato Head crack, or ask him how many channels he picked up on those satellite dishes disguised as ears.

In NBA guy-talk, this was high-level emotional discourse. Miller and Johnson were as close as a multimillionaire product of the MTV Rock & Jock generation and a middle-class kid could get. Somebody had to remind Miller of what the night could bring. Johnson was a natural. Miller was 11 points away from becoming the franchise's all-time leading scorer. He already had passed the storied ABA legends Freddie Lewis, Mel Daniels, George McGinnis and Roger Brown. The only name ahead of his was that of Billy Knight, currently the club's director of personnel and the only remnant of the difficult ABA-to-NBA transition years.

"I honestly didn't know about it until K.J. told me," Miller said. "I thought, 'That gives me something to shoot for'."

With a three-pointer to open the third quarter, Miller had his record, surpassing Knight's total of 10,780. But the Pacers were in no position to celebrate. The Pistons rolled over for no one at home. With big games from their best players — Isiah Thomas, Joe Dumars and Terry Mills combined for 60 points — the Pistons led through most of the second and third quarters and had a 79-78 advantage with 9:35 left. But Scott and Williams combined for 11 points in a 13-3 run that opened a 91-82 Indiana lead, and Detroit, which dropped to 20-59, did not mount a serious challenge thereafter.

On the night Miller stood alone atop the franchise scoring list, the Pacers clinched their fifth consecutive playoff berth. When it was over, though, the locker room attendants brought no champagne, just a platter full of hot dogs to the players. There was no celebrating, just food for an appetite that remained unsatisfied.

"I don't think we're really going to be accepted until we do something in the playoffs," said Miller. "It doesn't matter if we win 60 games. We've got to do something in the playoffs for this to be complete."

Still, from a season that started in so much darkness, this night offered a glimpse into the light. They had 43 wins with four games remaining. No Indiana team before them had won more than 44 in the NBA. If they continued their four-game winning streak, the Pacers would enter the playoffs with unprecedented momentum.

Into the midst of all these dreamy good times stepped a living nightmare: a 7-7, 330-pound monster from Transylvania.

Flash back to January 5. The Pacers go to Landover, Maryland, in desperate need of a road victory. They blow the game, 97- 95. Fast forward to February 1. Though they handle the Bullets at home the Pacers are unable to contend with Gheorghe Muresan.

This would be a combination of the worst of both games in what should be renamed the UScare Arena when the Pacers are in town.

Things were cruising along nicely, for a while. After a first half that consisted primarily of trading layups, the Pacers put together eight and one half minutes of solid defense that led to a 28-7 run and built an 88-62 lead with 3:30 left in the third quarter.

Just when another road blowout appeared in order, Muresan got in the way. Of everything. Blocking three shots and reaching in for four steals on defense, and tossing in remarkably soft baby hooks at the other — 13 points in the final 5:15 — Muresan left the Pacers reaching for solutions.

Smits, absolutely dwarfed for one of the rare times in his life, came up empty on three straight post-ups against Muresan down the stretch and wound up fouling out with 23 points — most against starter Kevin Duckworth, who challenges Muresan's weight, but not his height.

Neither Antonio nor Dale Davis could provide an answer, either. The same went for LaSalle Thompson. Four had been sent to scale the man-mountain, and none had planted a flag.

"I tried to front him, I tried to push him out, I tried to keep him from getting to the block, we double-teamed him, and nothing worked," said Antonio Davis. "Next time, we're just going to have to jump on his back to keep him from scoring. I jumped as high as I could and I barely touched his elbow."

McKey may have come up with the most efficient, if moderately illegal, strategy. "Get somebody to squat down behind him," McKey said, "then push him over."

Muresan was unbendingly dominant in the final minutes. The Pacers led 105-87 with 6:10 to go, but that was before he scored his first basket. He went on to score 10 of the Bullets' final 14, including the potential back-breakers.

When Smits fouled out holding Muresan on an inbounds pass, the biggest Bullet stepped to the free throw line and tossed one up that bounced off the rim four times before settling into the net, cutting the once-proud lead to 109-108. He left the second short and Dale Davis soared high for the crucial rebound. In swooped Muresan, grabbing the ball from Davis and tossing in a hook to put the Bullets up

110-109 with 9.6 seconds left. The fans couldn't have reacted more wildly if they had just witnessed the breaking of Wilt Chamberlain's 100-point record.

Two officiating wrongs then made a right, as far as the Pacers were concerned. Wrong No. 1: A driving Scott was driven into the floor by Muresan, but no foul was called. Wrong No. 2: McKey clearly tipped Scott's missed shot out of bounds, but the officials awarded the ball to the Pacers with five seconds left.

Miller, who scored 18 of his 34 in the first quarter, ran defender Mitchell Butler into a crushing Dale Davis screen, caught McKey's inbounds pass and buried much more than a game-winner. He exorcised the last-minute demons that had haunted the Pacers throughout the season.

When it all was over, Brown allowed himself a hint of a smile, and more than a glint of sarcasm. "Just a routine one-point win," he said. It had been that kind of season.

By sweeping the road trip through NBA hell, the Pacers tied the franchise record for NBA victories at 44, and set a new mark with 18 on the road. They were clinging to sixth place in the East, one game behind Cleveland but just a half-game ahead of New Jersey. Three games remained, two against teams in the playoff hunt.

None would be bigger than the April 20 game against Cleveland. A victory would clinch the season series, giving the Pacers a vital tie-breaker over the Cavs.

It came one night after the near-disaster against the Bullets, against a Cleveland team that had been off for four days. The Pacers looked at the bright side: none of their potential playoff opponents had a 7-7, 330-pound center that would provide a similar matchup problem. Not even Orlando.

If this was a big game, then it was time to look for Miller. He provided 29 points, including eight after the Cavs had cut the lead to 95-93 in the closing minutes, to provide the impetus for a 109-98 victory that left the Pacers' postseason fate squarely in their hands.

Not only had they set the franchise record for NBA wins, they kept two juicy carrots dangling. Victories in the final two games would wrap up fifth in the East, their highest finish, and extend their winning streak to a club-record eight straight.

Though the MSA crowd was a modest 13,072, it established a season record. The Pacers would average more than 13,000 for the first time ever — ABA or NBA. It wasn't much, to be sure, but it was a start.

All this talk of records slipped right past Miller. Quantity was one thing. Quality was another. "I don't know if we can be the best Pacer team ever," he said, "until we win a championship."

When it was over, the Pacers were left to ponder the possibility of a first-round matchup with Orlando, the made-for-TV team featuring center-rapper-movie star Shaquille O'Neal.

"No matter who we play," said Dale Davis, "it's not going to be an easy team."

Not to mention, vice versa.

* * *

For much of the season, Miller hadn't produced up to his normal standards. Neither had McKey. There had been the usual undulations from Smits.

And yet the Pacers were 45-35, with a bagful of franchise records, and realistic hopes of doing something other than watching the second round of the playoffs.

It hadn't been in the stars. It had been on the bench. This was a success made possible by a collection of willing role-players.

"They've made our whole season," said Brown. "Nobody even talked about them playing a minute, let alone being major contributors. You just can't lose two point guards and your big forward, but we did. That's what's been so much fun."

In losing players, the Pacers gained depth and character.

When Fleming went on the injured list 15 games into the season, Workman — who barely made the team after a poor preseason — was activated for insurance. Two games later, Richardson was lost with a stress fracture in his lower right leg, and Workman found himself in the starting lineup. In the 46 games he had started, the Pacers were 28-18.

When Dale Davis went down with a fractured bone in his left wrist, the Pacers were 12-17, and a collapse seemed imminent. Enter Mitchell, who had played sparingly to that point. With Mitchell playing exceptionally well, the Pacers won 11 of 18 games to start their turnaround.

Smits hadn't had any major problems but a handful of minor ones. In his stead, Antonio Davis averaged 16 points and 7.8 rebounds in four fill-in starts.

Scott was unemployed in Los Angeles when the season began. Since signing with the Pacers, he had been the leading scorer on a bench that desperately needed the offensive help, and the only threatening perimeter shooter beyond Miller.

Even Williams had done his part, providing what McKey would not: instant offense and energy.

The bench got them in position, but the starters were carrying them to the finish. The Pacers finally had found cohesion in the first unit. The same lineup started throughout the team's six-game winning streak. For the Pacers, that was virtually unprecedented stability.

It was reflected in the performances, both team and individual. Starting at the top with Miller and continuing through the roster, the Pacers at the moment had no weak links.

"The leaders have to step up, and it starts with myself," said Miller. "If the other guys see me stepping up, then Rik is going to start playing well as well as Derrick and Woody and the rest of the guys. It starts with me. I'm the one that has to go out there, dive on the floor, bust my behind, and I think that'll get everybody else going."

Less hesitant with his jumper and more aggressive with penetration, Miller had fed a team whose appetite for offense was reaching ravenous stages.

After a 13-game slump in which he scored more than 20 points just twice, Miller had found his groove. In the winning streak, he was averaging 23 points on 55 percent shooting. He had been particularly hot from three-point range, hitting 17 of 29.

"It's in our hands now," Miller said. "It's not over yet."

He sincerely hoped it had only just begun.

*   *   *

The final weekend of the season turned out to be anticlimactic. Philadelphia wasted plane fare coming to Indianapolis for its 133-88 loss, although the night wasn't a total writeoff. Smits continued his torrid offensive play by raising his career-best, for the second time in a week, to 40.

The 76ers offered no resistance, allowing the Pacers unanswered runs of 14 and 18 points to build a 43-17 lead in the first 16 minutes. The margin swelled to 56 twice in the fourth quarter before settling at 45 — tying yet another franchise mark set in 1980 against New York.

Indiana also racked up season highs in points, rebounds (64) and field goals (55). The Pacers shot better than 50 percent (.545) for the eighth straight game — that's right, a franchise NBA record.

"I think this is probably the best we've played," said Scott. "Even though that seven-game streak before (January 29 through February 9) was great, now we're playing well at both ends of the court. This is the best time of the year to be playing your best basketball."

For Smits, one personal obstacle remained uncleared. For whatever reason, he had struggled badly against Miami, whether the Heat started Seikaly or Salley. The final game would be his final test.

The Heat came to Indianapolis lacking motivation, for their playoff status had been secured the night before. Win or lose, they would finish eighth. They played like a team with nothing to gain in a 114-81 rout. Smits had 16 points, 10 rebounds and five assists in just 26 minutes.

And so this most irregular season came to a close in remarkable fashion. The Pacers had fifth place, a franchise victory record of 47, and an eight-game winning streak. In the process, they postponed potential matchups with New York or Chicago. Those teams were paired in the opposite playoff bracket. If the Pacers got past Orlando, they would face Atlanta in the second round. The Hawks won 57 games and were the top seed in the East, but they weren't quite scary. No one went into a game against the Hawks thinking they couldn't win.

* * *

Without Workman, none of it would've been possible.

He didn't have big numbers. He didn't have a polished all-around game. If you get right down to it, he really wasn't even a point guard.

You could find few in the locker room, however, who would offer an argument against Workman as the team's most valuable player.

Miller had his moments, as did Smits. For the first two months, a strong argument could've been made for Dale Davis. But the single most irreplaceable player proved to be the guy who barely made the team and, even then, didn't seem to have any role at all.

"He's not a point guard. He probably shouldn't be in the NBA," Brown said. "But they loved his effort and his toughness and they wanted badly for him to succeed. He just goes out and busts his ass, and that means something to the guy next to him. That's the way it should be."

Haywoode Workman.

His name said it all.

Wayward? His career had followed a fractured path, starting in the CBA, winding through Washington and Atlanta, then jumping to Italy.

Haywire? In training camp, his head was on a swivel as Brown displayed his trade-mark lack of tolerance for imperfect point guard play. He shot poorly, ran the offense tentatively and, had he not accepted the club's offer to open the season on the injured list, he might've found himself back in Europe.

Woodwork? He wasn't a master craftsman but, then again, he didn't have all the tools. When it came to the basics, though, his bubble was in plumb.

Injuries to Richardson and Fleming gave him his chance, and he made good. Now, guys like Miller could only wonder what would've become of this team if Workman had not come through.

"Personally," he said, "I think Woody has been our MVP."

He was not alone.

The Pacers, truly, were a Workman-like team.

Conquering The
11 Magic Kingdom

Houston won its first 15 games and bolted to a 22-1 start, so the Rockets were certified as championship contenders in December. Seattle fulfilled everyone's expectations early by winning its first 10 and cruising to a 26-3 record. The Knicks didn't lose in their first seven games. Atlanta's 14-game winning streak grabbed headlines. Chicago played far better than anyone had expected, winning 55 games without Michael Jordan.

All of those teams deserved the attention they had gotten since the early months of the season. The Pacers didn't begrudge that. They were a little confused, though, about why their remarkable finish had gone relatively unnoticed. Starting with that January 28 victory in Houston, the Pacers had gone 31-12. Only Seattle, at 32-11, had a better record in the same span.

Maybe no one else had noticed, but the Pacers had. Their confidence was at a peak.

"Our chances are as good as anybody else's," said Mitchell. "Right now, picking a favorite to come out of the East, I'd pick us."

"It's just so wide-open," said Miller. "All the other teams are probably saying the same things, as well. There is no clear-cut favorite: no Chicago, no Detroit. If a team gets hot and maintains it, anything is possible."

Though this was the club's fifth straight playoff trip, the Pacers were looking for their first series victory. They'd lost first-rounders to Philadelphia in 1981, Atlanta in 1987, Detroit in 1990, Boston in 1991 and 1992 and New York in 1993. Only once, in 1991, did they make it as far as a fifth game. Only three other NBA franchises had failed to advance in the playoffs — Minnesota, Orlando and Miami — and all three were in the league's most recent wave of expansion.

Brown, too, had the need to succeed. He hadn't coached a team past the first round since 1990, and that was a disappointing year because the Midwest Division champion Spurs were knocked out in the second round. Only one other time in the NBA, with Denver in 1978, had Brown made it out of the first round.

"Every year we don't win a championship, I feel unfulfilled," Brown said. "Last year (with the Clippers) we lost to Houston in the last seconds when they were the hottest team in the league. The year before, we lost to Utah in the last quarter and they were probably the hottest team in the league. After the season, I was proud of our team, but I didn't enjoy watching the rest of the NBA playoffs."

Brown knew what he wanted from the Pacers, but was uncertain what was realistic to expect.

* * *

Before the team could get on with its postseason, the roster had to be submitted. Brown wanted either Fleming or Richardson active, possibly both — even if that meant losing Conner.

There would be one practice where all would play. In it, Brown made his intentions clear. No matter what Richardson did, it was wrong. If he pulled up and hit an open jumper, he should've passed to a teammate. If he tried to beat his man off the dribble, he would be excoriated for not giving up the ball. If someone else made a bad cut or forgot to set a screen, it was Richardson's fault the play broke down. Richardson was clearly upset by this treatment, but he bit his tongue. After one of Brown's final outbursts, Richardson stalked to the other end of the court with only these words: "Yes, sir." He was being treated like a raw recruit, with Brown the grizzled drill instructor.

Though Richardson clearly was more physically ready than Fleming, who still had a noticeable limp, Richardson was left off the playoff roster. So was Sealy. Fleming and Conner would be kept instead. Richardson shrugged off the snub, which wasn't totally unexpected. Sealy could not. He felt he had been slighted and would not accompany the team to Orlando.

Brown explained the move by saying the team doctors couldn't assure him that Richardson's shoulder would hold up under the bump-and-grind of the postseason. The greater reality was that, if Richardson really wanted to be a part of the team in the playoffs, he needed to practice more than once, after the regular season had ended.

* * *

Smits already had squared off, for better or worse, against Bill Laimbeer, Robert Parish and Patrick Ewing in his playoff career. This time, the opposing center was Shaquille O'Neal, the NBA's No. 2 scorer and rebounder, not to mention runaway MVP "Most Valuable Product."

On paper, it was a mismatch of staggering proportions. In four regular-season games, O'Neal outscored Smits 150-73. No one expected any different. The Pacers had, after all, beaten the Magic twice easily at home. On the road, they had lost two close games. Even if O'Neal scored 50, they felt confident. He had scored 49 in one of their victories.

"He'll probably get 30 points a game," said Smits, "but we've got to try to contain everybody else. I'm sure they're going to keep going to him and going to him. I think I've shown I can score on him, and we've got to try to limit his points. But he's going to get his. Everybody knows that."

Brown dropped a few lines for the officials to chew on, basically daring them to give Smits respect. "One thing we have to see is if they let Rik play the guy," Brown said. "Physically and talent-wise, it's hard for anybody to be on the level of that kid, or David or Olajuwon or Alonzo or Patrick, but they can't guard Rik. They let him play. They cannot guard him. I think, if you ask all these centers, they feel like Rik is an offensive force. We've got to find a way to make him effective where Shaq has to guard him."

In Orlando, these words were read with great delight. The Orlando coaching staff, headed by Brian Hill with a great deal of help from Bob Hill, the former Pacer head coach, was obsessed with clippings that offered shreds of motivation for their players. Brown's words were somehow deciphered to mean that Smits was better than O'Neal.

Someone also had greatly exaggerated a scene at the end of the Pacers regular season finale against Miami. In Orlando, the story went like this: as the final minutes wound down, the Pacer players and coaches were all up out of their seats, waving towels and leading the MSA fans in a unison chant of "We want Shaq, We want Shaq."

The reality was far different. After the final buzzer sounded, a handful of fans tried to get that chant started and quickly were silenced.

No matter. The Magic propaganda machine had done its job.

"Shaq's pissed," said Bob Hill, "and it's not good to get him pissed. He wants this real bad."

There also was a somewhat amusing tug-of-war over the underdog role. A couple of national media outlets, USA Today and The Associated Press, had picked the Pacers to upset the Magic. This was taken by the hypersensitive Magic staff to mean the whole world expected the big, bad Pacers to blow into Orlando and humiliate the poor, overlooked Magic.

The Pacers felt some paranoia of their own. The NBA had gone through an image crisis in its first year without Magic, Michael and Larry. The best basketball was being played in the obscure Western markets of Seattle, Houston and San Antonio. Charles Barkley, the closest thing to a megastar the league had left, was laboring with a bad back that reduced Phoenix's appeal. The Knicks were media darlings in New York, but the rest of the country couldn't stomach their brand of plodding, bruising uglyball.

If the network ratings were to be salvaged in the postseason, Orlando was the most likely candidate. The Magic had O'Neal and Hardaway, "the two best young players in the game," according to Brown, and a large following among America's youth. Magic jerseys, caps and t-shirts were highly visible in every NBA arena. Orlando had made 17 appearances on network television. When in doubt, NBC's programming plan seemed to be, carry an Orlando game.

And the Pacers? They made their one NBA-mandated network appearance on TNT. That was all. They didn't need the Warren Commission to tell them which team the NBA on NBC would rather see in the second round.

The city of Orlando had gone nuts over the team's first playoff berth. Everywhere you looked, there were Magic banners and good-luck messages on signs. Radio and television stations dominated their broadcasts with coverage of anything related to the team. It was a dramatic contrast to what the Pacers left behind.

Though they played in a similarly small market, the Pacers still had a relatively apathetic public. Ticket sales for Game Three, the first of the postseason in Market Square Arena, were unexpectedly slow. No one in the organization would go out on a limb and forecast a sellout. Though the city had two metropolitan dailies, the afternoon News and the morning Star, they combined to send just three writers — two beat reporters and one columnist — on the road throughout the postseason

The city of Orlando, and its team, may have been too hyped. When Bob Hill spotted Indianapolis reporters in the Orlando Arena press room two hours before Game One, he walked right in and, after exchanging greetings, made an astonishing revelation. In the position-by-position matchups previewing the series that had appeared in the previous day's Star, reporter Dan Dunkin had referred to Tree Rollins as "ancient" and Anthony Bowie as "spindly." Rollins, 38, had come out of retirement when injuries decimated the front line. Bowie had but 190 pounds spread over a 6-foot-6-inch frame. So what?

To Hill, these were insults that simply could not be ignored. "You can't say that about a guy before a series like this," he said, smiling at what he felt was a motivational windfall. "I love it. You guys keep writing that stuff."

The writers were stunned by that, even more so after wandering into the Orlando locker room to check out the bulletin board full of photocopied stories from the Indianapolis newspapers. The "inflammatory" quotes were highlighted in yellow. The problem with this particular strategy was that the Pacers had made no rash comments, no bold predictions. They had nothing but the proper respect for the Magic. The days of Chuck "No-man-on-the-planet-can-guard-me" Person were long gone.

Asked if he ever tried that particular motivational methodology, Brown just shrugged. "Nah," he said. "I'm not smart enough."

The Indiana players had seen it all before, when Hill was their head coach, and expected as much. When it comes to words, often those who use the fewest say the most, Dale Davis being a perfect example. To him, the question was posed: Does that stuff work? His reply: "You see how far it got us."

The series had not yet started, but the games were well under way.

* * *

At one end of the spectrum, there was Boston Garden, the minimalist's delight. There were no dancers, no circus acts at halftime, no million-dollar sound system blaring at every opportunity. It had the degenerating parquet floor, a relic of an organ, and a basketball game. That's all, nothing else. And it was bound for the wrecking ball.

At the other end was Orlando Arena, which was something straight out of the Magic Kingdom just a few miles away. The dancers come out long before the game. The technopop music is loud and incessant. Even the team's uniforms, all pinstripes and glitter, are gaudily overdone. The public address announcer sounds like a top 40 disc jockey — the kind who talks over the music because he prefers the sound of his own voice — who's had a few too many cups of coffee. After the Orlando players were introduced, a procedure that only took about five times as long as necessary, a ridiculous amount of fireworks were set off inside the building, leaving a smoky pall that didn't clear until well into the first quarter.

That wasn't the only smoke blown, as it turned out. Orlando's coaching staff had a major surprise for the Pacers. Instead of risking foul trouble on O'Neal, they sent 6-foot-9-inch power forward Larry Krystkowiak to guard Smits. O'Neal would be given a far less challenging defensive assignment, Dale Davis.

It was a strategic coup.

Intent on exploiting the obvious mismatch, the Pacer players fell into the trap. They would bring the ball up, dump it into Smits and stand around. It was exactly what Brian and Bob Hill had hoped would happen. Smits had 10 points in the first quarter, but the Magic led 26-20, and not because of O'Neal. Nick Anderson and Dennis Scott both got off, scoring eight points each.

Donald Royal then came off the bench to torch the Pacers for 10 points in the second quarter as the deficit stretched to 17 late in the period. At the break, it was 54-42. Smits had 16 points, but no teammate had more than six. Miller hadn't scored in the second quarter. O'Neal, meanwhile, had a quiet 14.

Brown made the mandatory adjustment at halftime. Everyone would have to get involved, particularly Miller and Byron Scott. Those two had combined for more than 30 points a game during the season to carry the offense, but had just eight at the break.

Smits didn't attempt a shot in the third quarter, and would not score again. The Pacers looked elsewhere for offense, while their defense continued to swarm O'Neal and dare anyone else to beat them. Miller and Byron Scott combined for 15 in the quarter. When Scott relieved Miller with 3:27 left, the Pacers trailed 70-58. He hit a quick three then followed with another jumper to give the team life. The deficit was a workable eight points, 74-66, heading into the fourth quarter.

Though they trailed, the Pacers weren't rattled. Orlando did not have a deep bench, meaning the starters would be susceptible to fatigue the longer the game lasted. If it got close, there would be an inordinate amount of pressure on the home team.

"We understood that if it came down to the wire," said Miller, "their arms would feel a little heavy."

That was evident quickly. Over the first five minutes of the fourth quarter, Orlando scored just two points, a jumper by Anderson. Indiana tied the game when Antonio Davis dunked over O'Neal, then took a 78-76 lead on a pair of free throws from Miller.

Instead of building on their momentum, though, the Pacers relaxed, a potentially fatal mistake with more than six minutes remaining. They would miss their next seven shots as Orlando regained control. Consecutive drives by Hardaway put the home team ahead 84-78. The game appeared to be slipping away. But Miller stepped out and hit a huge three-pointer, than Antonio Davis beat the shot-clock buzzer with an improbable fadeaway jumper to cut it to 84-83.

O'Neal, a horrible free throw shooter, stepped to the line with 2:20 left and missed both, but Hardaway stole the rebound, saving a vital possession. Royal was fouled and the reserve made both. Orlando was ahead by three with 1:53 left and needed a couple of defensive stops to escape.

When O'Neal blocked Workman's drive, then Smits missed a followup 10-footer, Orlando had its first stop but couldn't capitalize. Going for an unnecessary knock-out punch, Hardaway missed a three-pointer with just over a minute left.

With the crowd in a frenzy, the Pacers worked the ball around but could not find a shot. The clock was dwindling, and so were they, until Miller snuck out beyond the arc again and just beat the buzzer with a tying trey.

Royal, the lone contributor off the little-used Orlando bench, drove into the lane but put the shot up too hard. O'Neal was there, though, tipping in the miss. Orlando led 88-86 with 25.7 seconds left.

Brown took a timeout to think about his options. Would he go for the win on the road? Would he make the safer play, try to force overtime and continue to wear down the tired Orlando starters? His first instinct was to go for the tie. When the Pacers couldn't get the ball inbounds and took a forced 20-second timeout, Brown inserted Byron Scott for Workman.

"We just wanted an extra shooter," Brown said. "And, for big games and crucial situations, we didn't have a lot of people who've been there before."

Scott had been the first to truly believe in this team. From the moment he joined the Pacers, he talked them into higher and higher goals. Once in a while, he would bring his three championship rings into the locker room, to fuel their desire.

"The first week I was here, I told them, "You guys — we — could be in the Eastern Conference finals. The number one thing we have to do is believe we can get there and then start playing like we can," Scott said. "We started doing both of those things and now all the guys on this team realize we do have a shot at it."

His performance had been admirable, but his presence immeasurable. Brown frequently turned to Scott for advice on how to handle a sticky situation, whether to practice or not, how the players would react to a certain approach. Scott was a resource Brown tapped regularly.

"I talked to him about Pat (Riley), about Magic, about why they won, about how they conducted themselves, how their practices were," Brown said. "I can't tell you how many things I asked him about. I talk to players a lot but, with Byron, I wanted to be like (the Lakers), basically."

Scott understood Brown's interest, but there was something about the old Lakers he did not want to remember. When the Lakers won a championship, the perception was that it was the product of the greatness of Magic Johnson, Kareem Abdul-Jabbar and James Worthy. When they lost, it was Byron's fault.

"In a city like Los Angeles, they have to have somebody to be a scapegoat," Scott said. "I could average 14 or 15 points during the season but, if that's what I did in the playoffs, it wasn't good enough. If we lost, Byron didn't do this or Byron didn't do that. It never really bothered me because I knew I contributed. I knew I had done everything I could possibly do to give our team a chance to win. I never bad-mouthed that organization, when a lot of people there said a lot of things. I've always said

Jerry Buss gave me an opportunity and I won three championships rings, so how could I say anything bad about the Laker organization?"

Brown had even borrowed a phrase from those Laker teams: winning time. Until late in the season, it meant nothing but frustration to the Pacers. Now, it was upon them once again, in the crucible of the playoffs.

Playing for the tie, the ball was worked into Smits, who tossed up a hook that missed. McKey beat the crowd to the ball for a tip but it, too, bounced out. The loose ball went out of bounds off an Orlando player, though, so the Pacers had another chance with 13.3 seconds left. It went to Miller, who put up another three-pointer, but this one was no good. This time, Dale Davis snared the offensive rebound and quickly passed to Scott, who sent it back to Miller, standing 28 feet from the basket with time running out.

He had hit two huge three-pointers down the stretch, and the Magic were determined not to let it happen again. Too determined.

When Miller started to drive, Nick Anderson left his man, Byron Scott, to turn what already was an effective double-team of Miller into a needless triple-team. In a crowd of defenders but composed, Miller kicked the ball over to his mentor, who rose up and nailed down a three-pointer with two seconds left.

This time, winning time belonged to Scott.

"I've always said signing Byron was the best move the Pacers have ever made in their NBA history," said Miller. But what about the first-round selection of a certain skinny shooter from UCLA in 1987 instead of a local legend named Alford? "OK," Miller said, cracking a smile, "the second-best move."

The Pacers led, 89-88, but nothing was won. This was a team, remember, that had found ways to lose games in far shorter amounts of time. There was little celebrating during the coming timeout.

So much had happened . . . Divac's two long jumpers, Barros' floater, Gugliotta's drive, Kukoc's three-pointer. If they survived these two seconds, they would have no more reason to doubt themselves. If they did not, their postseason nightmare would no doubt recur.

After two timeouts, the inbounds pass came to Anderson, who turned and was confronted with the long arms of the 6-7 Miller and the 6-10 McKey. With no time, or room, to pass, he hurled up a 25-footer that bounced hard off the back rim.

More than any other, those were the defining moments of Indiana's remarkable postseason run. The Pacers had not played particularly well. They shot 39 percent, were outrebounded 46-41 and had 12 shots blocked. But with the game on the line, they executed at both ends, coming up with big shots while holding Orlando to one basket — a tip-in, at that — in the final four minutes.

It represented a total reversal from much of the regular season when, with games on the line, they would find a way to lose. They had overcome a 17-point deficit in the first half, a 12-point deficit late in the third quarter, and found a way to win.

The victory did not come without cost. Thompson broke a bone in his left hand attempting to box out O'Neal in the first half. At the time, it was thought he would be lost for the rest of the playoffs. At the time, though, no one knew exactly how long the playoffs would last for this team.

As for those Orlando players who were so supremely motivated: O'Neal was so pissed he scored five points below his season average, 24; the ancient Rollins had four points in 16 minutes; the spindly Bowie didn't score.

Though the Pacers had snatched homecourt advantage, neither side expected this to be a quick series. "I expected this to go five games," said Brown. "I'm hopeful it will go five games. All we've done is win the first one."

The first half of Game Two was not unlike the opener. Orlando got a surprising outburst from an unexpected source — this time, 13 second-quarter points from Anthony Avent — to recover from an early deficit and lead 53-51 at the break. Considering O'Neal had scored a scant four points in a foul-plagued first half, Orlando's players were supremely confident. No team could keep O'Neal down for long.

The Krystkowiak-Smits strategy was working again. Smits had spent a week practicing for O'Neal, meaning more faceup jumpers and roaming away from the low post. Against Krystkowiak, he was planted on the blocks and having little success.

Indiana had a coaching ploy of its own in store, though. O'Neal's dunks produced much more than just two points, they were psychological manna for this young team and its fans. Brown implored his big men to keep O'Neal away from the rim, even if that meant constant fouling. Brown could send Smits and both Davises at O'Neal, meaning 18 fouls, if necessary.

The Magic came out intent on getting O'Neal involved, constantly dropping the ball inside to the big center. This produced little more than return trips to the free throw line, where he was relatively harmless. Though he scored 10 points in the quarter, he was six of 12 from the line. This time, Indiana's strategy had worked.

"I don't care if he shoots 50 free throws, as long as he doesn't dunk," said Antonio Davis, who was instrumental in the attack on O'Neal at both ends. "The thing is, he can dunk it 50 times, but he isn't going to make 50 free throws."

With Orlando stuck in a self-defeating offensive pattern, the Pacers gave the ball to Miller, who scored 11 straight points to break open a tight game and give them a 74-64 lead. Miller's outburst concluded a 23-7 run in which Orlando did not make a field goal, producing its points from six trips to the line, five for O'Neal.

Though they never pulled completely away, the Pacers maintained control of the game until the final three minutes, when Orlando's desperate three-pointers started falling. Dennis Scott hit one, then Anderson, to cut it to 101-98 at 1:34. Antonio Davis then took the ball right at O'Neal, scoring on the drive, to make it a five-point lead. After Hardaway missed a jumper, everything appeared wrapped up. The Pacers had a comfortable lead, and the ball, with less than a minute remaining.

Playing a little too comfortably, the Pacers didn't even take a look at the basket, dribbling out a 24-second clock violation that gave the ball back to Orlando. Two seconds after the turnover, Dennis Scott drilled a three-pointer, the 11th of the game for the Magic, an NBA record. Suddenly, it was 103-101 with 31.3 seconds left. Anything could happen, and something dramatic did.

Trying to avoid another 24-second violation, Workman's shot was blocked by Anderson. The loose ball wound up in O'Neal's hands with still one second left on the shot clock. O'Neal winged the ball to a streaking Hardaway, who dunked with 7.3 seconds left.

That touchdown pass, however, was called back. Official Dick Bavetta, anticipating the shot-clock buzzer, whistled play dead. The Pacers heard Bavetta's whistle and relaxed. The Magic, coaxed by their screaming fans, did not.

Orlando's players felt they had a potential game-tying basket taken away from them but, in reality, without Bavetta's whistle — poorly timed or not — Hardaway never would've been allowed to run from one end of the court to the other unmolested. "Otherwise," said Miller, "I would've been back on the play."

Still, the Magic had the ball with time to set up a play. They didn't want to go to O'Neal. That would bring a foul, and probably one point from the line, at best, so the ball was placed in Hardaway's hands. But the rookie's legs gave out on the drive. Hardaway, who had played every minute of the intense game, slipped and threw up an off-balance shot that wasn't close.

O'Neal grabbed the rebound and dunked, but it was well after the final buzzer. His only dunk of the evening didn't count.

Again, the Pacers had survived.

It was their 10th straight win overall and put them up 2-0. Just four teams in NBA history had recovered from that deficit to win a best-of-five series. One was Phoenix, just the year before, against Scott's Lakers. The veteran had a valuable frame of reference to share with his teammates. "Just because we're going home for two games, that doesn't guarantee anything, just like they weren't guaranteed to win their home games," he said. "We've got to keep everything in perspective. This series is not over. If you don't come ready to take care of business and try to put this series to an end, you give that team life. And if you give a team life, they're a dangerous team."

O'Neal had averaged 37.5 points against the Pacers in the regular season, but had totaled just 39 in the series. For his 36 minutes in Game Two, he had 15 points, seven rebounds, five fouls and no comment. His buddy, Dennis Scott, summed up Orlando's plight. "If this game was a must-win, I don't know what word to use to describe the next one," he said. "I guess the next one is life or death."

By now, the glowing embers of support in Indianapolis had been whipped into a blaze. Nearly 3,000 people greeted the team's charter jet upon its return to the airport in the wee hours of Sunday morning. Game Three on Monday night would be a sellout, as would every one to follow in Market Square Arena.

For a team needing to win just once on its homecourt to take its first playoff series ever, the Pacers were inordinately worried. O'Neal had yet to take over a game, and that weighed on their minds. They were braced for what they felt was inevitable. "I think," said Antonio Davis, "he's coming out to destroy somebody."

There was another problem for the Pacers to deal with. Now, they were expected to win. A team that thrived on adversity, that needed to feel like the underdog, had lost that valuable edge.

When the fans began pouring into MSA for Game Three, they were met at the doors by signs that read, "Sorry, No Brooms Allowed." Arena security personnel were worried about the potential for injuries. Brown was more concerned about how the Magic might react if they saw an arena full of broom-waving fans.

"I was dreading somebody coming out with a broom," Brown said. "I saw a guy sweeping the floor before the game and I about had a heart attack."

Sitting alone in his office before the game, Brown said he had never been quite this nervous. Unable to sleep the night before, unable to think of anything but the game that day, he showed up at the arena more than three hours before tipoff. "This is a different kind of nervousness," he said. "When you consider what this franchise has been through, you want so badly for it to turn out well. There's anxiety there. I'm more emotionally involved because of what these guys have gone through, the sacrifices they've made, the things Donnie and the Simons and George have been through. These are people I have relationships with."

Predictably, the team came out as tight as Brown. O'Neal had two dunks in the first six minutes, stating his presence with authority. Neither team, though, could get much going. With 3:27 left in the half, Workman and Anderson exchanged elbows, pushes and shoves — a typical NBA "fight" — and both were rewarded with technicals. Orlando's emotional young players used the altercation to fuel a 10-point run and closed the half with a 52-46 lead.

O'Neal had 14 points and 10 rebounds in the half. Though Miller got hot in the third quarter, scoring 10 points, the Pacers could not wrest the lead from the visitors. Entering the fourth quarter, Orlando led 72-68. O'Neal had 19 points and 12 rebounds, but he also had four fouls.

The Magic lead was 78-70 after a Dennis Scott drive with 10:23 left. Brown, trying to stave off a sense of impending doom, called a timeout. "When I took that timeout, I felt a dagger in my heart," he said. "They were playing with so much poise, and Shaquille was playing so unselfishly."

Byron Scott hit a jumper, then drove inside and drew O'Neal's fifth foul, making both free throws, with 9:22 left. O'Neal went to the bench with his team ahead 78-73. Though he stayed out just two minutes, the game changed completely in his brief absence. The run started by Scott was finished by Miller, who had eight points in an 18-2 spree that gave the Pacers an 88-80 lead.

O'Neal tried valiantly to bring his team back, converting a three-point play, then hitting one of two free throws to cut it to 88-84 with 3:49 left, but he missed a low-post shot, then threw a bad pass. Orlando would not score again until the final minute, after the Indiana advantage had swelled into double-digits. Over the last 10:20, the Pacers held the Magic to two field goals, forced six turnovers — four by the leg-weary Hardaway — and outscored them 29-8 to close out the sweep.

Workman's ability to harrass Hardaway into mistakes was pivotal to the series. The Pacers ranked 15th in the league in steals during the regular season but set an NBA playoff record with 38 thefts in the sweep of Orlando, led by Workman's 10. Hardaway committed 20 turnovers, 10 in Game Three, as Hill stubbornly refused to employ Scott Skiles for anything more than token minutes.

Orlando's postseason inexperience was consistently apparent down the stretch. In the fourth quarter, the Magic shot five of 19 in Game Three and 19 of 62 overall, just under 31 percent. Their man-mountain was turned into a relative molehill. O'Neal averaged just 20.7 points in the series. The dominant player had been the spindly Miller, who averaged 29 and was in the middle of every big Indiana run.

For this, O'Neal assumed his usual fall-back position of blaming the officiating. "I just hope the next time we play I get more respect," he said. "This is my third year (actually his second). I'm not a rookie anymore. I should get more respect." From a player who had appeared more on national television in two seasons than the Pacers had in their franchise history and who had been granted the privilege of the superstar's whistle from officials since the day he stepped into the NBA, it was a remarkably naive, not to mention ingracious, argument.

If any team knew the hard road to respect, it was the Pacers, and no one had traveled more of its miles than Fleming. When the final horn sounded, Miller headed straight for the veteran guard and embraced him as the rest of the team encircled them.

"We've gone through the ringer here. We're the sole survivors of the times with Chuck Person and Detlef Schrempf. If there's anyone I can laugh with or cry with, it's Vern," Miller said. "He deserves this more than anyone."

Credit was one thing. To the man who had played more games in a Pacers uniform than any other, 761, the layoff between the first and second rounds was the bigger reward. His sore knee could use the break.

* * *

Herb Simon delayed his exit in order to offer congratulations to some of those responsible for the team's success. When his car made it out of the MSA garage a half-hour after the game, the team's co-owner found unusually slow going.

Never had a man been quite so happy to be stuck in traffic.

The streets, empty all these years, finally were clogged with celebrating Pacer fans.

"People were all over the place, honking their horns and waving those towels," said Simon. "It was very exciting."

With a record-setting season on the court had come a corresponding set of marks just as significant. The club's tickets never had been hotter, their merchandise was flying off local shelves and a general fervor, missing since Simon bought the team along with brother Melvin in 1983, had gripped the community.

"There are markets our size that can support a team, and I've always believed that ours is one of them," said Simon. "We've tried everything. We've paid top-dollar for players and top-dollar for coaches, but the missing ingredient was winning. The way it looks now, that's the one we needed."

Though tickets initially were slow to sell for Game Three, the crowd (16,562) — and thus the total gate — wound up setting a Pacers record in Market Square Arena. Though the second-round opponent, Atlanta, wasn't a marquee team, tickets for that series would sell out quickly. The days of a public that bought its tickets based on the opposition were over.

"I knew we would sell out the second round, no matter who it was," said Walsh. "Then, the event becomes big and the people come to see us, not the other team."

For a franchise that never had hosted more than two postseason games, this represented a windfall.

Even with the lowest average ticket price in the NBA (about $24 for the playoffs), each sellout represented a total gate of roughly $360,000. Though that was divvied up between the Pacers, the NBA and the opposing team, it had the effect of found money for a franchise that entered the season with mild expectations.

The business side of the franchise was enjoying unprecedented success. The club's arena gift shop set its all-time sales record the day of Game Three and, according to merchandising director Rich Kapp, the following two business days "were every bit as strong as Christmas."

There were subtle signs that this might happen. Even in a regular season that had started poorly, the Pacers set an all-time attendance mark, averaging 13,264. Their total attendance (543,815) made them the city's second-biggest sports draw, behind only the Indianapolis 500.

To turn historically lukewarm interest up to a boil, though, required more than just making the playoffs. On their seventh try, the Pacers finally broke through that wall of the first round, and it would be downhill from there.

"It's a relief," said Simon. "That weight of not getting out of the first round was becoming heavy."

Though Simon wasn't ready to proclaim his franchise finally had turned the corner, he did sense "a feeling of legitimacy."

"I can't judge how long this will last," he said, "but I'm enjoying every minute."

12 From Shaq to Kak

The reward for their sweep was a dangerously long wait for the winner of the Atlanta-Miami series. The Heat had surprised the Hawks by taking the opener in Atlanta, then jumped to a 2-1 lead with a 90-86 win in Miami on May 3, the night after the Pacers concluded their series with Orlando.

This naturally got the team's hopes up. The Pacers had won three out of four from the Heat, who had yet to win in Market Square Arena, where Indiana would hold the homecourt advantage. Against Atlanta, they lost the season series 3-2. While the Heat would be glad just to be in the second round, the Hawks were on a mission to win a championship. No one would admit to a rooting interest, but it was clear who the Pacers wanted to see win.

Well, most of them, anyway. "It would be nice to have the homecourt advantage," said Miller, "but I think we'd play much better against Atlanta. That old mentality of having our backs to the wall, of being the underdog and taking on the No. 1 seed would probably give us a little more satisfaction in going against them."

No eighth seed had beaten a No. 1 seed since the current format was adopted in 1984. This would not be the exception. Miami blew its big chance in Game Four, losing 103-89 at home, then looked beaten from the beginning in Game Five, as Atlanta survived the series with a 102-91 victory.

While the Hawks and Heat were extending themselves in a tough series, the Pacers had six full days of practice, a virtual training camp redux. Brown was delighted with the extra time. His experience taught him that teams annually advancing in the postseason, be it the NCAA tournament or the NBA playoffs, benefited from the additional practice time as well as the experience of playing pressure games. Though he could not prepare for a specific opponent, that was less of a hindrance to Brown than other coaches. His primary concern was how the Pacers executed their own plan, not what plays the Hawks or Heat would run or what the matchups would be. He believed firmly in a team's ability to determine its own fate.

The team knew it needed the work. In spite of the sweep, they were struggling in several areas, most of them offensive. Smits (17 of 42) and McKey (seven of 26) both had shot poorly. Miller and Scott had carried them this far, but points from one position alone wouldn't be enough.

"We haven't really played our best, or up to our ability," Smits said. "I know we want to get that out of ourselves. It's kind of scary to think that we won those three games and we haven't really played all that well — not for four quarters, at least."

For six straight days of practice, they worked and waited until, finally, they knew where they were going: from Shaq to Kak. Atlanta's Jon Koncak was about as far as it gets from O'Neal. Though the matchup at center might offer Smits a chance to breathe a little easier, it represented a greater challenge for the team in general, and Brown in particular.

Brown had won a championship with Danny Manning. If he was going to win another this year, he would have to do it in spite of his former prodigy. Brown and Manning spent so many years together — four at the University of Kansas, where they won the NCAA title in 1988, and later one and one half seasons with the Los Angeles Clippers — their careers seemed inextricable.

Brown had coached Manning for 147 games in college, 125 more in the pros. They had gone against each other 17 times, 14 when Brown was with the Spurs, but never in the playoffs.

Now, they would be on opposite benches for the second round of the NBA playoffs. "It's not like he just got into the league. I coached against him when I was in San Antonio so I saw him a lot those first three or four years," Brown said. "But it is strange. I don't think too many college coaches are put in a position like this: coaching in the pros against a great player you coached, somebody that won a national championship for you. It is difficult. It's like I've been saying, I hope he does well, but I hope we win."

Like in many lengthy coach-player relationships, Brown and Manning wore on each other and the friendship became frayed. There was tumult, mostly in L.A., but those wounds were superficial and had healed. Since coming to the Hawks, Manning had offered nothing but praise for his former coach. At one point, he went so far as to say he wouldn't mind playing for Brown again, one day.

"We went through a lot together," Brown said, "and I understand that."

Brown had managed to bring out the best in Manning both as his coach, and his opponent.

After joining the Hawks in the trade for Dominique Wilkins on February 24, Manning produced decisive plays in both subsequent Atlanta victories over the Pacers.

He had a driving layup with 7.3 seconds left, then blocked Scott's drive to preserve a 90-88 victory in The Omni on March 5. Two weeks later, his dunk with 2.9 seconds left sealed an 81-78 victory in Market Square Arena. The first snapped a four-game Pacer win streak, the second an 11-game home streak.

Manning would get the chance to play spoiler once again. The Pacers would carry an 11-game streak into The Omni for Game One.

"Both teams are competitive and we played close games with them all year," said Miller. "They're going to have the advantage of the homecourt and, playing five games, they probably won't miss a beat coming into the second round."

On the other hand, Miller said, the strain of their difficult first-round victory might show on the Hawks "if this becomes a long series."

If anything, the Pacers were well-rested, maybe too much so. "I'm sure there's going to be some rust at first," Miller said, "but you really look forward to playing games after having a week of training camp."

The teams had a number of striking similarities beyond a history of playoff failure. Atlanta hadn't gotten past the quarterfinals since 1970, and the Pacers were there for the first time.

Each had: a legendary coach who breathed life into a struggling franchise by guiding the team on a record-setting course in his first season; a bald-headed, tough-minded, streak-shooting point guard who led by example; a lithe, brash shooting guard from the suburbs of Los Angeles capable of breathtaking performances; a soft-spoken, versatile small forward who didn't fit the positional prototype of a player who thinks mainly of scoring; a muscular power forward whose scowling countenance could be as intimidating as his physical game; a center who had spent most of his career as the object of the home fans' derision, only to rise above it all with the best play of his career this season; a bench bolstered by the additions of a veteran in the backcourt and an athletic big man up front.

The biggest difference between the teams had been their work schedules. Atlanta took five tough games to escape a first-round series with Miami and had one day of practice to prepare for the Pacers. After sweeping Orlando, the Pacers practiced for seven of the eight days between games.

Was Atlanta tired? Were the Pacers rusty? Was it much ado about nothing? "If you had told me at the beginning we'd win in three games, then have eight days off, I'd take it every time," said Brown. "But I personally feel like I've gone to war and there's been bad weather."

That angst, coupled with rust, led to a predictably slow start.

Kevin Willis was throwing in shots from everywhere but the low post, Blaylock and Augmon were running the floor and the Pacers continued to struggle for offense. Atlanta was a team that applied active pressure, extending their perimeter players for the specific purpose of forcing a mistake they could turn into a layup, and it was working splendidly.

The Hawks flashed to a 23-11 lead. It appeared they had learned their lesson from the previous series, when they had come out flat and wound up losing to Miami at home.

When both coaches went to their benches late in the first quarter, the Pacers found themselves, cutting the gap to 31-25 by the end of a quarter that was punctuated by a Dale Davis dunk. Davis, Smits and Scott kept the team close in the second quarter, combining for 19 points, but Atlanta had a 53-47 lead at the break.

The Pacers weren't worried. They had trailed at halftime in all four playoff games, and hadn't lost yet. They were a second-half team over the course of the regular season, when they overcame a 16-23 deficit to finish on a 31-12 run, and so it was going in the postseason.

Atlanta's strategy of chasing Miller all over the floor, keeping him from getting into the flow, worked for the Hawks in the first half, but against the Hawks in the second. Focusing so much on the perimeter, they left the inside wide open.

Antonio Davis hit all six of his third-quarter shots, picking up where Dale Davis had left off, as Indiana put together a 16-3 run that put them in the lead, 65-60. Five times in the period, the Hawks would cut it to one, but they never could reclaim the lead. After Atlanta closed to 73-72 on a Willis dunk, the Pacers scored the final six points of the quarter.

The Hawks proceeded to miss 11 of 12 shots, including nine in a row, to open the fourth quarter but, because the Pacers were similarly cool, the margin spread only to 85-76, when Workman beat the shot-clock with a jumper at the 4:42 mark.

Atlanta then put together its final challenge, as Stacey Augmon's three-point play was followed by a pair of Manning baskets that closed to 85-83 with 3:16 left.

The Hawks would score just one basket the rest of the way.

Miller hit a pair of free throws, drew a double-team and fed the open Antonio Davis for a dunk, then drained a three-pointer to make it 92-83 with 2:01 left. The Pacers won their 12th straight game, 96-85 and, in the process, had taken the homecourt advantage away from an Atlanta team that felt unbeatable in The Omni, where it was 36-5 during the regular season.

Though Miller had his lowest-scoring game of the postseason, 18 points, no one was calling it an off night. After averaging 29 against Orlando, Miller figured correctly he would be as much a decoy as anything against the Hawks, who double-teamed him — usually with a big man — every time he came off a baseline screen.

It did prevent Miller from getting his usual assortment of jumpers from either wing, but left the middle wide open. "That's the way I like it," said Miller. "If they're going to do that, our big guys are going to have a feast. It's kind of senseless, taking away a 25-footer but allowing all those tip-ins."

The Davises carved up the Hawks for combined totals of 29 points, 21 rebounds, seven dunks and 14 of 20 shooting. With those two doing the bulk of the work, the Pacers outrebounded the Hawks 48-33 and scored 19 second-chance points.

"Reggie didn't have a big scoring night but, if you look at the big men, we had a lot of easy baskets because of him," said Antonio Davis. "If you try to stop Reggie, you can't stop the rest of us inside, too."

Even when they did try, they didn't always succeed, as was demonstrated by his big plays late in the game.

Though the Pacers started slowly, they finished strong. They committed eight turnovers in the first 11 minutes, but just 10 more the rest of the night. Its offense unable to feed off Indiana mistakes, Atlanta produced its all-time postseason low of 32 points in the second half, just 13 in the fourth quarter. "When the game is on the line and you see the opportunity to win, it doesn't matter how tired you are," said Scott. "It's like with a shark: once you taste a little blood, you go after it even harder."

Willis and Blaylock, two players vital to the Atlanta cause, combined for 18 in the first quarter, but just seven thereafter. Blaylock missed his last 11 shots, six of which were three-pointers. Willis, who fell in love with his jumper in his hot first quarter, went two of nine the rest of the night. "I was hoping the short time off wouldn't hurt us," said Wilkens, "but, apparently, it did."

For both teams, the game represented a repeat of the first-round pattern. Both took that as a good sign. "We can come back," said Willis. "We've been in this situation before." So had the Pacers, with one difference. "We didn't steal this game," said Scott, referring to his closing three-pointer in the Orlando opener, "we came in here and took it."

* * *

For the Hawks, winning games was easier than winning fans. Though they won 57 games, the Central Division and the Eastern Conference, the Hawks were unable to overcome rampant apathy in the populace and indifference from the local media. In their six home playoff games, the Hawks would average 14,379 fans and sell out just once.

This was homecourt advantage?

"That would hurt my feelings, to do all this, have a great year and still not get the support," said Antonio Davis. "I love Atlanta as a city but I don't understand why they don't support the team. Homecourt advantage means you have all your fans behind you to give you that little extra boost you need to help push you over the hump. After 85 or 90 games, it's hard to get yourself up every night. You have to have somebody rooting for you, especially at home. I don't think they understand how much of a difference they can make."

The local mindset was reflected by the front page of the Atlanta Journal-Constitution after the 96-85 Game One loss, attended by 13,190. The paper stripped a headline about a Braves victory — even though 131 games remained in the season — across the top. In smaller type, beneath the heading, "Sports Score," the Hawks' result appeared.

"Why should you play hard and try to win first place in the Eastern Conference if no one's going to come and support you?" said Workman. "That sixth man is a big part of your play when you have the homecourt. I know, in that third game against Orlando, I don't think our crowd was going to let us lose. It helps. It keeps you going. When you come into that arena and you don't see the crowd there, you don't feel that support."

One of the most common copouts was the location of the Omni, downtown in the shadow of the CNN Center. Funny, the Georgia Dome was right next door and sold out regularly for Falcons games. Atlanta-Fulton County Stadium was in a far worse neighborhood and was packed on a nightly basis for the Braves. The greater reality was that Atlanta was a city where transients outnumbered natives. There simply was not much of a sports tradition rooted in the community. Until it became trendy to go to a Hawks game, the fans would stay away.

The local media apparently swallowed this mindset with little protest. One columnist went so far as to take pot-shots at Indianapolis because the city cared about its team. Steve Hummer wrote that Pacer tickets were so hot, "some scalpers are demanding as much as three tractors for a good ticket."

It was typical of the provincial, stereotypical cheap-shots that columnists often would exchange during the playoffs. During the Finals the year before, Chicago Tribune writers trashed the city of Phoenix on a daily basis, as if they wouldn't move there in a split-second, given the chance. They had given Portland much the same treatment the year before. When this practice started, no one knew, but it peaked in the Pistons-Lakers Finals, when Mike Downey of the L.A. Times and Mitch Albom of the Detroit Free Press waged a brilliant battle in side-by-side columns that appeared in both papers. Downey got the edge on the basis of one line. Explaining a list of reasons why the Lakers would beat the Pistons, Downey wrote, "We have the biggest Johnson." He meant the 6-foot-8 Magic over the 6-foot-2 Vinnie, but, then again, he really didn't.

* * *

The difference between Miller's approach to home and road games was marked by his introduction ritual. At home, he and Workman had a well-choreographed routine that, they said, was borrowed from the Jacksons, Michael and Janet. For the first two games in Atlanta, Miller was far more solitary. When the opponents' introductions began, so did Miller's march. Five steps out, five steps back. Starting on the sideline, ending on the sideline, each stride studiously retraced.

It wasn't a good sign. The offense was struggling, and Miller was putting too much of the responsibility for that on himself. His teammates noticed. When Miller believed he could play well, he usually did. On the other hand, he could talk himself into a bad game before it even began.

"I don't know Reggie that well, other than from what I've seen this season," said Antonio Davis. "But it's strange. He's so superstitious. If he feels like he's going to have a bad game or a bad series, he really does. He needs to get hold of himself and say, 'I'm going to miss some shots, I'm going to have a couple of bad games,' and find other ways to get it done. Even though he's a great shooter, he can do a lot of other good things. If he sets his mind to it, he could be the best defensive player on the court. But he thinks everybody wants him to score and needs him to score for him to be Reggie Miller."

Miller was tight, and the Hawks were desperate. Koncak summed up their situation by saying, "If you lose this game and go down 0-2, I don't know if you can see the end of the world from there, but you're pretty close to it."

That would prove an overwhelming combination.

If the Pacers had developed any delusions of invincibility in their 12-game winning streak, they were quickly brought back to earth, then planted beneath it by an Atlanta defense that held Indiana to the lowest postseason point total in NBA history. The Hawks didn't just regain their footing, they walked all over the Pacers, 92-69.

"It reminded us we can be beaten and it reminded us this isn't Orlando," said Scott. "This is the best team in the East right now. Nobody said it was going to be easy."

Reducing the double-teams of Miller and Smits that left holes in their defense in the opener, the Hawks took away the inside game one-on-one and thus were able to continually challenge the perimeter. The Pacers shot 32 percent and had more turnovers (20) than assists (15). Nearly half the baskets they did make (13 out of 27) were jumpers. The Hawks scored 36 of their points on dunks or layups.

Willis (20 points, 15 rebounds) and Manning (20 points, nine rebounds) took care of things inside while Blaylock bounced back to produce his fourth career triple-double (11 points, 10 rebounds, 13 assists).

The Hawks rolled to a 47-32 lead at halftime but, when the Pacers closed the third period with seven unanswered points in 1:09 to close the deficit to 65-57, it appeared another late-game comeback was brewing. Atlanta quickly perished any such thoughts. The Hawks opened the fourth quarter with six points in less than two minutes. The Pacers scored just six in the next eight minutes.

"It would've been a crime for us to come back after that, the way they had played," said Brown. "They showed why they're the conference champs."

The concerns about Miller were justified. He missed 11 of 13 shots and scored 12 points. As bad as his night was, Miller still led the team in scoring.

"I think this was good for us," he said. "Any time you're riding a high like we have been the last month, sometimes you need a loss like this to bring you down, give you a reality check. I think after Game One, in the back of a lot of guys' minds, we were taking Game Two for granted."

A big part of the problem, not just for Miller but also Scott, was that much of the offensive plan was predicated on what they thought was a mismatch in the middle between Smits and Koncak, but it wasn't working out that way. Banged around by Koncak, then backup Andrew Lang, Smits had not been a factor, totaling 22 points on nine of 28 shooting. He did not score for the first 18 minutes of Game One. It got worse in Game Two, as Smits missed 11 of 15 shots and pulled a scant two rebounds. Koncak and Lang concentrated on forcing Smits away from his favored right hand, and consistently rejected his soft lefty offerings. With Smits unable to draw a double-team, nothing opened up outside. Miller and Scott were 11 of 41 in the first two games.

His team had not yet played well from start to finish, which was a problem for Brown. He sensed the Pacers were settling into a comfort zone, convincing themselves they could coast for three quarters, then turn it on to win in the fourth.

When he gathered the team for practice on the Friday before Game Three at Market Square Arena, Brown decided to take them on a trip down short-term memory lane. It wasn't a pleasant jaunt. More like shock therapy. After practice, as the team was stretching, "he yelled and screamed and did his Larry Brown thing," said Antonio Davis. "Everybody was looking around, saying 'It wasn't me.' But then we went in and looked at the film and he said the same things all over again. He showed us we were doing those things. We weren't getting back. We weren't crashing the boards. We were letting them post up close to the basket. Everything we said we weren't going to do, we let them do."

A quirk in the schedule had Games Three and Four being played back-to-back, Saturday and Sunday, a rarity in the playoffs. The coming weekend would determine the series, and Brown knew his team needed an attitude adjustment. Normally not a film connoisseur, Brown showed the team Game Two in its entirety, uncut and uncensored. The practice, from beginning to bitter end, lasted more than three hours.

"If I'm looking at this, Saturday is going to be a war. If you're faced with back-to-backs, that first game is a monster because, Sunday, both teams are going to be tired and it's going to be a matter of who has, inside them, what it really takes," Brown said. "This is going to tell a lot about our team, a lot about individuals. It's a great, great chance."

There would be no slow start. Brown had seen to that.

Five minutes into the game, the Pacers had a 16-4 lead. Smits had scored three times on postups, and Miller had drained a pair of three-pointers. It was the perfect response to Brown's tirade the day before, and it put the Hawks on the defensive. "They had sent us a message in Game Two," said Brown, "and it was important that we re-establish ourselves."

That they did. Smits broke loose for 27 points and, according to plan, things opened up for the guards. Miller, Workman, Scott and Fleming combined for 52 points. Atlanta's guards had 31. That accounted for more than the difference in a 101-81 victory.

Smits didn't just score points, he made big plays. When the Hawks closed to 30-27, he dunked and drew a foul, converting a three-point play. When it was 33-29, he produced eight points in an 18-9 run that would result in a 53-42 halftime lead. The Hawks would trail by double digits the rest of the night.

Perhaps the most significant mental hurdle, though, was cleared by Miller. He did not shoot well once again, five of 12, and had 16 points. In the series, he was averaging just 15.3 points and shooting 31 percent. And yet the Pacers led 2-1. His self-imposed pressure, now, was relieved.

"It's not fair that Reggie feels he has to carry the team," said Mitchell. "It's not one guy's job, it's 12 guy's. That's what got us where we are, and that's what's going to get us where we're going."

Without a followup victory, though, the weekend would be a waste. "Once we got Game Three," said Scott, "Game Four became the most important game of the series."

With Atlanta focused on shutting down Smits, the perimeter was left open. The Pacers hit 11 three-pointers, with seemingly every one coming at an opportune moment, in a 102-86 victory.

Twice in the first quarter, Miller hit threes that put the Pacers ahead. After Atlanta had closed to 44-43 late in the second, Scott hit two, then Miller closed out the half with a bomb to open the margin to 55-48. McKey and Miller hit back-to-back threes midway through the fourth to quell an Atlanta rally, and even Antonio Davis threw one in late in the game, a heave at the shot-clock buzzer.

Atlanta opened the fourth quarter trailing by just six, 78-72. After Scott hit a three, Antonio Davis came up with the most spectacular defensive sequence of the series.

Lang tried to post him up, but he swatted it away. Craig Ehlo tried a followup drive, but Davis got that one, as well. The next time down, Ennis Whatley penetrated. Davis rose up again and recycled the shot. "They came in there three times in a row," he said. "What was I supposed to do, stand there?"

Miller, finally playing loosely, had 25 points and played to the crowd, pumping his arms throughout the celebratory final minutes. Davis, Scott, McKey and Smits also scored in double figures. Of the 34 baskets, 28 were set up by an assist. The defense had shut down everyone except Manning, who scored 35, and Lang, who had 17.

"As a coach, this is the best way I could've written the script," said Brown, "to have Danny play a great game on national TV and us win the game."

The Hawks, on the other hand, felt a sense of total loss. Willis had hyperextended his knee in a first-quarter collision with Manning. Though the injury was originally thought to be minor, Willis would not be a factor the rest of the series. Compounding the problem was that Willis was responsible for Ehlo's broken nose. When Willis threw a high elbow into Miller, the Pacer guard's head crashed into Ehlo's face.

As the fans filed out of the arena, honking horns and shouting, Koncak observed the scene. "Pacer-mania," he said, "is alive and well." Koncak could only wonder what it would be like to go back to Atlanta for Game Five and play before a crowd like this. Then again, he said, "half these people will probably be in Atlanta."

He wasn't far off.

Thanks to a special day trip offered by Indianapolis-based American Trans Air, nearly 1,000 Pacer fans would head down for Game Five.

The package, which included round-trip airfare, transportation to and from the arena and one game ticket, totaled $168 — a bargain, considering some scalpers were getting upwards of $250 for average seats in Market Square Arena. The venture was so successful, ATA needed three planes - two Lockheed L-1011s and one Boeing 757 — to accommodate the demand. A total of 940 seats were sold.

The airline had little trouble procuring the tickets. The Hawks were more than happy to sell to Indiana fans, since theirs weren't particularly interested.

A team that five weeks before faced a fight just to make the playoffs now was one victory away from the Eastern Conference finals.

* * *

For one veteran in the organization, it had been a particularly bittersweet season. Trainer David Craig had been with the franchise 24 years, but endured nothing like this.

Before training camp opened, Craig's wife, Linda, went to the doctor complaining of headaches and dizzy spells. She was diagnosed with a brain tumor. Walsh told Craig to take the year off to be with his wife and family, but the trainer wanted to stick to his routine. Work would distract him from his inner pain.

It turned out to be one of his busiest seasons. Twelve players missed at least one game. Eight spent time on the injured list. Even Brown had been sidelined with chest pains. Through it all, he kept the team taped together and now was succeeding beyond his wildest dreams.

"We've had such a dry spell here," Craig told Star columnist Bill Benner, whose wife was one of Linda's best friends. "It's like, let's baptize Market Square Arena with a winning team after all these years. I congratulate the fans who have stuck in there, like the old trainer, all these years. I look up in the stands and see those same fans who have been there all along, not the ones just coming out because we're winning. The greatest gift any team can give to a trainer is winning itself. It makes all the effort and the long days worthwhile."

Craig could not hide his pain, though. An effervescent personality lost much of its bubble. His work didn't suffer. The travel arrangements were made, the laundry washed, the expense money handed out, the practice sites coordinated. Craig did his best to hide it for the benefit of those he worked with, but his pain was obvious.

Even though the doctors offered his wife little hope of recovery, neither would they give up. She was in the doctor's office the afternoon of Game Three against Orlando, but was determined to make the game. She did.

It would be her last.

In and out of the hospital for weeks, Linda was in once again. This time, her condition was critical. Craig would not make the Monday afternoon flight to Atlanta but was so optimistic, he purchased a ticket on a commercial airline that would have him at the Omni before tipoff Tuesday night. It went unused.

Linda passed away Tuesday afternoon, May 17, from complications of chemotherapy. The medical battle lasted nine months.

"Linda's been with the Pacer family since it started, so this is a really sad day," said Walsh. "It puts what we're doing here in perspective." Brown told the team upon its arrival at The Omni. "I don't know how he's done this all year," he said.

Craig looked at it as the consummation of a heavenly deal made long ago.

"Before our first child was born, an X-ray showed a shadow in her brain," Craig said. "She told the doctor she would make a deal with God. If He let her live long enough to raise our children, then He could have her."

When He took her, it wasn't the only loss the franchise would feel that day but it was, by far, the most painful.

* * *

In the locker room before the game, Brown gave the team three instructions: play the best defensive game of the series, show better shot selection and control the boards.

The players then went out and did none of the above. They allowed the Hawks to shoot 50 percent while shooting 34 percent themselves, and had more turnovers (22) than assists (17). They did outrebound the Hawks, but only because they missed so many shots, there were numerous opportunities on the offensive glass.

"Our offense just kind of bogged down," said Workman. "It was like they knew what we were going to do the whole time."

Did they?

"Oh yeah, oh yeah," said Manning, who celebrated his 28th birthday with 20 points and nine rebounds. "We know our scouting report. They did throw a new play at us, but we'll have that one down by Thursday night."

Miller scored 22 and was complemented, finally, by McKey, who had his best play-off performance with 20 points, 13 rebounds and four assists. No other Pacer scored in double figures. Still, there were chances.

A six-point surge to start the third quarter put Indiana ahead 48-47, but Ehlo — inserted only because starter Stacey Augmon drew a seat on the bench for committing an untimely flagrant foul against Smits — stepped in and reversed momentum. Ehlo scored 10 straight points and 12 of the Hawks' next 14 while the Pacers managed just two buckets in nearly six minutes to fall behind 61-52.

The Pacers closed to 67-65 on an Antonio Davis basket with 10:03 left, then went dry for three possessions while the Hawks spread the lead to 73-65. The visitors didn't actually make a field goal in the final five minutes, but the only one that did count — a McKey putback that was goal-tended by Manning — cut it to 80-76 with 2:31 left.

From their final five possessions, the Pacers came up with four missed shots and a turnover. The Hawks, on the other hand, got something from every trip but one to close out the game with an eight-point run.

Though the Pacers still had a 3-2 advantage, the Hawks felt they had gained an edge. The pressure was now squarely on Indiana to wrap up the series at home in Game Six, because another trip to the Omni was an unattractive option.

As for those 1,000 rowdy Indiana fans? "We sent them home," said Manning, "on the red-eye."

If the Hawks were trying to put pressure on the Pacers, it wasn't working.

After the off-day practice before Game Six, Workman voiced the team's confidence when he said, "I don't think they can beat us here."

Overhearing those bold words, McKey interjected, "That's going to be a headline tomorrow."

The Pacers didn't particularly care. They weren't supposed to be here, after all, but would reach the conference finals with one more victory. In their minds, all the pressure was on Atlanta, the regular season conference champs. The Hawks needed this series to fulfill expectations.

There was pressure, though, and it got to Miller. On the drive to the arena for Game Six, he talked himself into taking over. "No way am I going to let this one slip out of my hands," he said to himself. "If I've got to shoot it 30 times, I will."

That's exactly how Miller took the floor. He hit his first shot, a three-pointer, but went cold, missing five of the next six. If not for Smits, who got off to his usual fast start at home with 10, the Pacers wouldn't have ended the period with a 24-23 lead.

Nothing could've prepared either team for the ugliness that was to follow.

The Hawks and Pacers, two of the elite eight still playing and therefore presumed to be among the best, put forth one of the worst periods in playoff history. The Pacers missed 10 of 17 shots, went zero of four from the line, committed five turnovers, and produced 14 points.

And they actually extended their lead.

Atlanta scored a single basket in the first six minutes of the quarter, then squeezed out 10 more points. The Hawks' 12-point second quarter tied the third-fewest ever scored. Combined, the teams' 26 points tied the second-lowest scoring quarter in NBA history. On April 22, 1977, the Lakers and Golden State Warriors produced 25.

At halftime, the score was 38-35, Pacers.

Brown, quite naturally, had little to say about the offense. "I wasn't really concerned with that," he said. "With this team, it's something I don't get caught up in."

Instead, he reminded the players of their options: win at home, watch the city erupt and take a few days off before heading to the conference finals, or head back to Atlanta for Game Seven and risk having this joyride come to an end.

"They talked a lot about the pressure being on us," said Brown. "I didn't buy that, but I think, had we gone down to Atlanta, I wasn't that excited about staying in that same hotel, and I had already seen every mall that was close by."

When the second half started, so did the Indiana offense. The Pacers grabbed momentum with a 12-2 run to start a surge that would not end until the third quarter was over, when the lead had swelled from three at the break to a full 21. Smits scored 11 in the period. McKey hit a pair of three-pointers. Miller, who apparently drank a cup of decaf at the break, settled down and took just two shots, making both.

The Hawks, already reeling, had to cope with Willis' inability to perform. Wilkens had no choice but to turn to little-used Adam Keefe early in the third period when Willis limped off.

Atlanta opened the fourth quarter with eight straight points and got as close as 12 twice, but the Pacers had too many answers.

Miller, McKey and Smits combined for 18 in the fourth quarter, and Scott provided the exclamation point with a soaring dunk in the face of Ehlo to make it 91-75.

That turned the final three minutes into an intense celebration for the crowd of 16,552. When the game concluded with a 98-79 final, the party spilled out of the arena and into the streets, where fans abandoned their logjammed cars to seize a moment nearly two decades in the making.

And still under construction.

Even with Willis limited to 17 minutes and four points by injuries to his left thumb and right knee, and with Jon Koncak held to 12 minutes by a swollen left knee, the Hawks forced the Pacers to play all their cards. Fortunately for the home team, it was a full house.

Smits (27 points) took care of things inside, Miller (18) and Byron Scott (14) the outside and McKey (17 points, 10 rebounds) everything in between. The list hardly stopped there. The Davises combined for 20 rebounds while Workman had 11 points and 10 assists.

"It's pretty hard to imagine," Brown said. "I think our staff is so proud of this team because so many people have made a contribution and tonight was a perfect example."

The Pacers' universe would now expand to include either the three-time defending champion Chicago Bulls or the bigger, badder New York Knicks. Whichever team won that glamour series would earn the privilege of facing the Pacers, who had won seven of nine playoff games and 38 of 52 overall.

Miller, naturally, had to express a controversial preference.

"We match up better with Chicago, but I'd rather get New York," he said. "It's the media capitol of the world. Plus, I'd get to see my old friend John Starks."

It all was so unreal to Miller, he needed evidence. Not until he read about it in the next day's newspaper would he be sure this wasn't some kind of dream. Then, he might take a little victory stroll.

"Finally," he said. "Finally, I can walk around the city, and little kids, the elderly, dogs, birds, fishes . . . everyone knows what's going on."

Or, to be more precise, who was going on: the Pacers, to the conference finals.

13 Miller Time

As compelling as the Orlando series had been, it was overshadowed by another first-round matchup between small-market teams, Seattle and Denver. The eighth-seeded Nuggets knocked off the prohibitive Western Conference favorites in five games and quickly became media darlings, with the scene of Dikembe Mutombo on the floor clutching the ball in celebration after Game Five indelibly etched in the memories of TV watchers from coast to coast.

Their second-round series, too, took place out of the national spotlight. The Knicks and Bulls squared off in what New York Times columnist Harvey Araton described as "the de facto Eastern Conference finals." There was a marquee matchup in the West, as well, with Charles Barkley's Phoenix Suns against Hakeem Olajuwon's Houston Rockets.

Now, finally, the Pacers would be under the full heat of the national spotlight. Hundreds of reporters from across the country would descend upon Indianapolis, if they could find hotel space. It happened that the Pacers' first two home games would take place the same weekend as the Indianapolis 500. This wasn't just for the conference championship, it was for the conference championship New York felt it already owned.

The brighter the lights, the more Reggie Miller shined. In the postseason, his personality transformed. He needed an image, any image. So he took to wearing a bandanna on his head during off-day practices. Coupled with an assortment of funky sunglasses, Miller was fostering the look of an outlaw.

Brown thought something else entirely: "Oh, he's wacko."

One of the leading conspiracy theorists in the locker room, Miller had annually explained the strange bad luck that seemed to befall the team — unfortunate whistles, inexplicable scheduling, all-star snubs, etc. — as some mysterious master plan hatched in a closed boardroom in the NBA offices in New York. The league had no use for the Pacers, and probably preferred them to relocate to a bigger market. That's why bad things happened to the Pacers; the league wanted it that way.

Illogical though his thinking was, it served Miller well. He took on the aura of a player the league, and most of its fans, would loathe, and hoped it would serve his team. He played to the boos on the road.

"This ain't a very nice team to like," he said. "We have a lot of attitudes on this team and if they don't like us, who cares, as long as we come to play every night. We're not worried about people liking us. It's the last thing on our minds. It's great. It's fantastic. I love when they're chanting "Reg-gie" or "Cher-yl." I encourage that. Maybe sometimes that's why I do things, just to rub 'em the wrong way. It's the best feeling anyone could feel. You guys don't know what it feels like to me to be booed, to be cursed at, have my name chanted, hear little kids chanting my name because they're taught that from adults. They're taught that.

"I love it. It's the best. It's the odds of being the underdog, 12 vs. 16,000. We're supposed to lose, supposed to get hammered. To come in and kick some behind, that's what it's all about. I love being the underdog. It's the best feeling. I don't like playing at home. I'd rather play all my games on the road."

Brown didn't particularly like Miller promoting that attitude, in part because it was so dramatically different from reality. Miller was anything but an outlaw. He had been a coach's delight, a player willing to make sacrifices, who became more of a leader, and he did it without complaint.

After Game Two of the Orlando series, Miller was asked to address his new rebel image, then did so at length. As Miller stood up to leave the room, though, Brown leaned over and said, "That stuff's a bunch of malarkey. Reggie's as nice a kid as you'd ever want to know."

The problem was, Miller really didn't want to let anyone into his world. He wanted to be famous, but he didn't want to be known. It wasn't the only dichotomy in his life.

His ability to score is what got him into the league, then made him an All-Star and Dream Team II member. He chafed, though, when described as a scorer. "The first impression is the last impression," he said. "All they remember is the jump shot."

The adjustment to national stardom wasn't coming easily. It was as though this player who had spent most of his basketball life in someone else's shadow was blinded by the sudden glare of the spotlight.

This would be just the latest in the series of challenges that faced Miller from the day he was born. Early in life, in fact, Miller could only hope that he would one day have the skill to be called for walking.

Born with pronated hips that caused splayed feet — instead of both pointing north, one went east, the other west — and an open chest cavity, Miller's parents were told by doctors not to expect him ever to walk unassisted.

Through the age of four, he wore braces on both legs. His only mobility came with crutches or a wheelchair. The treatment for the open chest cavity, though not as severe, was no less traumatic for a child. "I had to eat liver twice a day, every day, till I was five," he said, shaking his head at the memory. "That's why you can't get me anywhere near liver today."

Now, he can joke about it. Then, it was much more serious. "I just remember Cheryl always being by my side," he said. "She couldn't pronounce my name, so she called me "Ready." That became my nickname in the family."

His recovery and subsequent rise to basketball fame left an indelible mark on Cheryl, now the women's basketball coach at USC. "I want Reggie to talk to my players one day about the work ethic, because he's a prime example," she told the Los Angeles Times. "You know, at one point Reggie was 6-foot-7 and 160 pounds and all kinds of people told him he'd never be able to play college ball. Reggie never argued with anyone about it, he just worked. People who told him he couldn't play — when they were getting out of bed in the morning, Reggie had been shooting for two or three hours. And when they went to bed, he was still shooting."

He was, no doubt, making up for the lost time of his childhood. The braces came off when he was five. He didn't take to the court, he said, "for another four or five years" because he was too busy having fun hanging out with his brothers and sisters.

"I was just happy to be able to go out and play," he said, "instead of staying in the house all the time with my mom and the dog."

Though his story of perseverance was inspirational, Miller has chosen to keep it largely private. "I really don't talk about it," he said, almost at a whisper. "There's not much for people to know."

For most lifetimes, learning to walk would've been challenge enough. For Miller, it was only the first.

Though he got a late start, he soon gained ground in an athletic family. Cheryl may have been the best woman player ever. His brother Darrell had a long major league baseball career as a catcher. Another sister, Tammy, played volleyball at Cal State-Fullerton. The best athlete in the family, according to Reggie, was Saul Jr., but he chose the Air Force.

Initially, Reggie preferred baseball. "We would've all said he would be a major league baseball player," said Saul, father and captain of Team Miller. "All of the boys played baseball, but Reggie exceeded them all, including Darrell. As a 12-

year-old in Little League, he batted over .500 and was a pitcher who no one could hit. High school coaches were licking their chops."

He didn't exactly stray from basketball, keeping his jump shot sharp on the family's backyard court. As he grew into competitive play, Miller found himself motivated by the constant action and the roar of the crowd. Baseball was challenging, but it also was slow. The fans were more pastoral than in basketball, where every good move was rewarded with a roar.

By his sophomore year at Riverside (California) Poly High, Miller was committed to basketball. But it wasn't easy. As good as he became, he wasn't even the best in his family.

On the night of his first high school start, the sophomore came home elated after scoring 39 points. The same night, Cheryl scored 105 for the girls' team.

"He picked up the ball," said Cheryl, "went outside, and started shooting."

As close as Reggie and Cheryl were, he would eventually leave her shadow. After she chose USC, he went to rival UCLA.

There, Miller found his best wasn't enough to satisfy everyone. He scored 2,095 points, still good for third on the school's all-time list. He was a three-time John Wooden Award winner. And the Bruins won their first Pacific-10 Conference championship in years. But at UCLA, the standards are higher. Anything short of a national championship is failure. The frustration got to Miller.

He developed a negative image, centered largely around an incident during a game with Brigham Young. When a BYU player spit on one of Miller's teammates, he spat back. Already a focal point of criticism for his tendency toward trash-talking and general on-court exuberance, Miller was labeled a head case. It got so bad, he eventually quit talking to the media in his hometown.

When he interviewed with the Pacers, Walsh was braced for the worst. "All I'd heard was he was a bad kid, he had an attitude, he spit on a guy, whatever," Walsh said. "After I sat down with him face-to-face, I knew all that stuff was wrong. Reggie was an intelligent, honest, hard-working kid." Walsh scrapped his plans to use the 11th pick on St. John's point guard Mark Jackson. Miller was his man.

When the Pacers called his name in the 1987 draft, it should've been a joyous occasion for Miller. Instead, he was haunted by boos from Hoosier fans who wanted the team to draft the squeaky-clean but marginally talented Alford.

The irony was that Miller and Alford were very much alike. Both were pure shooters who had to work at the other areas of their game. Both were self-made players who would rather spend the summer in the gym than at the beach. Both led disciplined lifestyles; Miller's biggest vices, it seemed, were occasional horror movies, or high-stakes card games at the back of the team plane.

But Alford was a known commodity. Miller was something of a mystery. Once again, Miller would have to prove himself.

It didn't take long.

In his first year, he averaged 10 points and broke none other than Larry Bird's record for three-pointers by a rookie with 61. The team struggled, though, failing to make the playoffs his first two years. His breakthrough came in the 1989-90 season, when Miller averaged a career-best 24.6 points and made the All-Star team.

No longer just a three-point shooter, Miller's game had expanded with slashing drives to the basket and a trademark move known as "the floater," when he ball-fakes an opponent into the air, leans under and softly flips the ball into the hoop, often drawing a foul.

The Pacers returned to the playoffs in 1990 but were swept out of the first round by Detroit. Two consecutive first-round losses to Boston were followed by the past year's 3-1 loss to New York.

Entering this season, the team had been rebuilt largely around Miller. Gone were two primary scorers, Person and Schrempf. Miller looked around the locker room and quickly knew what he had to do. If the team was to accept Brown's defensive philosophy, it had to start with Miller. His personal life had settled with marriage to model-actress Marita Stavrou the previous summer. Now, his professional life would undergo a similar maturation process.

"When they made the (Schrempf) trade, I really knew then it was all going to change for me, and there was no one else I could rely on. It was just me," Miller said. "There was no more Chuck, no more Det, no more Micheal Williams. I knew I was going to be out there by myself, so I was the one that was going to have to sacrifice the points, I was going to be the one that moved the basketball, I was going to be the one that had to get on guys out there. I knew after the trade that was what they were looking for. I had to accept it. If I didn't, we wouldn't have been 47-35 and the fifth seed. No way. There was no way I could be selfish."

Miller's greatest growth had been his role within the team. The responsibility of leadership was thrust upon him when Schrempf was dealt away, and he accepted it willingly. Scott helped show him the way in the role of mentor.

"I always felt Reggie was a great competitor and a team player but I didn't think he was a leader, verbally," Brown said. "He learned a lot from Byron. I thought that was one of the biggest blessings. As much as you think you can teach Reggie, well, having a guy that Reggie watched play and win championships was as important as bringing Byron here as a player."

Scott established a theme with Miller. "The way you make your mark in this league is by winning championships and advancing in the playoffs," said Scott. "You can score 20,000 points in your career, but if you're always losing in the first round, no one will remember you, and they probably don't even know who you are."

Brown didn't put it quite that harshly. Whether the team won a championship or not would have little bearing on his opinion of Miller.

"I don't know of many guys who are more of a winner than him," said Brown. "The thing that has impressed me more about Reggie every day I'm with him is he wants to do everything right, and he's completely unselfish. You're proud of a lot of things that went on, but I admire him and what he's done. He's let everybody know he'll make sacrifices on the court, he'll do whatever it takes to win. That's infectious, when your best player has that mentality."

It should've come as no surprise, then, that given a choice between the Knicks and Bulls, Miller voiced a preference for New York. Against them, his team would be the bigger underdog, and he would have a greater challenge.

* * *

Even though they had reached the conference finals, the Pacers wondered aloud if the basketball world was taking them seriously.

The more pressing issue, at the moment, was how seriously they took themselves. They'd won 54 games, sent home a pair of 50-win teams and advanced through two rounds of the playoffs with startling authority. Even if swept by the Knicks, the Pacers' memorable season would be untarnished.

Such unprecedented achievement could work both ways; it might serve to diminish their hunger and make them a more placid opponent, or allow them to play with the freedom of a team with absolutely nothing to lose. "This team has shocked me," said Brown, "but that doesn't mean we can't continue to win."

As good as they'd been, the Pacers realized they hadn't been quite good enough, primarily on offense. Their top six scorers had combined to shoot 42 percent. Miller had a great series against Orlando, but more often than not struggled against Atlanta. Smits had been a home-only entity. McKey was invisible until the last two games. Workman and Scott had shooting percentages that more closely resembled batting averages.

The defense had been brilliant, arguably the best in the league in the playoffs. Opponents had averaged 87 points on 42 percent shooting. Seven times in nine games, they held teams to less than 90 points. The only two times they did not, the Pacers were beaten.

Points would not come easily against the Knicks, but the Pacers weren't a team to worry about the opposition. Their strength had come from focusing only upon themselves. "We've played maybe two good games," said Miller. "A lot of that has to do with the teams we've been playing, but we still haven't put a total 48 minutes together. Hopefully, the best is yet to come for us."

Maybe that was asking a bit much, but this was a team never short on ambition.

They entered Game One fully convinced they would repeat their pattern of the first two rounds, steal a game on the road, then control the series the rest of the way.

That confidence was shaken quickly. On the first possession, Miller slashed through the lane and scored. On his way back inbounds, he was greeted impolitely by Charles Oakley, who intentionally collided with the 180-pound guard, adding a forearm to the chest for effect. Just 17 seconds into the game, Oakley had drawn a technical foul. Given its impact, the Knicks might've wondered what took him so long.

It was the basketball equivalent of a knockdown pitch, and served its intended purpose: Miller did not dig in the rest of the night. Settling for jumpers and thereby playing right into the teeth of a voracious New York defense, Miller did not score another basket for nearly 20 minutes.

By then, the Pacers were facing a 45-30 deficit against the best defensive team in the league. Though they rallied in the second half to whittle the margin down to 85-83 with 4:09 left, the Pacers committed five turnovers and missed six of seven shots thereafter to help New York close the game with a 15-6 run for a 100-89 victory.

The biggest play came from reserve guard Hubert Davis. After Fleming had driven for the basket that cut it to two, coach Pat Riley took a time out to regroup his team. It worked wonders, as Davis came out and hit a quick three-pointer. "That three was a killer," said Fleming. "It was a heartbreaker."

Miller, the player who said he wanted this challenge, did not rise to it. He was virtually invisible with just 14 widely spaced points, primarily because he made himself easy to defend. Knicks starter John Starks wore a brace on a surgically repaired left knee that kept him out the final six weeks of the regular season. His jumping ability and lateral movement remained hindered, and Starks was vulnerable to being beaten off the dribble. It was a vulnerability that went largely unexplored by Miller.

"In the playoffs, they take away your first two or three moves, then they want to see what you have in your kitty," Miller said. "That's OK with me."

Though Smits scored 27, it didn't have its usual effect of opening up the floor for the perimeter players. The Knicks rarely double-team the low post and, with Patrick Ewing inside, would not in this series.

"If he gets 27 and they get 89," said Riley, "I have no problem with that."

Until Miller shook loose, the Pacers would have the problem.

But for that to happen, someone other than Smits had to produce. McKey continued his abysmal offensive play by missing all seven of his shots. "I'm not a shooter," he said, shrugging off his performance. "I can score sometimes, if I'm lucky." Brown wasn't quite as ambivalent, saying, "We've got to get his hands on the ball. We have to have him involved."

Workman, rattled because he did not start, missed all eight of his attempts. Brown gave Fleming the honor of a hometown start, which was viewed as a monumental gaffe by the New York press. Brown, though, apologized to no one. "If it hurt, then it's on me but I'd do the same thing again," Brown said. "Vern's been in the league 10 years, a Pacer for 10 years. It's been a dream of his, and I thought we owed it to him."

Brown was questioned over another move that, in retrospect, was counterproductive. He replaced Smits with Antonio Davis with 2:58 remaining and the Pacers trailing 88-83. The Pacers wouldn't get another basket until the closing seconds, when it was far too late.

Both fountains of controversy — the hometown start for Fleming and the late benching of Smits — were standard operating procedure for Brown during the season. It's just that this was a team, and a coach, few had taken the trouble to get to know.

The biggest mystery within the locker room was McKey. Everyone knew he was capable of far more, especially in a matchup against Charles Smith, who was playing out of position at small forward. Miller and Smits had demonstrated they would accept the challenge. Would McKey?

Not in Game Two.

Though Miller scored 23 and Smits 22, McKey remained invisible. He scored four points and missed seven of his nine shots. His teammates seemed baffled by his offensive indifference, and how he might be snapped out of it.

"I don't think that's up to us. That's up to Derrick," said Scott. "He has to decide to be more aggressive. We need Derrick. That's an understatement."

Asked if the team missed McKey's offense, Miller replied, "You need to go ask Derrick McKey those questions."

McKey had his usual answers. "I've got to go out and play my game," he said. "If the shot's not falling, I've got to do other things. They're playing good defense, but I'm getting some good looks. My shot's not falling. I feel like I can make things happen out there, I can be valuable to the team. We've won a lot of games with me playing my game, helping to get other guys going. I don't feel any pressure. I go out and try to do things, but it's just not working."

The Pacers looked like a team seizing the moment for most of the second quarter, outscoring the Knicks 18-6 to take a 39-31 lead with 3:42 left. New York missed its first eight shots and 15 of 16 in the quarter. And yet, thanks to a 9-1 run in the closing minutes, they escaped with a tie, 40-40, at the half.

The Pacers made another move in the third quarter. With Miller and Smits combining for 16, they built a 62-57 lead with 3:39 left. Six minutes later, New York had a 71-62 lead as the Pacers missed 10 straight shots and were outscored 14-0 in what turned out to be the game's decisive run. The Knicks went on to win 89-78 to build a 2-0 lead.

"The bottom line is we're expecting Rik and Reggie to beat them," said Brown. "We're expecting Rik to play Patrick to a standstill and we're expecting Reggie to beat all the rest of them." Smits and Miller combined for 45 points and attempted exactly half the team's 78 shots.

Ewing won the battle of the low post decisively, racking up 32 points and 13 rebounds. He made his last eight shots in a brilliant clutch performance. Oakley, singled out by Brown prior to the series as the key player for the Knicks, was proving the coach correct. In two games, he had 37 points and 19 rebounds. "I've been watching the Knicks play all year and I know how good Patrick is," Brown said, "but I keep looking at Oakley. I read the MVP votes and stuff like that, and I don't see too many players who do more for their team than he does."

Only five teams had come back from a 2-0 deficit to win a best-of-seven series. One of those was Chicago, which had done it to the Knicks in last year's East finals. Surely, the Knicks had learned from that lesson.

"They're going after everything. They're leaving it all out on the court," said Scott. "It seems like they're on a mission to win a championship."

And the Pacers?

"We have to get on the plane," he said, "take a hard look at ourselves and see what direction we want to go."

At the moment, there was only one alternative.

The Pacers returned to Indianapolis disappointed not as much in the results, as in their methods. When Brown gathered them for an off-day film session, the veterans turned it into a team meeting. For aging players like Thompson, Fleming and Mitchell, it was more than a chance to advance to the Finals. It might well be their last chance. They impressed that upon the younger players who, they felt, were acting like the team had somehow earned an automatic bid to next year's conference finals.

"Nothing can describe the looks those guys had on their faces," said Antonio Davis. "They were serious."

As was the team's situation.

"Hell, yes, we had some things to say," said Thompson. "It's one thing to play hard and get beat, but when you let somebody kick your ass, that ain't what it's all about. That ain't what got us here."

"You don't get a trophy for competing, or trying hard, or almost winning," said Miller. "I want to win. There's no other consolation."

"It's like with a bully," said Brown. "They keep beating you up and pushing you around unless you fight back. They're going to continue to do it. Now, we've got to fight back."

Both Indianapolis newspapers billed it as the biggest sports weekend in the city's history. The two conference final games, Saturday and Monday, would sandwich Sunday's Indianapolis 500. "People will be in a frenzied state," Riley said. "We have to go back there with a very focused, very businesslike mentality and find a way to get a win."

The first half of Game Three was brutal. The teams combined for nearly as many turnovers (25) as baskets (28), before it mercifully ended with the Knicks ahead 39-37.

Considering Ewing was scoreless and Starks had been likewise until hitting a late three-pointer, the Knicks felt like they were in pretty good shape. They couldn't play that badly for another half, or so they thought. The Pacers had a little motivation of their own, though. McKey had shown up. He scored eight points in the first seven and one half minutes, more than he had totaled in the first two games combined. If he would remain a threat, eventually, things would fall into place.

The third quarter was plodding along at about the same pace, though. After Anthony Mason worked into the lane for a basket that cut the Indiana lead to 52-47 with 3:30 left in the period, the Knicks were still comfortable. They had established, through the course of their first two playoff series, that they would assume control of a game in the final minutes of the third quarter and maintain the stranglehold with defense throughout the fourth.

This time, though, they went dry. Mason's bucket would be their last for more than six minutes, during which the Pacers put together a 15-6 run to open a 67-53 lead. With both Ewing and Oakley in foul trouble, the Knicks not only failed to come back, they fell completely apart. In the final 15:29, they were outscored 36-21 and lost 88-68.

Ewing finished with one point, missing all 10 of his shots. He could not remember a worse game at any level of his basketball career. "That was an aberration," said Riley. "I'm not even going to think about that." Brown was similarly stunned. "I never thought I'd coach a game where he scores one point," he said. "He'll probably come back and get 40 in the next one."

The Knicks established a record for fewest points in a playoff game. It was one the Pacers were keenly aware of, since they had been the bearers of that ignominious distinction since their 92-69 loss to Atlanta in Game Two. The players weren't about to pretend they didn't care. "We knew," said Scott, "exactly what it was." When Hubert Davis went to the line with 1:07 left, he had a chance to give the Knicks their 69th point, but he missed, and the bench erupted.

For Indiana, it was a nearly perfect result. The defense dominated the Knicks, who had 21 turnovers and shot 34 percent, and held a dominating 46-30 advantage on the boards. And, for the first time in 12 playoff games, McKey had led the team in scoring, with a modest 15 points. Wherever he had been in Games One and Two, he was back.

* * *

Whither the mouths that roared?

Miller and Starks, those trash-talking, sweet-shooting, high-profile guards, had taken on another hyphenated role: low-profile.

"I don't know what you guys were expecting," said Miller, addressing the media's inquisitions. "I think you guys were expecting something else. You were expecting me and John, when the jump ball went up, to start head-butting one another."

If that happened, it would've been less of a surprise than what had instead transpired. The most celebrated, not to mention volatile, matchup of the conference finals had been positively serene. Miller wasn't talking to Starks during the games. Starks said he wouldn't be listening, anyway.

While Miller's offense at least had moments, Starks had been barely a flicker. The New York All-Star — chosen at Miller's expense — and the team's No. 2 scorer during the regular season, was averaging just eight points on 30 percent shooting through three games.

"I really haven't been looking to score that much, and it has hurt us, at times," Starks said. "I have to get my aggressiveness back."

Miller had long droughts in each of the three games. He went 20 minutes between baskets in Game One, then was shut out for 17 straight minutes in Game Two, both Pacer losses in New York. The confines of Market Square Arena weren't much friendlier. Though the Pacers won Game Three, Miller had his longest dry spell. More than 27 minutes elapsed between his second basket, early in the first quarter, and his next, midway through the third.

"It's been tough," Miller said. "They've been going with pretty much single coverage on Rik, and they're sending three guys out at me."

It may have worked to the Pacers' advantage. Brown had been preaching the need for more widespread involvement in the offense. With Miller on the bench for more than half the game, others had to step forward.

"It took 12 guys to get us here," said Miller, "and we needed all 12 of them."

For the Pacers to go farther, though, Miller knew he had to be the man. He was averaging 17 points and shooting 43 percent. That wouldn't get it done, especially with the health of his reliable backup, Scott, in doubt. Scott was taken down hard by Oakley in the third quarter and suffered a severely bruised lower back that would, at the very least, restrict his minutes in the upcoming games.

Beyond all that, though, he wasn't being himself. So concerned with doing the right thing, he had muzzled his competitive spirit. If he was suspicious of this, it was confirmed when he got a phone call from Cheryl. She had seen the same things. He wasn't talking trash. He wasn't pumping his arms. He wasn't even exchanging jabs with Spike Lee, a taunt waiting to happen in his courtside seat at the Garden.

This model behavior would come to an end. Miller was going to be himself, like it or not.

"Reggie Miller's best," he said, "is yet to come."

That line prompted an interjection from Brown: "Now, you're talking."

* * *

Something other than Miller's cocky personality was missing from this series: drama. The first three games had moments, but all were decided by double-digit margins. As the stakes got higher, though, the scores would get closer, starting with Game Four.

The first half wasn't much different than Game Three. It was ugly, neither team could buy a basket, and nothing was established, though the Pacers led 42-39. The most interesting morsel was that the Knicks, nine of 29 in the second half of Game Three and 12 of 38 in the first half of Game Four, had managed to shoot 31 percent over four consecutive quarters. The Knicks were finding good shots harder to come by than hotel space in Indianapolis on 500 weekend.

It wouldn't get much better.

New York scored just four points in the first six minutes of the third quarter while the Pacers finally found a groove. McKey and Miller combined for nine of the points in the 14-4 run that opened a 56-43 lead and whipped the crowd into a frenzy. The celebration was a bit premature.

The Knicks cut it to 62-55 by the end of the third quarter, then went on a 15-6 run over the first six minutes of the fourth. When Greg Anthony beat the shot-clock buzzer with an off-balance three-pointer to tie it, then Hubert Davis hit a three to push the visitors into the lead, it was starting to look like the Knicks' night.

"I don't know how everybody else felt," said Antonio Davis, "but, in my mind, it was 'Oh, my God.' " It wasn't a statement of panic, but of determination. Davis, who guarded Ewing down the stretch, helped keep New York's center from getting up a shot in the final six minutes. With Ewing — whose 25 points up until then represented the only threat to the Pacers — surrounded, the Knicks blindly looked elsewhere.

They came up empty on four straight possessions while Miller got rolling. He hit a jumper from the right wing, fed Rik Smits for a 10-footer, drained a left-to-right fallaway, then drew three straight shooting fouls from New York defensive specialist Derek Harper. Miller made all six free throws, putting the Pacers ahead 80-72 with 2:20 left.

It wasn't quite over, though. The Pacers wouldn't make a basket the rest of the way, and when McKey missed a pair of free throws with 28.4 seconds left, New York trailed 80-77 and the door was wide open. The Knicks wanted to go to Ewing, but he wound up with the ball 25 feet from the basket, not exactly ideal post position. Ewing spotted Hubert Davis open behind the three-point line in front of the Pacer bench, but the pass skipped off the rookie's fingertips and out of bounds.

Haywoode Workman rattled in one free throw before the Knicks got that one, last turnover — number 26 on the night — out of their systems, and Miller went back to the line to cap his brilliant clutch performance. He scored 13 of his 31 in the fourth quarter, all in the final 7:17.

The Pacers had much more than an 83-77 victory. They had life. Miller was his old self. McKey was back. Smits had been consistent. The defense was relentless.

New York was showing cracks in its facade of invincibility. Oakley, already bothered by a sore right foot, rolled that ankle in the fourth quarter, complicating the problem. "We just have to do it the hard way," said Riley, disdain in his voice.

"Maybe he thought it was going to be easy," said Antonio Davis. Those thoughts, like New York's once commanding series lead, had vanished.

To sum up his night, Miller turned to his Hollywood roots and came up with a cinematic reference.

"I remember in the movie Fatal Attraction, when Glenn Close's character said, 'I will not be ignored' " he said. "Well, we are not going to be ignored."

They were bold words, perhaps, but thoroughly in character from the man who had just boiled New York's bunnies.

The Pacers were starting to take themselves a little more seriously. The Knicks considered themselves the rightful heirs to the throne, but the Pacers no longer genuflected toward the crown. Both franchises won their last league championships in 1973, the Pacers in the ABA. Since then, neither had even played for a title. "We have just as much right to it as they do," said Miller. "It's not like they've been there every year for the last 10 years. It just seems that way."

They had started thinking ahead. Six more victories, and they would be the world champions. "That," said Brown, "is mind-boggling to me."

At least one of those, however, would have to come in Madison Square Garden, and this form of MSG had been hazardous to the Pacers' health. They had lost 11 straight, 20 of 21, and 31 of 33 there. In 11 years, they had won there just twice. For the last three years, they had been shut out.

In the first two games, the Pacers played as if they expected the league to suddenly change the rules and forbid the Knicks to practice their trademark thuggery. They were experts in throwing hard elbows to the kidneys, holding jerseys to keep a player from jumping, swatting arms away from a rebound, slapping hands that had just claimed one, moving picks, trips and shoves. It was ugly, but it was their style. To many coaches, it was detrimental to the game that a team be allowed to play that way. Brown just shrugged it off and demanded that his team adjust.

"If you don't play the way they play, you're going to get killed," he said. "They're so physical, so aggressive, when you're not used to that, it affects you." Now, we're starting to say, 'Hell, if they're going to play that way, we're a pretty physical team, we're capable of playing that way.' It's the only way we're going to have a chance. The league has allowed this stuff to go on, this kind of play. That's the way they want it played. You have to accept it and deal with it."

As he sat in Madison Square Garden before Game Five, Brown pondered the disparate public perceptions of his Pacers and the Knicks. "I feel like we're some small private-school team, something that ends with Country Day," he said, "and we're going up against Power Memorial."

For three quarters, that's how the game was played. New York, playing with total confidence at home, dictated the tempo. The Pacers were so overcome with nerves they couldn't even hit a free throw, missing 13 of their first 18. Ewing and Oakley were dominating Smits and Dale Davis. Scott, barely able to run, wasn't physically capable of bailing out his young team.

When the fourth quarter began, the Pacers trailed 70-58, teetering on the brink of disaster.

*   *   *

It started innocently enough. Miller tossed in a three-pointer, but then Smits committed his fifth foul, sending Oakley to the line for a pair of free throws that kept the Knicks in control, 72-61.

Then, Miller hit another three, and suddenly the Knicks tightened, as though they could sense what was coming. They committed six straight turnovers, and the Pacers knew exactly what to do with them.

"They were yelling from the bench, 'Just throw him the ball, it doesn't matter where he catches it,' " said Workman. "We'd bring the ball up and all I'd be thinking is, 'Where's Reggie?' "

He was in his backyard, in Riverside, California, shooting baskets all by himself. He'd hit one, back up a step and hit another, then back up again. Eventually, he'd run out of concrete and into his mother's carefully tended flower beds. In his fantasy games, Miller went beyond the usual boundaries, testing his limits.

In the hothouse of Madison Square Garden, Miller stepped back into a three-pointer that must've come from somewhere between the petunias and the geraniums. When it planted at the bottom of the bucket, putting the Pacers ahead for the first time, 75-72, there was no question what was happening.

He was, as never before, in full bloom.

Playing the kind of game that seems possible only in a child's imagination, Miller drove a spike squarely through the heart of New York with one of the greatest clutch performances in playoff history. He scored 25 of his 39 points in the fourth quarter — 19 in less than six minutes — to rally the Pacers to a 93-86 victory.

"That," said Walsh, "was Jordanesque."

Only one other player had scored more in one playoff period — not Jordan, but Sleepy Floyd, who produced 29 for Golden State against the Los Angeles Lakers in 1987. This was slightly less prolific, but far more impressive, for it came against the best defensive team in the league not just this season, but for the last three.

The Knicks had owned the fourth quarter — Miller scored more in the period than the Bulls ever managed in a seven-game second-round loss — but had it broken into and ransacked by the Pacers, who outscored them 35-16, allowed three baskets and forced nine turnovers.

They also had owned the Pacers in this building, winning 11 straight and 31 of the last 33, but had to sublet.

"We're shocked, they're shocked, everybody watching on TV is shocked, our fans are shocked," said Antonio Davis, "and I'm shocked."

The one player who didn't seem to be was Miller. "It all started," he said, "with defense." The defense started, improbably, with Thompson.

Playing only because foul trouble forced Brown to dig deep into the bench, the veteran with the broken bone in his left hand thrice stepped around Ewing to intercept passes intended for the post to help fuel the comeback.

Miller's third consecutive three-pointer concluded a 23-3 turnaround in which he provided 19 of the points, hitting seven of eight shots — five of them treys from a garden variety of locations. The killer was the bomb that, if the NBA wanted a four-point line, would establish the distance, and pushed his team into the lead for the first time. It may have been a 27-footer, but the distance it really covered was immeasurable.

Through it all, Miller used Spike Lee as his willing foil, singling him out for verbal exchanges after virtually every one of his jumpers. After one, Miller gave Lee the choke sign. After another, he said, "put that in your movie," sprinkling in the usual colloquial invectives each time.

"It's the kind of friendly chit-chat we've had over the years. He brings out the best in me in New York," Miller said. "He's their biggest fan and you can't fault him for that, but sometimes he opens his mouth a little too much and gets the other guys going. I think tonight was one of those nights."

Every great show needs drama at the end, and the Knicks provided it by scoring six straight points to cut the deficit to 81-79 on a pair of Ewing free throws with 4:11 left. Ewing was three of four from the field in the fourth quarter; none of the other Knicks made a basket. That was more a condemnation than a statistic.

After a couple of minutes out of the spotlight, Miller stepped back in and dropped a jumper from the top of the key to start a six-point counterpunch, and the Knicks were done.

Until then, Lee had not been particularly welcome in Market Square Arena. That had changed. "If he wants to," said Walsh, "he can sit at half-court."

As impressive as Miller had been, it wasn't something his teammates hadn't seen before. "In practice one day, Reggie and Sam got to bickering, and Sam had to guard him," said Workman. "Reggie hit eight in a row and we had to stop practice. The only difference was, we couldn't stop this game."

Much to New York's chagrin.

* * *

The Pacers had won 10 straight at home, including six in the playoffs. They hadn't been beaten there since April 8, a span of nearly two months and, in fact, had been close to dominant. Their average margin of victory at home, in the postseason, had been 16 points.

In order to enhance their sense of urgency, as they had before Game Six of the Atlanta series, the Pacers described their situation as more desperate than it actually was. Remember, this was a team that thrived primarily when the odds were against it. Now, they were expected to win, at least in Indianapolis.

"We can't go back to the Garden," said Miller. "We did what we had to do. We can't win two in the Garden, I don't think. We were lucky to escape with one."

"I don't think there are too many people in the league who think we could come in there and win two in a row, and there aren't many people who would let that happen," said Scott. "I think they all want to see a New York-Houston matchup in the Finals because of the media coverage. So, we have to take care of business at home."

For the Knicks, the motivational tools had a sharper edge. An aging team that had spent three years working toward one elusive goal must win the next two games or awaken, perhaps once and for all, from the championship dream.

"It comes down to this: three years of a push," said Riley. "This team has invested a tremendous amount of mental, physical and spiritual energy into accomplishing the goal of winning a championship. If this is the way it has to be, then that's the way it's going to be. We've been in these situations before and not handled them well. We're going to have to handle it differently, period."

The New York tabloids stoked the players' flames with vicious back-page headlines the day after Game Five. "Gag City," said the Daily News. "Chokers," said the Post. "Collapse," said Newsday.

The front pages were devoted to Lee, who absorbed a disproportionate share of blame for the defeat. In the process, he lashed out at Miller, who had grabbed his crotch during one gesture. Lee, suddenly becoming politically correct, said "I thought the brother had more class," and threatened to file a complaint with the league office.

By now, Miller had grown weary of the monster he created, and would talk about it no longer. "I'm not playing Spike Lee. I'm playing the New York Knicks," he said. "This is the biggest game of my life. I've got to worry about John Starks and Patrick Ewing, not Spike."

The Knicks, not surprisingly, weren't talking. Their intention was to have the last word.

In the meantime, the seed planted long ago by Hummer in the Atlanta Constitution had sprouted into full-blown civic paranoia. Sensitive to its sleepy, rural image, Indianapolis, through its columnists and television anchors, had built this series into a clash of cultures. Outside the arena prior to Game Six, there were tractor rides, a hillbilly band, cloggers and hordes of fans dressed in bib overalls. Instead of trying to shed its image, the city was reveling in it.

"I've never seen anything like this," said Brown, "except maybe in college. But even in college, March Madness lasts maybe three weeks. Here, it's been, it seems like, two months."

In the locker room, the players tried to stay loose by trading insults about the t-shirts that represented their respective "gangs." On one side, there were "The Regulators," consisting of veterans Scott, Thompson, McKey, Fleming, Conner and Mitchell. On the other there was "The Dog Pound," with both Davises, Miller, Sealy, and Williams. New shirts had been printed, featuring the faces of the members, and left on each player's chair.

"The Regulators control the Dog Pound," said Thompson.

"They try, but they can't," said Miller.

Was this a sign of division, however slight? Anything but.

"There's a lot of unity in this room," said Antonio Davis. "It's better that we separate two ways than 12 ways."

For the Pacers, the pregame hype was unprecedented. For New York, it was old hat. The Knicks handled it well, jumping out to leads of 15-4, then 25-14, then 48-37, before settling in with a 58-51 edge at the half. Starks, trying to answer Miller's challenge, took off for 11 in the first quarter. Ewing had eight in the second. The Knicks were also doing something out of the ordinary: running. They had 17 fastbreak points, a remarkable total for this plodding, unathletic team.

Despite the exhortations from the crowd, the situation would only deteriorate in the third quarter. Starks got hot again, scoring 10 more, and the Knicks built an 80-69 lead going into the fourth.

In the Pacers' three straight victories, Miller had racked up 46 points in the fourth quarter alone, certifying himself as one of the most threatening clutch scorers in the league. When the final 12 minutes of the season in MSA began, the question was: Could he do it again?

He opened the quarter with a trey that cut it to eight. Sound familiar? After a 21-footer, the deficit was six. After two free throws, it was four. After a driving leaner, it was two. After a pair of free throws, it was one.

When Ewing lost the ball, the Knicks' seventh turnover of the period, the ball wound up in Miller's hands on the right wing, giving him the chance to push the Pacers into the lead. But his jumper rimmed out. Small matter. He reached in to steal Charles Smith's pass to Starks and was promptly fouled by his New York counterpart.

When he stepped to the free throw line with 2:06 remaining and the Pacers trailing 91-90, he held the series in his hands. If ever there was a sure thing, this was it. Miller was one of the game's deadliest free throw shooters and was at his best in the postseason. He ranked fourth among active players, hitting 88 percent from the line in his playoff career. In this series, he had made 90 percent.

When he missed the first, said Starks, "I knew we would win the game." Though Miller hit the second to tie it, the Knicks had their reprieve, and made it stick. Miller would not get another shot, and New York scored the final seven points to win, 98-91, and force a seventh game the Pacers desperately wanted to avoid.

"This is it," said Antonio Davis. "The whole year, we've made it hard on ourselves. When we've been presented opportunities to do something special, we haven't gotten it done. This is just another one of those instances. Now, everything has to be perfect. We have 48 minutes left. Either you play hard the whole 48 minutes, or you go home. We're going to have to make it happen. We didn't want to go back, but now we have to. I think we can go up there and win a ballgame, but it's going to take a whole lot of effort.

"No matter what, win, lose or draw, when the game's over, I hope we can say we gave it our best shot. If we can say that, everybody will be happy. If we can't say it, we sold ourselves short."

*   *   *

For some, Game Seven in New York represented a second chance 24 years in the making.

More than two decades before, the Pacers and Knicks met in what theoretically was an exhibition. Realistically, it was not only the biggest game in town, but one of the biggest in the pro basketball world. It was the brash, unappreciated ABA Midwesterners attempting to rattle the staid Eastern arrogance of the NBA.

In so many ways, it was just like new times.

The Knicks were the reigning NBA champions, one of the great teams in league history, with a roster full of future Hall of Famers: Willis Reed, Walt Frazier, Dave DeBusschere, Bill Bradley, and coach Red Holzman.

The Pacers were the reigning ABA champions, but none of their players were destined for Springfield, Massachusetts, an unjust, yet apparently permanent, sentence. The legends of Roger Brown, Mel Daniels and George McGinnis lived on only in Market Square Arena, where their retired numbers hang, and in the minds of the fans who still cherished the memories of those three magnificent championship seasons.

Before the 1970-71 season, the Knicks descended upon Indianapolis to meet the Pacers on their turf, the rowdy State Fairgrounds Coliseum.

"It was no such thing as an exhibition game," said Daniels. "It was for real. There was a lot to prove, that we were as good as the people in the NBA, and I think we proved it."

On Sunday, June 5, 1994, the Pacers would descend upon the Knicks' turf, pungent Madison Square Garden, with the chance to become the first of the four surviving ABA teams to reach the NBA Finals.

This time, though, there could be no moral victory.

"They were out to prove that they could play with us," said Frazier, a Knicks broadcaster. "We wanted to prove that we were still the premiere league."

Though the Knicks escaped with a 98-96 victory, the Pacers hardly considered it a loss.

"They were a cocky, proud ballclub, but they didn't know how cocky and proud we were," said Slick Leonard, the former coach. "In the middle of the fourth quarter we had 'em down 14 and I think everybody was shocked, even though it was an exhibition game. Roger Brown gave Bill Bradley a lesson in basketball. Mel Daniels outplayed Willis Reed. George McGinnis was the best big forward on the floor. Red went to his bench - I think he figured it was over — so I sent in some rookies I wanted to see, and it wound up being a close game.

"They won it by a basket, but they knew who the Indiana Pacers were. My starters beat that Knick ballclub's starters."

At least one of the Pacers' key players — then — didn't take it quite so seriously.

"It was still an exhibition, so they were lucky I was even there," said Brown. "I wasn't playing hard. I didn't think you went hard for an exhibition."

This prompted a grunt from Daniels, who pointed at Brown and said, "McKey."

Frazier remembered the game well, particularly the enthusiasm in the community beforehand. It was much like the euphoria that preceded Game Six.

"The atmosphere was festive. This place was bedlam," Frazier said. "It was a lot like a college crowd. You didn't get crowds like this often in the pros. It just didn't happen. But I had played in Evansville (while a collegian at Southern Illinois), so I was prepared for it."

Though he was, by most accounts, the hero of the game, the protector of the NBA's precious pride, there was another memory stronger in Frazier's mind.

"I really don't remember (making the last shot)," he said. "All I remember was how good they were. After that, I had a lot of respect for them. Those guys could play in the NBA."

Most of them never got the chance. A victory in Game Seven, though, would help bring back their faded memories, and allow them to bask in reflected glory.

* * *

When the Pacers walked onto the Garden floor for the deciding game, they were confronted with the enormity of the event. This was a chance to either become another stone in history's path, or to change its course. For the last 12 years, no home team had ever lost a seventh game, 18 visitors tried, all failed.

It seemed the perfect opportunity for this team that had done nothing according to plan. All of its accomplishments had come against great odds, and there would be none greater.

"First six minutes," said Slick Leonard, who hadn't coached for 14 years but still lived and died with the team. "Stay in the game for six minutes, then anything can happen."

Playing as though they had heard Leonard's words, the Pacers began the game loose, and the offense clicked right away. That wasn't enough. Though they were shooting 60 percent, the Pacers trailed, 30-24, early in the third, because the Knicks had turned the missed shot into their best offensive weapon. Ewing, in particular, was relentlessly crashing the boards, either scoring on putbacks or passing out to team-mates for second-chance shots.

The Pacers had a proud, noble veteran of their own, though. Scott entered the play-offs with 2,172 postseason points, 19th all-time. During their course, he moved past Elvin Hayes, then Bob Pettit and finally Isiah Thomas, to rank 16th, right behind Bill Russell. Three of his former Laker teammates, Abdul-Jabbar, Johnson and Worthy, were among the 15 that remained ahead. A fourth, Michael Cooper, was No. 2 on the postseason three-point list with 124. Scott was third.

It was apparent, then, why he didn't stand out in Los Angeles. With the Pacers, he stood tall, and never more so than in the second quarter of their biggest game. He scored nine points to ignite a 15-4 run that pushed the Pacers into a 39-34 lead. When the Knicks tried to challenge, Scott and Miller both were there to repel the assault. Scott wound up hitting all five of his shots in the quarter, totaling 13 points. Miller scored the final eight to give Indiana a 51-47 lead at the half.

The defense hadn't been bad, but the rebounding was atrocious. The Knicks kept themselves in the game with 18 second-chance points. To win, the Pacers were told they would have to keep Ewing, Oakley, and Mason off the glass.

When the third quarter began, the Pacers were nearly flawless. Five different players scored, while the defense held the Knicks to just five points in nearly eight minutes. Antonio Davis made two free throws with 4:39 left in the quarter to build the lead to 65-53, and the Knicks had to wonder what was happening. Ewing, the man who had carried them to that point, picked up his fourth foul on the play.

Conventional wisdom would've sent Ewing to the bench. Riley, though, loved to flaunt convention. He left Ewing in, a huge gamble that paid big. The Knicks regrouped with a 14-4 run that was wrapped up by Ewing's three-point play. The Pacers had put them on the ropes, but they had counterpunched. This one would go the distance.

The game would be analagous to a boxing match in one other way. Even though the Knicks weren't the champions, they would be treated as such by the officials. That meant the Pacers, the brash challengers, would have to win a clear knockout.

Leonard, sitting upstairs at the visitors' radio perch, couldn't bear to watch. He took off his headset, turned to play-by-play man Mark Boyle, and said, "Do you mind if I leave for a few minutes? I can't take this anymore." He then headed out to calm his nerves, but returned with six minutes left.

He didn't miss much.

Ewing managed to play more than 11 consecutive minutes before picking up his fifth, a double foul when he became entangled with Antonio Davis with 4:52 remaining. Again, he would not come out. The Knicks led, 85-80, but hardly had control.

A New York nightmare recurred when Miller rose up and threw down a three-pointer from the top of the arc to make it 85-83, then, two minutes later, he swished a 20-footer from the right wing to cut it to 89-88. Less than two minutes remained, and the Pacers had become the aggressors.

Two Knick turnovers gave Indiana two chances to retake the lead. After Oakley traveled, Smits got excellent position against Ewing on the left block, spun to the baseline and had a virtual lay-in. But the ball hit both sides of the rim, then bounced out. The Knicks then seemed too intent on letting Ewing win it for them, throwing the ball into the post, where he was inevitably doubled. He kept passing back out before Starks finally tossed a desperation three-pointer that didn't draw iron, and the 24-second clock expired.

The Pacers then went to their bread-and-butter play. Miller would set up under the basket, push Starks into one screen, then run him into another. If the defense chased Miller outside, a big man would be open underneath. If it didn't, Miller would be open. When Miller curled around Dale Davis' screen to the left wing, both Oakley and Starks responded to the threat and jumped out at the guard. Davis was left wide open in the lane. Workman whipped a pass through the heart of the New York defense to Davis, who rose up for a dunk.

Ewing, the weakside help, was late to arrive. When he did, he whacked Davis across both arms with his left and bumped his body with such force that the Pacer power forward turned 45 degrees but still was able to force the ball through the hoop. When Davis landed, he turned, looked, and listened. Silence. No whistle. Though officials Hugh Evans, from the baseline, and Mike Mathis, from the right wing, both had a clear view of the play, neither would call Ewing's sixth foul. Even the NBC analyst, former Orlando coach Matt Guokas, thought it a strange no-call. "It should've been a foul on Ewing," he said. It would've been his sixth.

Still, the Pacers led 90-89 with 34.5 seconds left. They were one defensive stop away from the NBA Finals. During the timeout, Brown reminded the players that they had a foul to give. No matter what, he said, they could not allow themselves to get beat off the dribble. A foul would force the Knicks to set up another play and drain precious seconds from the clock.

Brown's instructions went unheeded. Riley didn't throw any new wrinkle at the Pacers. It was a simple high pick-and-roll with Ewing and Starks. When Ewing bumped Miller at the top of the key, Antonio Davis hesitated before stepping away from Ewing in a vain attempt to block Starks' path to the basket. Not only did he fail that, he left Ewing free to attack the exposed glass. Starks drove hard and shot hard but when the ball spun out, Ewing rose up, caught it with his left hand, then dunked it back through. It was his 22nd rebound of the night, the Knicks' 28th on the offensive glass.

Still, 26.9 seconds remained, an eternity by NBA standards. The Pacers had a play that had worked all night, and they would run it again, this time to the right side. Miller ran Starks into Antonio Davis, this time, and was fed the ball by Workman. When both Oakley and Starks jumped out at Miller again, Davis was alone under the basket, his hands pleading for a pass. But Miller already had committed to shoot, the worst option, under the circumstances. With Oakley in his face, Miller's 20-footer wasn't close and deflected out of bounds off Dale Davis.

They were down, but they weren't out, until Mathis brought the game to a premature, bitter end with what could generously be called a questionable call. Starks caught the ensuing inbounds pass and went into a semi-crouch to protect the ball. Miller, rushing from midcourt, put two hands into Starks' chest and shoved. It was a hard foul designed to stop the clock. Mathis saw it as something else. After Starks, ever the thespian, took an exaggerated flop to the floor, Mathis called it a flagrant foul.

When Starks missed one of the free throws with 3.2 seconds left, it would've left the Pacers a three-pointer away from the NBA Finals — a desperate chance, maybe, but at the very least a chance — Mathis' call took on even greater significance. The players would not be allowed to decide the outcome. Mathis had seen to that. On the gift possession, Starks was fouled again and, this time, made both.

Scott had predicted as much. His team would have little chance beating the Knicks in New York, he said before Game Six, because "not many people are going to let that happen." Asked if that was indeed the case, Scott said, "Basically."

The Pacers didn't feel cheated out of a victory, but robbed of an opportunity. They had come too far, overcome too many obstacles, played too hard, for one official's opinion to take the ball out of their hands in the closing seconds of their ultimate game.

Mathis' call even took Starks by surprise. "I thought it was an aggressive push on his part," Starks said, "but the referee made the call and you have to live with it."

For the winner, that was easy to say.

For Miller, it proved impossible to swallow. "I was just trying to get to him quick before he took another step," he said in a hushed voice, beyond despair. "In the conference finals, you can't make that call. I was trying to go for the ball. I thought maybe I could pry it loose." He would only answer a few more questions before looking to the floor and losing control of his emotions. The tears that had welled in his eyes now streamed down his face.

There now was compelling circumstantial evidence to support Miller's conspiracy theory. Ewing should've picked up his sixth foul before providing the game-winning putback. Miller's foul on Starks hardly was flagrant. It reminded some of Game Five of the previous round, when Scottie Pippen jumped into Hubert Davis after the Knick guard released an errant three-point attempt in the closing seconds. In any other situation, in any other arena, that call is never made. In the Garden, a whistle was blown, Davis made both free throws, and the Knicks escaped with a pivotal 87-86 win.

If the league would give that call to an unheralded reserve and against one of the game's great players, a three-time defending champion, certainly there was nothing to prevent similar misfortune from befalling the Pacers.

"I don't think they wanted to see the Indiana Pacers play the Houston Rockets," said Antonio Davis. "With that on their minds, we started the game down a few points." And finished that way.

Brown would not take the bait. He refused to criticize the officiating, instead heaping praise on Ewing, who had played a brilliant game with 24 points, 22 rebounds, seven assists and five blocked shots, while giving his own team credit for its remarkable postseason run.

"I'm not going to take anything away from this game or this series to talk about (the controversy)," he said, showing equal amounts of restraint and class. "These guys played great. It was a great basketball game and they won with a great player making a tremendous play. I'm proud of both teams. I'm proud of the way the series went. I'm disappointed as hell that we lost, but they made the plays down the stretch. They got second shots to keep them in the game and they got second shots to win the game.

"I'm proud of my team. I think we're a credit to the league and we play the right way. I wouldn't walk in that dressing room disappointed by anybody or our effort. We just got beat by a better team tonight. My perspective won't change on this team. It's a great group. What they did, and what the city showed in appreciation, it made the season even more special."

Though the New York players avoided questions that would've given the Pacers credit — "I don't really care about them," Ewing said, as the local mob cackled — Riley did not. He knew the pain the Pacers were feeling because he had been there before, with other teams.

"I want to give the Indiana Pacers a tremendous amount of credit," Riley said. "They were a great basketball team, a well-coached team. Larry Brown did something that was beyond coaching. I mean this from the bottom of my heart: beating that team is something I'll always remember. It was a harrowing, harrowing experience playing against them. We got the job done. I have great respect for them and wish them the best. They have nothing to be ashamed of. They have everything to be proud of in their accomplishments. They're very small words because they lost the game, but they were more than a formidable opponent."

And they fully expected to remain so, in the coming season. Few teams win championships in their first try. Detroit was taught that lesson by Boston before breaking through to win two titles. The Pistons, in turn, stood in Chicago's way. If a team had to suffer before it could truly expect to win, then the Pacers had paid their dues.

"The pain we take from this series," said Scott, "will make us a better team next year."

"We'll be back," said Antonio Davis. "And we'll be a little stronger, a little wiser."

As bad as they felt that night, the Pacers must've been surprised at what happened the next morning.

The sun rose.

With it, they hoped, would come the dawn of a new era.

Epilogue

As glorious as she had looked, in the heat of the moment, her flaws became more apparent in the days after. Cinderella would need a facelift.

Walsh, always cautious with the scalpel, would have to be doubly so in the summer of 1994. He was going to work on the most successful Pacer team in the franchise's NBA history.

"We have a team we need to treat carefully," he said. "We've got the ingredients to make a championship. But anybody we invite into the private club of this team, we need to make sure they fit. Our choices have to be based on talent, and a willingness to sacrifice to be a part of this group. They have to accept what we're all about."

Walsh's first move, as if there had been little doubt, was dictated by the players. When they met to divide up their $427,500 in playoff earnings, they sent Walsh a clear message. Of the players on the roster, 14 were voted full shares of $28,500 apiece. Richardson was voted a one-third share of $9,500. The rest of his share, as well as roughly $15,000 in daily fine money accrued over the course of the season, was divided up among assistant trainer Kevin Johnson, equipment manager Bill Hart and the ball boys.

Richardson was done with the Pacers, and they with him. He was traded to the Clippers, with Sealy and the No. 15 pick in the June draft, Nebraska forward Eric Piatkowski, for Brown favorite Mark Jackson and No. 25 pick Greg Minor, a swingman from Louisville.

Richardson was anything but bitter about his departure from the Pacers. He handled the exit with class.

"They're sending me home," he said. "I'm happy. I'm not upset at all. They couldn't have done anything better. I think it's going to work out for both teams. Coach Brown always wanted to have Mark Jackson. It's hard to play when the coach has his eyes on other people. He's got to get people he wants and people he feels he can win with. Coach Brown didn't want me. It's hard to play for somebody under those conditions. It's no sour grapes. I'm not mad at all. I understand now what was going on all year long. He wanted to trade me."

Sealy was less ambivalent. When he was introduced to the L.A. media, he said he and Brown had a love-hate relationship. "We loved," he said, "to hate each other."

In his first eight years atop the Pacers organization, Walsh had employed 12 point guards. Jackson became the 13th. That just happened to be his jersey number.

Was it coincidence or kismet? Either way, the union between Jackson and the Pacers seemed inevitable.

Had Miller not been available when the Pacers picked at No. 11 in the 1987 draft, Walsh planned to take Jackson, who wound up going to New York at the 18th pick and was the NBA's rookie of the year.

A few years later, the Knicks offered Jackson to the Pacers for Chuck Person, but Walsh opted not to pursue the deal.

Finally, the Pacers got their man. Jackson was expected to do what the dozen before him had not: solve the Pacers' perpetual problem at the point.

"It is a joy and a thrill to be a member of the Indiana Pacers right now," Jackson said. "It's something I've thought about for a long time. Watching those guys in the playoffs, the terrific run they made toward the NBA championship, as a player in the league I couldn't help but root for them. I know coach Brown well and I know what he's capable of doing with a team. I almost felt a part of it. This place is all about the Indiana Pacers right now. . . . I missed that feeling. It's great to be here."

Brown had pushed hard for the deal since February.

"Mark's the kind of player we needed to solidify our team," said Brown. "I know his strength and I know his character. We're trying to build something here with people like him. He's like the guys on our team. He's a born leader, a selfless guy and he has a lot of respect for his teammates."

Four players started at the point in the 1993-94 season: Workman (52 games), Richardson (25), Vern Fleming (four) and Byron Scott (one). Though Workman performed admirably as a fill-in, the franchise had little pretense about his future as a starter. Fleming, 32, is entering the final year of his contract.

Finding a quality starter was the first priority in the off-season. Jackson's acquisition, in Brown's words, makes it "a position you don't have to concern yourself with any more."

Walsh equated it to "getting a great quarterback in football."

Jackson, 29, played five seasons with the Knicks before joining Brown with the Clippers for the 1992-93 season.

"A lot of people say he's hard on point guards but I had a tremendous relationship with him," said Jackson. "He's going to yell at me the same way he yells at the other point guards. But, the thing is, I understand it. That's pure affection. He wants me to be the best and he wants the Pacers to be the best. That's why he's the best."

He holds both the New York (868) and Clipper (724) single-season assist records and is eighth on the active list with 4,639 career assists, an average of 8.4 per game. No Pacer ever has totaled more than 685 or averaged better than 8.5 in a season (both set by Don Buse in 1976-77). Jackson has posted a better average five times in his seven seasons and a higher total four times.

In short, an average year from Jackson could well be the best this franchise ever has seen.

He also has 10 triple-doubles, tied for fifth among active players.

"I'd be the first to tell you I'm not the fastest point guard in the league, and a whole lot of other things, but I try to be an extension of the coach on the floor," Jackson said. "I think one of the greatest things is I'm a leader. I'm a guy that can put the ball in the right hands."

What Jackson hasn't done is experienced much postseason success, never advancing past the second round.

"Without me, the Indiana Pacers have a heck of a basketball team. With me, I think we can be even better," he said. "What you want, before the season starts, is to have the opportunity, at the end, to hold the trophy up, wear the ring and be crowned the champions. This team has the capability of doing just that, as much as anybody in the league."

The Pacers have left no doubt about their intentions.

"You reach a point where you either build for the future or you go for it now," Walsh said. "We're at the stage where we're going for it."

The busy draft week offered Walsh one last chance to placate the local fans. Damon Bailey, the latest local legend to be produced by Bob Knight's program in Bloomington, would most certainly be available to the Pacers.

Though Bailey had an excellent senior season, averaging 19.6 points, 4.3 rebounds and 4.3 assists, he struggled in the postseason camps. In the Phoenix Desert Classic, he shot 30 percent and missed all six of his three-point tries. Shooting was one of the expected strengths of his game. He did not show well in the Chicago pre-draft camp, either. His stock fell drastically.

The Pacers had two second-round picks, Nos. 41 and 44 overall. Because the draft was hosted by Indianapolis, nearly 20,000 fans had packed the Hoosier Dome, many in red and white, more than a few wearing a replica of Bailey's college jersey. When

NBA vice president Rod Thorn stepped to the microphone to announce the 41st pick, there was great anticipation. . . . "the Indiana Pacers select . . . William Njoku of Canada." This was heresy. Instead of Bailey, Walsh had selected some unknown center from Ghana by way of Canada. The Hoosier Dome thundered with boos.

It was Walsh's way of working the crowd. He knew Bailey would be available at No. 44. The next time Thorn announced an Indiana pick, the place went crazy.

It didn't take Bailey long to have an impact. Brown decided to throw open the third day of the July rookie and free agent camp for a public scrimmage. Nearly 5,000 fans paid a $2 admission for Bailey's debut, unofficial though it was.

It was not the largest crowd Brown had seen for an intrasquad scrimmage, but it left an impression. In the summer of 1989, prior to David Robinson's rookie year, Brown's San Antonio Spurs scrimmaged before a packed house. "We could've drawn 50,000 for that one, but they had two years to wait for David," Brown said. "We only had two days to get ready for this."

It was an awful lot of fuss over a guy picked No. 44, whose chances of making the roster are long. Maybe too much, by Brown's standards. To the coach, Bailey was just another player trying to make the team, and the distractions that come with his local celebrity can be counterproductive.

"I played at North Carolina and I know how the people down there feel about those players," Brown said, "but I haven't seen anything quite like the way the people here feel about him."

This may have been new to Brown, but it was more of the same for Bailey.

"It gets frustrating," he said. "I'm here to work on my game and I'm going to have to spend a half-hour here, a half-hour there. It kind of comes with the territory."

In the NBA-sanctioned scouting camps, Bailey did not impress scouts because his weight was up, his conditioning down and he had not fully recovered from a pulled abdominal muscle that hampered him throughout much of his senior season. He hired a personal trainer in Phoenix to prepare for the opening of training camp in October.

"I was impressed with him," said Brown. "I was impressed watching him at I.U. I think, on our level, a lot of people get caught up in what a kid can't do. I think if you harp on what he can do, you'll see he has a better chance of making the league, and possibly our team."

He has a far greater level of local celebrity than the players he's competing with, but Bailey was taking nothing for granted.

"It's very exciting," Bailey said. "Ever since you're a little kid, this is what you've dreamed of. I'm not an Indiana Pacer as of right now. I'm here trying to make the team, show that I can contribute in some way. I've got to go out, prove a point and make a statement about myself and my game."

Somebody asked Bailey if Bobby Knight had any advice on making this transition. In answering, Bailey demonstrated he needed none.

"Coach Knight's a great college coach. I'm not sure Coach Knight would make it at the professional level, and he's said that he's not sure he'd really want to," Bailey said. "It's two different types of game. They're not anything alike. I've got to do the things the coaching staff here wants me to do. I'm going to rely more on their advice than anybody's because they're the ones I have to please."

Hearing those words, Brown couldn't help but smile. Bailey always has had a way of doing that to coaches.

* * *

With Bailey attracting all the attention, two other potentially significant acquisitions went about their business in relative anonymity, Minor and John Williams.

At Louisville, Minor played in the shadows of two far more widely known teammates, forward Clifford Rozier and guard Dwayne Morton. But NBA scouts who made the journey to check those two out marked another name in their ledgers, hoping no one else had spotted the athletically gifted, hard-nosed guard-forward.

"Most of the scouts that came to visit were there to see Dwayne or Cliff," said Minor. "It just so happened that I was having a good season."

Good, sure. But 13.8 points, 6.1 rebounds and 2.5 assists aren't the kinds of numbers that jump off a stat sheet and scream, "Draft me!" When it came time to line up for postseason honors, Minor went home relatively empty-handed. He was voted first team all-Metro, and that conference's players named him the league's best clutch performer but, nationally, he was anonymous.

Basketball Weekly didn't list him on any of its three All-America teams or even its first two all-Southeast teams. His name was buried, with 49 others, as an honorable mention pick.

At least that publication noticed. Basketball Times didn't give him any mention, honorable or otherwise.

The Sporting News published a list of the 30 most underexposed, underappreciated and underrated players in the nation, which should've been right up Minor's alley. It wasn't. He didn't even make that list.

The only people who seemed to know about Minor, outside of Louisville, were the ones who mattered most, the scouts, who wanted to see him as much as possible in the postseason. He didn't disappoint them, making the all-tournament teams at both the Portsmouth Invitational and the Phoenix Desert Classic.

A versatile swingman who played shooting guard on offense and small forward on defense for the Cardinals, Minor exhibited his full range of offensive skills in the tournaments. In five games in those two events, he averaged 17.4 points, 6.4 rebounds, three assists and shot 55 percent. His stock rose dramatically.

"He's the kind of player we want on our team," said Walsh, "because he gives effort and does the dirty work. He'll definitely fit in with us."

Whether Williams would was another question. Released by the Clippers, Williams answered Brown's invitation to the rookie and free agent camp but showed up weighing 320 pounds.

"This is virtually his last chance," said Brown. "He knows that, and he knows how we feel about him. I love him. I want him on our team, but I don't want to see him hurt himself. He's got to start now."

Williams sounded willing, and ready, to return Brown's favor.

"He's going out on a limb for me. It's time to start backing him up and making him look right," Williams said. "People look at him like he's crazy when he says good things about me. It's time to go out and prove everyone wrong and get this thing turned around."

After one practice, Williams strained a knee and was unable to participate in rookie league games.

"He's the most talented kid I ever coached, as far as understanding the game and trying to play the right way," Brown said. "He's a great person. I like him. I like what he stands for. I'm just frustrated by it because I know how good he is and I hope people recognize that. But as good as he is, he can't do it at this weight. It's just too tough for him. If he was on our team at a reasonable weight, he'd be the greatest addition we could have because he does all the things to help other players."

After three solid years with the Washington Bullets, Williams played in just 51 games from 1989-92, spending the entire '91-92 season on the suspended list. The Clippers acquired Williams prior to the '92-93 season, spawning a strong relationship between the player and Brown. Williams was a productive reserve that year, averaging 6.6 points and 7.4 rebounds in 74 games.

When Brown left the Clippers for the Pacers last summer, "I felt real lost," Williams said. "That took a huge hunk out of my motivation."

Though he was reunited with Brown, there were no guarantees.

And so they headed to North Carolina, where it all began for Brown, with a new point guard, a couple of interesting rookies, and an overweight veteran trying to make the most of his last chance.

There was, of course, something else. Unfinished business.